BOAT DATA BOOK

Fourth Edition

IAN NICOLSON

SHERIDAN HOUSE

To Jeremy and Claire Lines

Other books by Ian Nicolson

The Log of the *Maken*

Sea Saint

Building the *St Mary*

Outboard Boats and Engines

Dinghy Cruising

Small Steel Craft

Surveying Small Craft

Marinise Your Boat

Designer's Notebook

Yacht Designer's Sketchbook

Comfort in the Cruising Yacht

Guide to Boat Buying

Roving in Open Boats

The Ian Nicolson Omnibus

Cold Moulded and Strip Planked
    Wood Boatbuilding

Build Your Own Boat

Improve Your Own Boat

Build a Simple Dinghy (with Alasdair
    Reynolds)

Race Winner (with Richard Nicolson)

A Sail for All Seasons

Fourth edition 1999
Published by Sheridan House Inc.
145 Palisade Street,
Dobbs Ferry, NY 10522

Copyright © Ian Nicolson 1978, 1985, 1994, 1999

First edition published 1978
Second edition published 1985 by
Sheridan House
Third edition published 1995 by
Sheridan House

While all reasonable care has been taken in the publication of this book, the publisher takes no responsibility for the use of the methods or products described in the book.

Library of Congress Cataloging-in-Publication Data
Nicolson, Ian, 1928-
    Boat data book/Ian Nicolson-4th ed.
        p.   cm
    Includes index.
    ISBN 1-57409-044-5
        1. Boats and boating—
Equipment and supplies—Handbooks,
manuals, etc.   I. Title
VM321.N49   1999   98-46365
623.8'2—dc21   CIP

Printed in Great Britain
ISBN 1-57409-044-5

INTRODUCTION

This book is for owners, crew, boatbuyers, charterers, chandlers, builders, repairers, designers, draughtsmen and students. In fact, for anyone concerned with boats and ships.

One of its most valuable uses is saving time and trouble when specifying anything. By simply quoting a page anyone can order equipment without having to look up the correct size and write out lengthy details. An owner can phone a marina or chandler and simply say: 'Put a new anchor on my boat. Size as specified in *Boat Data Book*'. Designers can reduce long lists of rigging to: 'As detailed in *Boat Data Book*, page 115, column for yachts between 9 m and 11 m'.

Anyone buying a boat can check the standard of its equipment by referring to the lists in this book. There is a widespread practice of fitting boats with totally inadequate anchors, chain, winches and so on. Many second-hand boats offered for sale are found to have inadequate safety gear, and much of what is on board is often out of date. Reference to pages 26 to 35 will show what is needed.

When designing or acquiring a boat it is important to check dimensions of berths, galley top heights and so on. There is a tendency also to save on building costs by fitting furniture which is under-size and as a result inconvenient, besides being uncomfortable to use. Chapter 6 on Design gives many basic dimensions, standard, recommended minimum sizes and so on.

Dimensions are given in metres (or millimetres) as well as feet and inches. Speed is in knots because this is still the universal unit at sea, but there are conversion tables from knots to kilometres per hour and miles per hour.

CONTENTS

3 FASTENINGS

4 SPARS AND RIGGING

5   ENGINES AND POWERING

6 DESIGN

7 TABLES AND FORMULAE

INDEX

Acknowledgements
My thanks are due to the people, often unknown, who devised many of the
formulae in this book, and to McKechnie Metals of Walsall for permitting me
to use many of their tables. Thanks are also due to those who have kindly
given permission to use data, graphs and lists including the British Standards
Institute, Calor Gas, Camping Gaz, Caterpillar, Harken, Ian Proctor Metal
Masts, International Paints Ltd, Lewmar, Marlow Ropes, Murray Cormack
Associates, Norseman Ropes, Ormiston, Riggarna, RNLI, Simpson-Lawrence,
South Western Marine Factors, J Thompson Timber, XM Yachting, *Yachts
and Yachting*, and Bernard Hayman. Apologies are offered for inadvertently
omitting any company or person whose data has been used.

1 BOAT EQUIPMENT

Fisherman anchors – proportions

A folding Fisherman anchor has the virtue of being effective in all types of holding ground. Where the seabed is covered with layers of kelp it is one of the few types of anchor that may penetrate the weed and obtain a firm grip on the bottom.

    This graph shows the proportions which have in practice been found to give an effective anchor. It is important that the palms are sharp and there must be good fillets where the shank meets the arms to ensure adequate strength.

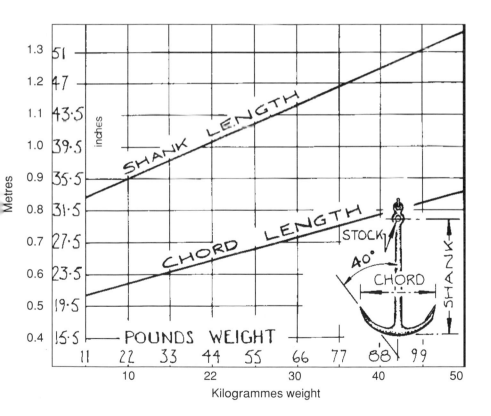

Danforth anchors – proportions

These figures are based on the standard Danforth anchor which has been developed and tested extensively. Wide variations from these proportions may be treated with caution. A side elevation is shown below.

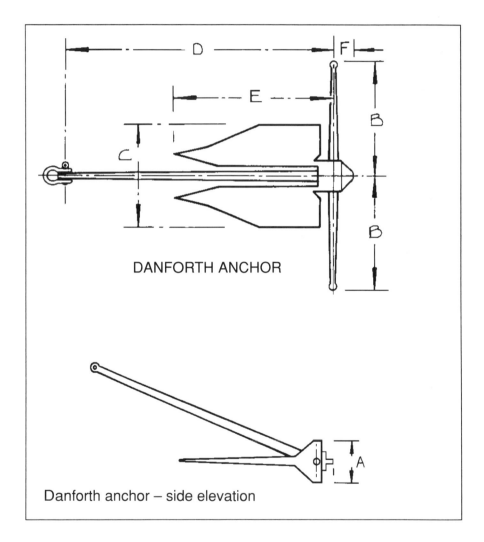

DANFORTH ANCHOR

Danforth anchor – side elevation

Dimensions and weights: imperial units (Danforth)

Anchor size: pounds	17	30	43	55	75	100	150	200
Dimensions: inches								
A	$4\,^1/_4$	$5\,^3/_4$	$6\,^3/_8$	$7\,^1/_8$	8	$8\,^3/_8$	9	$9\,^3/_4$
B	$10\,^3/_8$	$13\,^3/_4$	$15\,^9/_{16}$	$17\,^5/_{16}$	$19\,^3/_4$	$20\,^9/_{16}$	$21\,^1/_4$	$22\,^3/_4$
C	$9\,^5/_{16}$	$12\,^1/_8$	$13\,^7/_{16}$	$14\,^7/_8$	$16\,^{13}/_{16}$	$17\,^1/_2$	$18\,^7/_8$	$20\,^9/_{16}$
D	24	32	36	40	$45\,^5/_8$	$47\,^1/_2$	49	$52\,^1/_2$
E	$14\,^5/_8$	$19\,^5/_8$	$21\,^{15}/_{16}$	$24\,^3/_8$	$24\,^7/_8$	$28\,^{15}/_{16}$	$29\,^7/_8$	$32\,^1/_{16}$
F	$1\,^7/_8$	$2\,^1/_4$	$2\,^9/_{16}$	$2\,^5/_{16}$	$2\,^{15}/_{32}$	$1\,^{19}/_{32}$	$1\,^{29}/_{32}$	$2\,^5/_{32}$
Shackle inches	$^3/_8$	$^1/_2$	$^1/_2$	$^1/_2$	$^1/_2$	$^5/_8$	$^3/_4$	$^7/_8$

Dimensions and weights: metric units (Danforth)

Anchor size: kilos	7·7	13·6	19·5	25	34	45	68	90
Dimensions: millimetres								
A	108	146	162	181	203	213	229	248
B	264	349	395	440	502	521	540	578
C	237	308	341	378	427	445	479	522
D	610	813	914	1016	1159	1207	1245	1334
E	372	499	558	619	708	736	759	813
F	48	57	64	58	62	41	49	54
Shackle millimetres	9·53	12·7	12·7	12·7	12·7	15·9	19	22·2

CQR anchors

A CQR anchor is sometimes left hanging over a bow roller when a vessel goes to sea. It is important that there are at least three strong lashings on it: two on the shank and one to prevent the plough end from moving in severe conditions. These lashings are usually needed even if the anchor chain has been hauled in very tight by the anchor windlass.

It may be necessary to fit a pad between the sharp point of the plough and the hull, or have stainless steel plates on the stem-head to deal with wear caused by the anchor when stowed on the stem-head roller.

Dimensions in millimetres

Weight in kilos	*A*	*B*	*C*	*D*	*E*	*F*	*G*	*H*	*I*	*J*	*K*	*L*	*M*	*N Diameter*
7	337	235	692	273	457	22	14	33	57	565	50	305	121	67
9	357	270	803	314	533	28	16	44	60	660	50	368	152	76
11	419	305	857	343	559	32	16	48	65	689	50	381	159	79
16	464	349	965	356	635	35	21	57	76	775	50	445	178	82
20	508	381	1029	371	676	38	25	60	83	819	64	470	191	89
27	559	419	1156	406	765	41	25	70	89	914	64	533	210	102
34	603	451	1235	441	825	44	25	76	95	971	70	572	229	113
48	690	485	1152	396	660	47	30	114	120	838	70	495	208	66
64	763	537	1274	438	730	52	33	126	128	927	70	548	230	73
80	826	582	1379	474	790	56	36	137	138	1003	70	593	248	79
110	910	641	1519	522	870	62	40	151	146	1105	83	653	273	87
135	983	693	1641	564	940	67	43	163	154	1194	83	705	296	94
180	1079	763	1801	619	1032	74	47	179	164	1310	92	774	325	104
225	1157	825	2054	665	1112	79	49	186	174	1421	102	834	348	110
270	1236	870	2063	709	1118	84	54	205	184	1501	104	887	372	118

Dimensions in inches

Weight in pounds	*A*	*B*	*C*	*D*	*E*	*F*	*G*	*H*	*I*	*J*	*K*	*L*	*M*	*N Diameter*
15	13 1/4	9 1/4	27 1/4	10 3/4	18	7/8	9/16	1 5/16	2 1/4	22 1/4	2	12	4 3/4	2 5/8
20	15 1/4	10 5/8	31 5/8	12 3/8	21	1 1/8	5/8	1 3/4	2 3/8	26	2	14 1/2	6	3
25	16 1/2	12	33 3/4	13 1/2	22	1 1/4	5/8	1 7/8	2 9/16	27 1/8	2	15	6 1/4	3 1/8
35	18 1/4	13 3/4	38	14	25	1 3/8	13/16	2 1/4	3	30 1/2	2	17 1/2	7	3 1/4
45	20	15	40 1/2	14 5/8	26 5/8	1 1/2	1	2 3/8	3 1/4	32 1/4	2 1/2	18 1/2	7 1/2	3 1/2
60	22	16 1/2	45 1/2	16	30 1/8	1 5/8	1	2 3/4	3 1/2	36	2 1/2	21	8 1/4	4
75	23 3/4	17 3/4	48 5/8	17 3/8	32 1/2	1 3/4	1	3	3 3/4	38 1/4	2 3/4	22 1/2	9	4 7/16
105	27 1/8	19	45 3/8	15 1/2	26	1 7/8	1 3/16	4 1/2	4 3/4	33	2 3/4	19 1/2	8 3/16	2 1/2
140	30	21 1/8	50 1/8	17 1/4	28 3/4	2	1 1/4	5	5	36 1/2	2 3/4	21 1/2	9	2 7/8
180	30 1/2	23	54 1/4	18 5/8	31	2 1/4	1 1/2	5 1/8	5 1/2	39 1/2	2 3/4	23 1/8	9 3/4	3 1/8
240	35 3/4	25 1/4	59 3/4	20 1/2	34 1/4	2 1/2	1 1/2	6	5 3/4	43 1/2	3 1/4	25 3/4	10 3/4	3 7/16
300	38 3/4	27 1/4	64 5/8	22 1/4	37	2 5/8	1 5/8	6 3/8	6	47	3 1/4	27 3/4	11 5/8	3 3/4
400	42 1/2	30	70 7/8	24 3/8	40 5/8	2 7/8	1 7/8	7	6 1/2	51 1/2	3 5/8	30 1/2	12 3/4	4
500	45 1/2	32 1/2	80 7/8	26 1/8	43 3/4	3 1/8	2	7 3/8	6 7/8	56	4	32 7/8	13 3/4	4 3/8
600	48 3/4	34 1/4	81 1/4	27 7/8	46 1/2	3 5/16	2 1/8	8	7 1/4	59	4	35	14 5/8	4 5/8

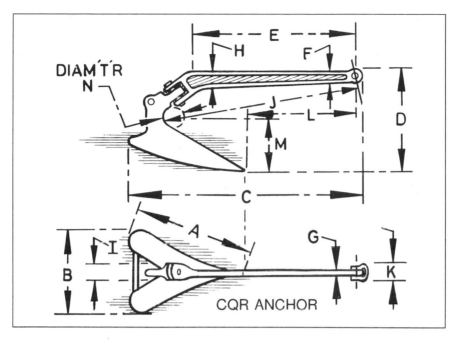

CQR ANCHOR

Delta anchors

The advantages of the Delta anchor include excellent holding power, no moving parts, and the ability to self-stow and self-launch on and off a steam-head roller. The two bends in the shank are the secret of its self-stowing ability. Dimensions are shown overleaf.

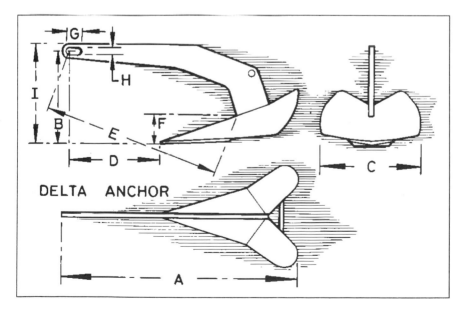

DELTA ANCHOR

Dimensions and weights: imperial units (Delta)

Anchor size: pounds	9	14	22	35	55	88
Dimensions: inches						
A	20 1/8	23 7/8	27 7/8	32 5/8	36 1/8	40 3/8
B	7 7/8	9 1/8	10 5/8	12 3/8	14 3/8	15 1/2
C	8 7/8	10	11 5/8	13 5/8	15 7/8	17 7/8
D	7 3/4	8 5/8	10 1/8	11 3/4	13 5/8	15
E	15 1/4	17 3/4	20 5/8	24 1/8	28	30 5/8
F	2 1/2	2 3/4	3 1/8	3 3/4	4 1/4	4 7/8
G	1 3/8	1 3/8	1 5/8	1 5/8	1 7/8	1 7/8
H	5/8	5/8	3/4	3/4	1	1
I	8 1/2	9 3/4	11 3/8	13 1/4	15 1/2	16 1/2

Dimensions and weights: metric units (Delta)

Anchor size: kilos	4	6	10	16	25	40
Dimensions: millimetres						
A	512	607	708	828	961	1025
B	201	231	270	315	366	393
C	224	254	296	347	402	455
D	196	219	256	299	347	382
E	387	450	525	614	712	777
F	64	69	80	94	109	124
G	35	25	42	42	48	48
H	16	16	19	19	24	24
I	217	247	289	337	392	420

Anchor ropes and mooring warps – sizes

- Anchor ropes – polyamide (nylon) or polyester (Terylene/Dacron).
- Warps should be of the same material or polypropylene (Courlene etc).
- All ropes and chains are detailed by *diameter*.
- Protect against chafing at the bow fairlead.
- *Never* use a floating rope (such as polypropylene) on an anchor.

Yacht's length overall	up to 5·5 m 18 ft	5·5–7·3 m 18–24 ft	7·3–9 m 24–30 ft	9–11 m 30–36 ft	11–13·5 m 36–44 ft	13·5–16·5 m 44–54 ft
*Thames tonnage**	Dayboats and dinghies	2–4 tons	4–8 tons	8–12 tons	12–18 tons	18–30 tons
Anchor rope with short length of chain	30 m of 10 mm plaited plus 5 m of 5 mm chain or 100 ft of ⅜ inch diam plaited plus 18 ft of ³⁄₁₆ inch chain	42 m of 13 mm plaited plus 5 m of 6·5 mm chain or 140 ft of ½ inch diam plaited plus 18 ft of ¼ inch chain	55 m of 13 mm 3-strand plus 5 m of 8 mm chain or 180 ft of ½ inch diam 3-strand plus 18 ft of ⁵⁄₁₆ inch chain	70 m of 16 mm 3-strand plus 7 m of 10 mm chain or 240 ft of ⅝ inch diam 3-strand plus 24 ft of ⅜ inch chain	90 m of 16 mm 3-strand plus 7 m of 11 mm chain or 300 ft of ⅝ inch diam 3-strand plus 24 ft of ⁷⁄₁₆ inch chain	120 m of 19 mm 3-strand plus 7 m of 13 mm chain or 400 ft of ¾ inch diam 3-strand plus 24 ft of ½ inch chain
Mooring warps 3-strand or plaited	2, 3 or 4 required each 9 m of 10 mm or 30 ft of ⅜ inch diam	3 or 4 required each 14 m of 11 mm or 45 ft of ⁷⁄₁₆ inch diam	4 required each 18 m of 13 mm or 60 ft of ½ inch diam	4 required each 23 m of 13 mm or 75 ft of ½ inch diam	4 or 5 required each 27 m of 16 mm or 90 ft of ⅝ inch diam	5 or 6 required each 30 m of 19 mm or 100 ft of ¾ inch diam

*See page 204 for the formula which gives Thames tonnage.

Anchor sizes relative to boat length and type

- Recommended sizes of 'patent' anchors such as Delta, Danforth, Bruce, CQR, Plough etc. For Fisherman types increase the weight by 20%.
- Tested anchors are recommended.
- For inshore racing a light kedging anchor is likely to prove inadequate if the yacht has to anchor in severe weather in an unprotected anchorage.

- Long-range cruising assumes that the yacht may have to ride out a hurricane. In these conditions a modest increase in weight and size of anchor over the average will sometimes save the boat.

ANCHOR SIZES

Dimensions and weights: imperial units

Boat length overall: feet	20	26	33	39	46	52	59	66	72
For inshore racing: lbs	10	15	20	30	40	65	80	50	65
								90	150
For coastal cruising: lbs	10	15	22	35	45	56	2@70	2@85	2@120
	30	40	50	60	75	95	1@125	1@175	1@250
For long range cruising: lbs							80	90	100
	20	25	35	50	60	70	2@120	2@140	2@160
	30	45	2@70	2@90	2@130	2@170	2@220	2@280	2@350

ANCHOR SIZES

Dimensions and weights: metric units

Boat length overall: metres	6	8	10	12	14	16	18	20	22
For inshore racing: kilos	5	7	9	14	18	29	36	23	29
								41	68
For coastal cruising: kilos	5	7	10	16	20	25	2@32	2@39	2@54
	14	18	23	27	34	43	1@57	1@79	1@113
For long range cruising: kilos					27	32	36	41	45
	9	11	16	23	36	45	2@54	2@64	2@73
	14	20	2@32	2@41	2@59	2@77	2@100	2@127	2@159

Sheet winches – power ratio

There is a good deal of controversy about the correct size of sheet winch to fit on a boat. This is because crew strengths vary, different yachts are used for different purposes, and some are much harder driven than others. Dominating all is the high cost of powerful winches, which is the reason why so many standard boats are marketed with winches of inadequate power.

The graph shows upper and lower limits for winches to suit the sail area of the largest genoa to be set, which should be taken as the basis. If the crew is weak or if the boat is to be raced hard in all weathers, go for the larger size of winch. If in doubt use the right hand side of the graph curve. For multihulls increase the power ratio by 20%.

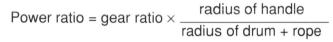

$$\text{Power ratio} = \text{gear ratio} \times \frac{\text{radius of handle}}{\text{radius of drum} + \text{rope}}$$

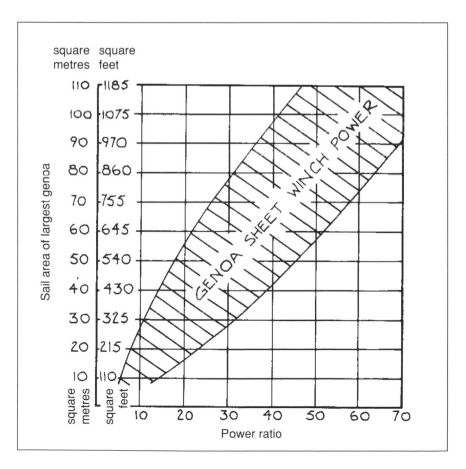

Winch sizes

See data on pages 20 and 21.
Winches are catalogued by their size number. This number is an

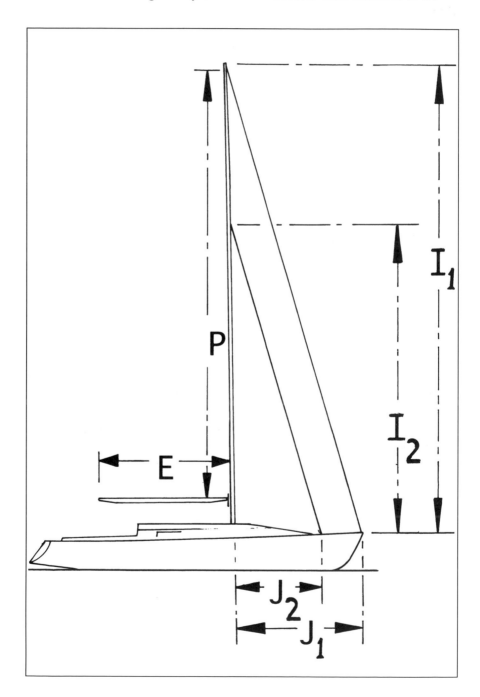

indication of the winch's power or mechanical advantage. Thus a size 42 winch gives a power ratio of about 42:1. This ratio will be obtained when the winch is being used in its highest gearing.
The table of winch sizes overleaf is based on the standard sail plan dimensions, namely:

I_1 = Distance from the deck to the top of the foretriangle, that is the point where the forestay meets the fore side of the mast.

I_2 = Distance from deck to top of inner forestay, where it meets the fore side of the mast. This is roughly at the staysail halyard block.

J_1 = The distance from the front of the mast at deck level to the bottom of the forestay.

P = Length of mainsail luff.

E = Length of mainsail foot.

In each case two figures are given for the Max sail area, or Max 'I', or Max 'P' etc. The upper figure of each pair on pages 20 and 21 is in square feet, or feet; the lower one is square metres or metres.

The winch sizes given in the tables on the next two pages should be taken as the minimum because:
- Winches wear and become less efficient in time.
- Anyone who is tired, seasick, working in an awkward position or inexperienced needs an extra powerful winch, and therefore one larger than the basic minimum.
- In severe conditions the efficiency of the crew is decreased at a time when the winch power may be of particular importance.
- Whereas many craft have been under-equipped with winches, few have been over-equipped.
- Some winchmakers give their products numbers which do not exactly correspond to the winch power.

Winch size	Genoa		Mainsail		
	Sheet	Halyard	Mainsheet	Halyard	
	Max sail area 100% Foretriangle $(I \times J \times \cdot5)$ $\dfrac{ft^2}{m^2}$	Max 'I' $\dfrac{ft}{m}$	4:1 Sheet Max sail area $(P \times E \times \cdot5)$ $\dfrac{ft^2}{m^2}$	Max 'P' $\dfrac{ft}{m}$	
6	75 7	25 7·6	—	25 7·6	
8	120 11	36 11	150 14	32 9·8	
16	165 15	42 12·8	245 22·7	40 12·2	
32	240 22	48 14·6	350 33	45 13·7	
40	275 25	54 16·5	425 40	51 15·5	
42	320 30	59 18	520 48	56 17	
44	350 33	64 19·5	575 53	62 18·9	
46	375 35	69 21	650 60	67 20·4	
48	400 37	73 22·2	725 67	72 22	
53	435 40	77 23·5	790 73	76 23·2	
56	570 53	82 25	860 80	82 25	
64	610 57	86 26·2	1000 93	87 26·5	
66	700 65	92 28	1200 111	95 29	
74	875 81	100 30·5	1350 125	102 31·1	

This table is based on information supplied courtesy of Peter Fairley, formerly of Harken UK Ltd.

| | Spinnaker | | Topping lift & Foreguy | Staysail |
Reef	Sheet	Halyard		Halyard
Max 'P' $\frac{ft}{m}$	Max sail area $(I \times J \times 1\cdot8)$ $\frac{ft^2}{m^2}$	Max 'I' $\frac{ft}{m}$	Max 'I' $\frac{ft}{m}$	Max 'I₂' $\frac{ft}{m}$
34 / 10·4	500 / 46	26 / 8	35 / 10·7	25 / 7·6
40 / 12·2	800 / 74	37 / 11·3	44 / 13·4	37 / 11·3
46 / 14	975 / 91	42 / 12·8	50 / 15·2	42 / 12·8
53 / 16·2	1135 / 105	48 / 14·6	56 / 17	48 / 14·6
57 / 17·4	1240 / 115	54 / 16·5	61 / 18·6	54 / 16·5
63 / 19·2	1315 / 122	59 / 18	66 / 20·1	59 / 18
68 / 20·7	1400 / 130	64 / 19·5	73 / 22·2	64 / 19·5
73 / 22·2	1530 / 142	69 / 21	78 / 23·8	69 / 21
78 / 23·8	1750 / 162	73 / 22·2	82 / 25	73 / 22·2
85 / 25·9	1960 / 182	77 / 23·5	90 / 27·4	77 / 23·5
92 / 28	2200 / 204	82 / 25	98 / 29·9	82 / 25
97 / 29·6	3000 / 279	86 / 26·2	108 / 33	86 / 26·2
106 / 32·3	3500 / 325	90 / 27·4	—	—
—	—	100 / 30·5	—	—

Cleat sizes

The majority of cleats on standard and production boats are too
small, especially for use in severe conditions. Broken and loose

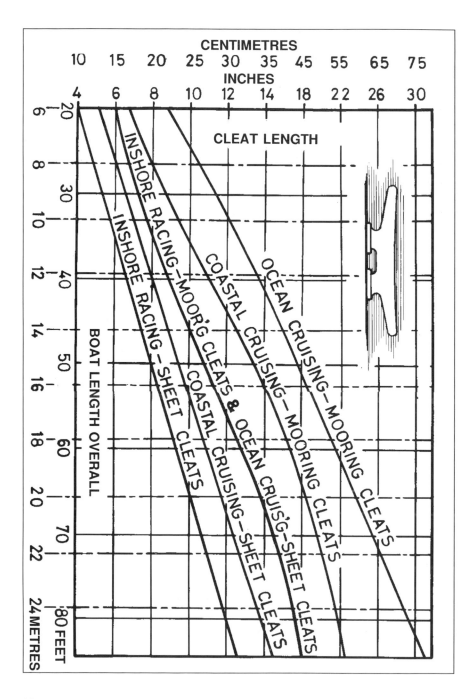

cleats are commonly found during surveys, which confirms that cleats on a wide range of craft should be larger. These graphs show cleat sizes for different types of craft and different purposes. In general, halyard cleats should be the same size as sheet cleats.

Tools for small craft

The selection of hand tools carried on board is at least partly a matter of personal preference and experience The available space for stowage and working will also affect the size of the list.

Racing boats are usually skinned out and carry only the minimum equipment to deal with emergencies. At the other end of the scale boats which have to be entirely self reliant will carry all the tools listed here up to List E, even when the craft's overall length is 12 metres, 40 ft overall.

These lists are based on the need to deal with emergencies afloat, including damage control and repair. They are also worked out on the principle that some maintenance will be done afloat, and on larger craft alterations will be carried out on board without extensive shore facilities. The dividing line between these requirements will be a matter of owners' preference.

Only the best tools are adequate for work afloat and even the best lack proper corrosion resistance. It seldom pays to buy second best even on the principle that annual replacement of tools is part of the ship's maintenance schedule. When tools are wanted afloat they are needed badly and breakages are intolerable.

Chisels, screwdrivers, saws etc. should have hard plastic handles. Full corrosion protection should be carried out including the use of oil impregnated tool-kit lining papers, the use of Lanolin etc on blades and edges.

List A is for boats up to 6 metres (20 ft) overall.

List B is for boats up to 9 metres (30 ft) overall.

List C is for boats up to 12 metres (40 ft) overall.

List D is for boats up to 15 metres (50 ft) overall.

List E is for boats up to 18 metres (60 ft) overall.

List A

Knife, with marline spike or multi-purpose blades
Medium-large screwdriver (size 330 mm or 13 in overall length)
    or multi-type screwdriver with several blades.
Mini-mole grip or pliers
Oil can
If the vessel has an engine – set of engine tools

List B

List A plus:

Wire cutters for largest size of rigging (only required if the vessel is
    a sailing yacht)
Junior hacksaw and 4 spare blades
Surform
Hand-drill
Set of about 8 twist drills (from 2 mm to 6 mm; $^1/_{16}$ in to $^1/_4$ in)
Counter-sink for steel (12 mm; $^1/_2$ in size), with shank to fit hand
    drill. This tool can be used for wood or soft metals in
    emergencies
Pair of pliers, single joint side-cutting type (180 mm; 7 in length)
Small screwdriver set (handle and various accessories)
Metre rule (folding type which shows millimetres and inches)
Adjustable spanner to open up to 40 mm; 1½ in or big enough for
    stern gland etc

List C

Lists A and B plus:

Portable or table vice
Engineer's ball pein hammer (0·75 kg; 1½ lb size)
Ratchet brace with assorted drill bits (8 mm to 30 mm; $^3/_8$ in to
    1¼ in)
Two screwdriver bits (6 mm and 9 mm; $^1/_4$ in and $^3/_8$ in)
Centre punch
Chisel (12 mm; $^1/_2$ in)
Mole grip
Full size hacksaw, of the type which will take any size of blade
Packet of assorted fine, medium and coarse hacksaw blades
Special wood cutting hacksaw blade

List D

Lists A, B and C plus:

Hand saw (500 mm; 20 in)
Full set of counter-sinks for ratchet brace
Swedish file (medium cut on one side, smooth on the other)
Rat-tail file
Round (cylindrical) surform
Large screwdriver
Square (250 mm; 10 in)
Pinch bar or wrecking bar
Plane (50 mm; 2 in cutter width)
Electric drill to work off ship's power, shore power or the cordless
    type precharged ashore. To take up to 8 mm; 3/8 in drills
Set of twist drills from 6 mm to 9 mm; 1/4 in to 3/8 in
Carborundum stone – double sided, coarse and fine
Chisels, 6 mm; 1/4 in and 18 mm; 3/4 in
Mole grip with bench cramp on handle
2 small cramps
Expanding bit (size 12 mm to 35 mm; 1/2 in to 1 1/2 in)
Adjustable spanner to fit largest nut on board
Cold chisel (8 mm; 3/8 in)
Stubby screwdriver
Wood scraper(s)
Full packets of fine, medium and coarse hacksaw blades

List E

Lists A, B, C and D plus:

Pad saw
Tenon saw
Adjustable spokeshave
Mallet
'Soft' hammer with a selection of faces or tips
Large hammer, eg 2 kilos; 5 lb
Small hammer, eg 0·2 kg; 1/2 lb
Full set of files
Set of bradawls
Set of gouges up to 20 mm; 3/4 in
Set of cold chisels from 6 mm to 25 mm; 1/4 in to 1 in
Set of socket spanners and/or ring spanners, and/or open ended
    spanners   *cont*

Set of Allen keys
Spanner to fit keel bolt nuts where applicable
Chain type pipe wrench
Nail punch 1½ mm; ¹/₁₆ in
Inside/outside calipers
2 large clamps (jaw opening at least 250 mm; 10 in)
Mechanic's vice with swivel base – 90 mm; 3½ in jaw width
Woodworker's vice
Soldering iron (electric to work off ship's supply, or traditional
    type heated by an external source)
Blow-lamp (to use the same fuel as other items on board, eg calor
    or paraffin)
Adaptor to turn electric drill into a reciprocating saw
Bench pedestal to turn electric drill into grinder etc

Safety equipment – craft under 5·5 m (18 ft) LOA

Item no	Safety item	Number required	Status	Type and size
1	Lifejacket	1 for each person	Essential. To be worn when conditions are dangerous	To BSI specification. Children's size where appropriate. BMIF or similar approved buoyancy aid may be used in sheltered waters
2	Lifebuoy	1	Recommended. 2 are recommended where possible especially on motor cruisers. A rescue quoit of DoT approved pattern may be substituted for one	Horseshoe type. Orange or yellow
3	Anchor with warp and/or chain	1	Recommended. 2 recommended for sea-angling and 2 suggested for extended cruising	See Tables on pages 9 *et seq*
4	Bilge pump	1	Recommended	Non-choke diaphragm ty 45 litres (10 galls) per minute
5	Bucket or bailer	1	Essential	Even with a self-bailer a hand bailer or bucket is required except on racing dinghies

Set of tools for electric drill including wire brushes, grinding points, buffs etc

Adjustable cutters or set of hole cutters

Magnet with lanyard

Breast drill with chuck opening to 15 mm; 5/8 in

Metal drills up to 15 mm; 5/8 in

Set of wood drills up to 15 mm; 5/8 in, which have shanks to fit 8 mm; 3/8 in electric drill

Paint brushes, two each size: 12 mm, 25 mm, 35 mm and 50 mm; 1/2 in, 1 in, 1 1/2 in and 2 in

Bevel gauge

Spirit level – at least 300 mm; 12 in and plumb gauge

Tap wrench and set of taps, 4 mm to 16 mm; 3/16 in to 5/8 in

Stocks and dies, 4 mm to 16 mm; 3/16 in to 5/8 in

Equipment	Stowage	Overhaul or test frequency
Whistle recommended. Waterproof light self-activated by seawater recommended	Away from engine, exhaust pipe etc. Preferably not in extreme bow	Annually
30 m (100 ft) of buoyant line of at least 115 kg (250 lb) breaking strain – eg 4 mm (5/32 in) diam. Ulstron-tied to one lifebuoy. Self-igniting light if sailing at night. A lifebuoy without a heaving line must have a drogue	On deck close to helmsman	Annually
Chocks and lashings on deck where appropriate	End of warp secured inboard. Anchor(s) on foredeck or ready for instant use	Annually
Strum box to prevent pipe choking	Bolted down near helmsman is normally best. However a portable pump which can draw water from the sea can sometimes be used for fire fighting	Each voyage
Lanyard		Annually

Safety equipment – craft under 5·5 m (18 ft) LOA (continued)

Item no	Safety item	Number required	Status	Type and size
6	Paddle or oars with rowlocks	1 paddle or 2 oars at least	Recommended by DoT but 2 suggested certainly if oars are carried and even if paddles are carried	To suit size and freeboard of craft
7	Distress signals	2 at least	Essential. It is suggested that for serious cruising the requirements for 13·7 m (45 ft) craft be followed	5-star red hand-held flares for night use. Orange smoke flares for day use
8	Compass	1	Recommended. For serious cruising a second or hand-bearing compass is suggested	Marine type with a card at least 75 mm (3 in) across
9	First Aid kit	1	Recommended	See next column
10	Torch	1	Recommended; 2 suggested for serious cruising	Waterproof type at least large enough to take 2 U-2 batteries
11	Radar reflector	1	Essential in shipping lanes at night or thick weather	At least 300 mm (12 in) cube
12	Radio receiver	1	Recommended for weather forecasts	For extended cruising a DF type is an asset in many areas
13	Engine tool kit	1	Essential whenever there is an engine on board	To suit engine and to include essential spares such as pump impeller etc
14	Firefighting equipment	2	Extinguishers essential. 1 may be carried but if there is no galley or engine an extinguisher may be omitted	1·5 kg (3 lb) dry powder. Carbon dioxide or foam extinguishers of equal capacity may be fitted. BCF & BTM should not be fitted for use in confined spaces as they give off toxic fumes
15.	Auxiliary firefighting equipment	1 1 1	Should only be carried **in addition** to the above equipment	Bucket with lanyard Blanket or rug Asbestos blanket

All the above items are on the British DoT list.

Equipment	Stowage	Overhaul or test frequency
Lanyards on rowlocks. Leather on oars	Locate oars and paddles where they cannot be trodden upon etc or accidentally broken	Annually
Waterproof container. A polythene bag alone is not enough as it is too vulnerable	Away from engine heat, and not in a locker with sharp or heavy items. Near helmsman	See the 'Shelf-life' stamped on the flares. It is usually about 3 years
Gimbals on a sailing craft. Correction card. Light and dimmer switch	Near helmsman and away from steel fittings, instruments which generate a magnetic field	Whenever opportunity offers. Certainly every 2 months
Instruction book and contents as recommended by current medical authorities	In a waterproof container	Half yearly
Spare batteries and bulbs	One near helmsman. Well clear of drips, bilge water etc	Each voyage
At least two securing points (top and bottom) if portable; 3 or more securing bolts or screws if permanently fixed	'Flat' side up at least 3 m (10 ft) above sea level. Rigidly secured at masthead or other high point if possible	Annually
Spare batteries	Away from drips, bilge water and rigidly secured	Each voyage
Tools with moving parts such as pliers need coating with grease or similar treatment to prevent rusting and seizure	In a waterproof container	Monthly
Operating instructions posted up by extinguishers. Also a notice warning crew of dangerous fumes if BCF or BTM types are carried	In a securing bracket on bulkhead or similar location away from drips etc. Also not close to probable source of fire such as galley or engine	Half yearly
This is often carried for bailing in any case Soaked in seawater Specially made for firefighting		Annually

Experience suggests the items on pages 30–35 are almost always as important

Safety equipment – craft under 5·5 m (18 ft) LOA (continued)

Item no	Safety item	Number required	Status	Type and size
16	Charts	As required to cover cruising area	Essential in strange waters, in thick weather in home waters	Large scale Admiralty or yachtsmen's
17	Depth gauge. Either echo-sounder or lead and line	1	Frequently most valuable, often essential	Yacht size echo-sounder sounder. 1·5 kilos (3 lbs) lead and 25 m (12 fathoms) of 5 mm ($^3/_{16}$ in) plaited terylene rope
18	Signalling cloth	1	Suggested since it shows up at a considerable distance. May also be used as weather protection, as a storm sail etc	Day-glo orange waterproof cloth 2 m x 2 m (6 ft x 6 ft)
19	Storm canvas		Essential for sailing craft making passages more than 5 miles from base	To suit vessel. Consult designer or builder for recommended size
20	Warm and waterproof clothing	1 set for each person on board	Essential	Good quality well fitting oilskins and seaboots
21	Portable VHF radio	1	Becoming the most effective safety device	Waterproof hand-held with all essential and local channels

For craft between 5·5 m (18 ft) and 13·7 m (45 ft) LOA

Item no	Safety item	Number required	Status	Type and size
22	Safety harness	One for each person on board For power craft only those on deck are likely to need harnesses so 2 may do	Essential. To be worn in rough weather or medium weather at night	To BSI specification. Children's size where appropriate
23	Lifebuoys	2 or more	Recommended	Horseshoe type. Orange or yellow

Equipment	Stowage	Overhaul or test frequency
A flat working surface, parallel rulers or equivalent, pencil and rubber etc	Away from drips etc. Stowed flat not rolled	Annually
Spare batteries	Within sight of helmsman	Each voyage
Eyeholes at 500 mm (18 in) intervals all round with lanyards	Kept away from engine etc	Annually
		Half yearly
Safety harness integral is a great advantage		Monthly
Spare batteries	In dry location	Monthly

Equipment	Stowage	Overhaul or test frequency
A long safety line is needed for use with short line or extra clip at half line length for use when the vessel is doing more than 8 knots since it can be dangerous to fall overboard at this speed	Generally near the companionway	Monthly
One should have a 30 m (100 ft) buoyant line with a breaking strain of 1150 kg (2500 lb) eg 10 mm ($^3/_8$ in) diam Ulstron (polypropylene multifilament). A self igniting light and smoke signal should be attached to one	Near helmsman	Annually

For craft between 5·5 m (18 ft) and 13·7 m (45 ft) LOA

Item no	Safety item	Number required	Status	Type and size
24	Inflatable liferaft or rigid dInghy or Inflatable dInghy	1	Recommended	DoT type or equivalent With permanent not inflated buoyancy and oars and rowlocks sec- ured. May be collapsible type, with at least 2 sep- arate inflatable compart- ments,one to be kept permanently inflated
25	Bilge pump	1, 2 or 3	Recommended	
26	Flares	6	This is an absolute minimum number	Two to be the rocket parachute type. The rest to be '5-Star' reds
27	Daylight distress smoke signals	2	This is an absolute minimum number	The smallest size acceptable is 180 mm (7 in) x 90 mm (3^{1}/$_{2}$ in) diameter
28	Towrope	1	Recommended	Normally a pair of mooring warps or the anchor warp will do
29	Lifelines	1 or 2 3	Recommended. Far better when children are on board	All round vessel so far as possible. 5 mm ^{3}/$_{16}$ in wire minimum diameter
30	Recognition **name** and/or **number**	1 each side 1 on deck	Recommended Optional	Figures and letters at least 220 mm (9 in) high and 300 mm (12 in) much to be preferred
31	Firefighting equipment	1 2 3 2 1	Recommended for vessel under 9 m (30 ft) if it has only an engine but no cooking facilities or vice versa. Recommended for vessel under 9 m (30 ft) if it has both engine and cooking facilities. Recommended for vessels of between 9 m and 13· 7 m (30 ft & 45 ft) Recommended for all craft over 9 m (30 ft). Recommended in engine space	1·5 kilos (3 pounds) capacity dry powder. See notes on item 14 As above Two, each 1·5 kg (3 lb) capacity dry powder or equivalent and one or more of 2·5 kg (5 lb) capacity dry powder or equivalent Buckets Automatic extinguisher operated by heat

Equipment	Stowage	Overhaul or test frequency
Bailer, painter, oars and rowlocks or paddles. Duplications of many of the parent yacht's safety equipment such as flares etc are found in inflatable life-raft packs and are recommended for inflatable dinghies or rigid dinghies. Also recommended: CO_2 inflation and an overall canopy	On deck or in a locker opening directly on to the deck	Annually
A separate strum box needed on each pump suction pipe to prevent the pipe becoming choked	One near the helmsman If 2 are fitted one should be below deck	Each voyage
A tube fixed on deck is needed for some types of rocket. In a water-proof container. A polythene bag alone is not rugged enough	Away from engine heat and and not in a locker with sharp or heavy objects	See the 'Shelf-life' stamped on the flares. It is usually 3 years after date of manufacture
	Near helmsman	See the 'Shelf-life' stamped on the signals. It is usually 3 years after date of manufacture
A smooth fairlead at the bow and well bolted. Strongly based mooring post or cleat. Also chafing gear to wrap round the warp		Annually
Threaded through stanchions at 1·8 metres (6 ft) intervals	Permanently rigged and kept taut	Annually
	Name and/or number on dodgers or on topsides and/or numbers on sail	Annually
See notes on item 14	See notes on item 14	Half yearly
	When 2 or more extinguishers are carried they should be located at different points throughout the vessel	
	Secured over engine electrics	Half yearly

For craft between 5·5 m (18 ft) and 13·7 m (45 ft) LOA

Item no	Safety item	Number required	Status	Type and size
32	Anchors	2	See item 3	
33	Compass	2	Recommended. One arranged for taking bearings	Marine type with a card of at least 100 mm (4 in) across
34	First Aid box	1	Recommended	See item 9 for size
35	Charts		See item 16	
36	Torch		See item 10	
37	Radar reflector		See item 11	
38	Radio		See item 12	
39	Softwood bungs	1 per seacock	Essential	To fit each seacock
40	2nd VHF radio	1	Recommended	25 watt with usual local channels
41	Engine tool kit		See item 13	

Lights and shapes

Masthead

These show from 22·5 degrees aft of the beam on the port side right round forward to 22·5 degrees aft of the beam on the starboard side, making a total arc of 225 degrees showing forward and on to the beam.

Side

These are green on the starboard side and red on the port side and shine from dead ahead to 22·5 degrees aft of the beam making the arc for each light 112·5 degrees.

Stern

This is a white light placed at or near the aft end of the vessel and showing over an arc from 67·5 degrees on the port side round aft to

Equipment	Stowage	Overhaul or test frequency
Gimballed on a sailing craft. Correction card. Light and dimmer switch	Near helmsman and away from all steel etc as well as away from instruments and electric wiring which generates a magnetic field	Whenever opportunity permits. Certainly every two months
Each bung needs a hole through the top and securing line	Secured to seacock with light lashing	Annually
Spare batteries and emergency aerial	Near chart table	Monthly

67·5 degrees on the starboard side, making a total arc facing aft of 135 degrees.

Towing
This is yellow and shows over the same arc as the stern light.

All-round
This shows a light to a total arc of 360 degrees.

Arc restrictions
Sometimes lights have to be mounted so they are partly obscured by adjacent spars, instruments and so on. For instance, 'not under command' lights are mounted well below masthead height, so the mast must obscure part of the arc of the lights. It is required that the arc which is obscured is 6 degrees or less and this often means setting such lights out on platforms or brackets to clear the mast.

Location and spacing of lights

- On a power-driven vessel of 20 metres (65 ft 7 in) or more in length, the forward masthead light must be at least 6 metres (19 ft 8 in) above the hull. If the beam exceeds 6 metres, then the height above the hull is to be the same as, or greater than, the beam. However, the light need not be more than 12 metres (39 ft 4 in) above the hull.
- When two masthead lights are carried, the after one shall be at least 4·5 metres (14 ft 9 in) higher than the forward one.
- The masthead light of a power vessel of 12 metres length, but less than 20 metres length, shall be placed at a height of 2·5 metres (8 ft 2 in) above the rail.
- On a vessel of less than 12 metres overall length, the masthead light must be at least 1 metre (3 ft 4 in) above the sidelights.
- On a power-driven vessel the sidelights must be located at a height above the hull not greater than three-quarters of the height of the forward masthead light and not so low as to interfere with the deck lights.
- On a power-driven vessel of less than 20 metres overall length, where the sidelights are in a combined lantern, they shall be more than 1 metre below the masthead light.

Shapes displayed during daylight

- On a towing vessel, and on the vessel being towed, when the overall length of the two exceeds 200 metres (656 ft) the diamond shape is carried on the towing vessel and on the towed vessel.
- An auxiliary sailing vessel with sails up and motoring exhibits a conical shape located forward, apex down.
- A vessel fishing exhibits two cones with the apexes together in a vertical line, one above the other. If the vessel is less than 20 metres in length, she may exhibit a basket instead.
- A vessel 'not under command' exhibits two balls in a vertical line.
- A vessel restricted in her ability to manoeuvre exhibits two balls with a diamond between, all in a vertical line.
- A vessel dredging, or engaged in underwater operations, exhibits two balls in a vertical line on the side where an obstruction exists and two diamonds on the side where other vessels may safely pass.
- A small vessel which cannot exhibit the correct shapes owing to her size, when engaged in diving operations exhibits a rigid international code flag A which is at least 1 metre high. This flag is swallow-tailed, the half nearest the pole being white and the other half blue.
- Vessels constrained by draught display a cylinder.

Continued on page 41

Lights and shapes needed on small craft

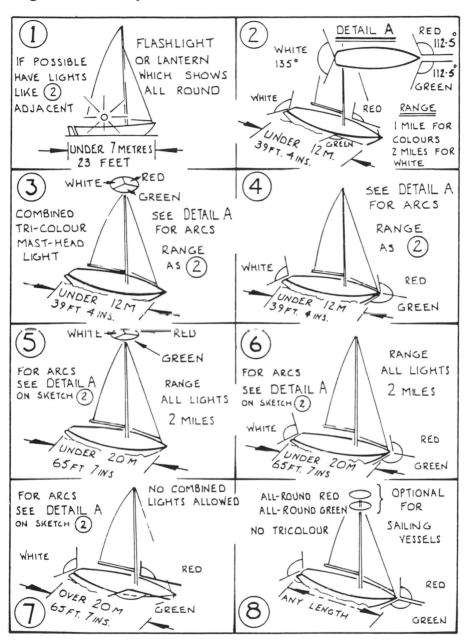

1 IF POSSIBLE HAVE LIGHTS LIKE ② ADJACENT — FLASHLIGHT OR LANTERN WHICH SHOWS ALL ROUND

UNDER 7 METRES 23 FEET

2 DETAIL A — RED 112·5° — GREEN 112·5°

WHITE 135° — WHITE — RED — GREEN

UNDER 39 FT. 4 INS. 12 M.

RANGE — 1 MILE FOR COLOURS — 2 MILES FOR WHITE

3 WHITE — RED — GREEN

COMBINED TRI-COLOUR MAST-HEAD LIGHT — SEE DETAIL A FOR ARCS — RANGE AS ②

UNDER 12 M 39 FT. 4 INS.

4 SEE DETAIL A FOR ARCS — RANGE AS ②

WHITE — RED — GREEN

UNDER 12 M 39 FT. 4 INS.

5 WHITE — RED — GREEN

FOR ARCS SEE DETAIL A ON SKETCH ② — RANGE ALL LIGHTS 2 MILES

UNDER 20 M 65 FT. 7 INS

6 FOR ARCS SEE DETAIL A ON SKETCH ② — RANGE ALL LIGHTS 2 MILES

WHITE — RED — GREEN

UNDER 20 M 65 FT. 7 INS

7 FOR ARCS SEE DETAIL A ON SKETCH ② — NO COMBINED LIGHTS ALLOWED

WHITE — RED — GREEN

OVER 20 M 65 FT. 7 INS.

8 ALL-ROUND RED — ALL-ROUND GREEN — OPTIONAL FOR SAILING VESSELS — NO TRICOLOUR

RED — GREEN

ANY LENGTH

Lights and shapes needed on small craft (continued)

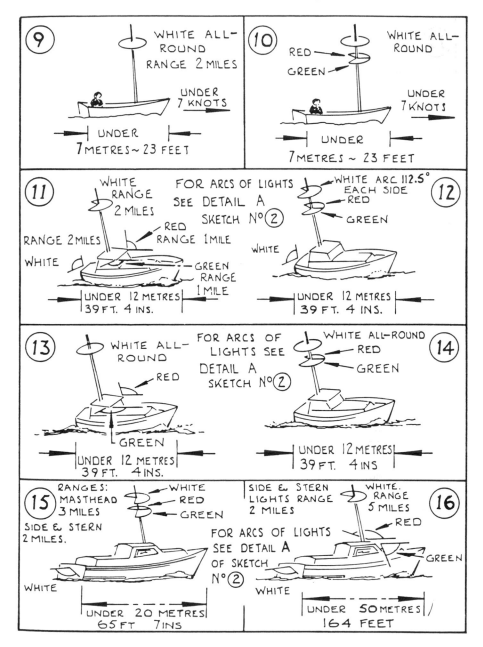

⑨ WHITE ALL-ROUND RANGE 2 MILES
UNDER 7 KNOTS
UNDER 7 METRES ~ 23 FEET

⑩ RED GREEN WHITE ALL-ROUND
UNDER 7 KNOTS
UNDER 7 METRES ~ 23 FEET

⑪ WHITE RANGE 2 MILES
RANGE 2 MILES
WHITE
RED RANGE 1 MILE
GREEN RANGE 1 MILE
UNDER 12 METRES 39 FT. 4 INS.

FOR ARCS OF LIGHTS SEE DETAIL A SKETCH N°②

⑫ WHITE ARC 112.5° EACH SIDE
RED
GREEN
WHITE
UNDER 12 METRES 39 FT. 4 INS.

⑬ WHITE ALL-ROUND
RED
GREEN
UNDER 12 METRES 39 FT. 4 INS.

FOR ARCS OF LIGHTS SEE DETAIL A SKETCH N°②

⑭ WHITE ALL-ROUND
RED
GREEN
UNDER 12 METRES 39 FT. 4 INS

⑮ RANGES: MASTHEAD 3 MILES
SIDE & STERN 2 MILES.
WHITE
RED
GREEN
WHITE
UNDER 20 METRES 65 FT 7 INS

SIDE & STERN LIGHTS RANGE 2 MILES
FOR ARCS OF LIGHTS SEE DETAIL A OF SKETCH N°②

⑯ WHITE. RANGE 5 MILES
RED
GREEN
WHITE
UNDER 50 METRES 164 FEET

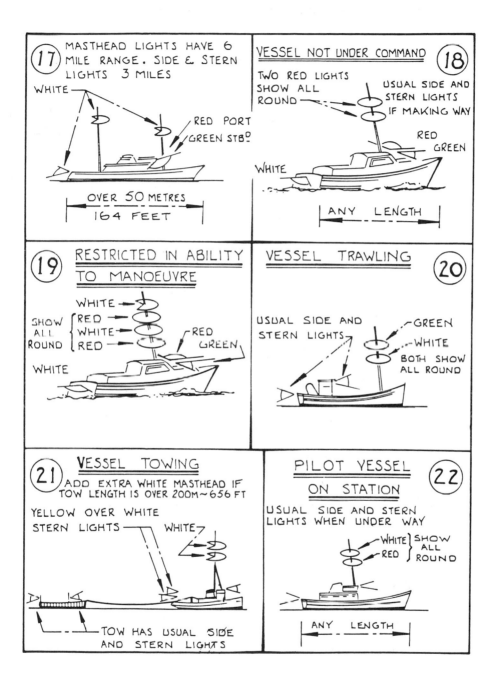

17 MASTHEAD LIGHTS HAVE 6 MILE RANGE. SIDE & STERN LIGHTS 3 MILES

WHITE

RED PORT
GREEN STBD

OVER 50 METRES
164 FEET

18 VESSEL NOT UNDER COMMAND

TWO RED LIGHTS SHOW ALL ROUND

USUAL SIDE AND STERN LIGHTS IF MAKING WAY

RED
GREEN

WHITE

ANY LENGTH

19 RESTRICTED IN ABILITY TO MANOEUVRE

WHITE
SHOW { RED
ALL { WHITE
ROUND { RED

WHITE

RED
GREEN

20 VESSEL TRAWLING

USUAL SIDE AND STERN LIGHTS

GREEN
WHITE
BOTH SHOW ALL ROUND

21 VESSEL TOWING
ADD EXTRA WHITE MASTHEAD IF TOW LENGTH IS OVER 200m~656 FT

YELLOW OVER WHITE STERN LIGHTS

WHITE

TOW HAS USUAL SIDE AND STERN LIGHTS

22 PILOT VESSEL ON STATION

USUAL SIDE AND STERN LIGHTS WHEN UNDER WAY

WHITE } SHOW
RED } ALL ROUND

ANY LENGTH

Lights and shapes needed on small craft (continued)

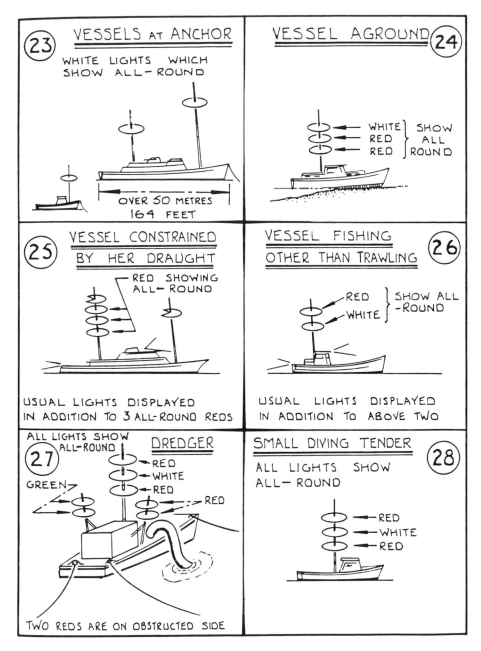

- A vessel at anchor displays a ball and a vessel aground displays three balls in a vertical line.
- When two or three lights are to be carried in a vertical line, they are spaced as follows:
    On a vessel over 20 metres overall length, lights are to be at least 2 metres apart and the lowest light is to be at least 4 metres (13 ft 1 in) above the hull, except where a towing light is required.
    On a vessel of less than 20 metres overall length, lights are to be not less than 1 metre apart and the lowest of these is to be at least 2 metres above the hull, except where a towing light is required.
- When three lights are carried, they are to be equally spaced.
- The lower of the two all-round lights on a fishing vessel shall be at a height above the sidelights not less than twice the distance between the two vertical lights.
- When at anchor, and two anchor lights are carried, the forward light is to be at least 4·5 metres (14 ft 9 in) above the aft one.
- On a vessel of 50 metres (164 ft) or more in length, the forward anchor light is to be at least 6 metres (19 ft 8 in) above the hull.
- When two masthead lights are fitted on a power-driven vessel, the horizontal distance between them shall be not less than one half the overall length of the vessel, but need not be more than 100 metres (328 ft).
- The forward light is not to be more than one-quarter of the length of the vessel from the stem.
- On a power-driven vessel of 20 metres overall length, the sidelights shall not be placed in front of the forward masthead light. They shall be placed at or near the side of the vessel.

Shapes - dimensions
These are to have the following dimensions:
- The ball is to have a diameter of not less than 0·6 metres (2 ft).
- The cone shall have a diameter at the base of not less than 0·6 metres (2 ft) and a height equal to its diameter.
- A cylinder shall have a diameter of not less than 0·6 metres (2 ft) and a height of twice the diameter.
- A diamond shape consists of two cones as defined above, having a common base.
- The vertical distance between shapes shall be at least 1·5 metres (5 ft).
- In vessels of less than 20 metres overall length, smaller shapes may be acceptable commensurate with the size of the vessel.

2 MATERIALS

Brass and steel rod* (metric measure) — weight in kg/m and lb/ft

Diameter or width across flats millimetres	Decimal equivalent inches	d ○ Weight kg/m	Weight lb/ft	d ⬡ Weight kg/m	Weight lb/ft	d ▢ Weight kg/m	Weight lb/ft
1	.0394	.0067	.0045	.0073	.0049	.0085	.0057
2	.0787	.0266	.0179	.0293	.0197	.0339	.0228
3	.1181	.0598	.0402	.0659	.0443	.0762	.0512
4	.1575	.1064	.0715	.1173	.0788	.1354	.0910
5	.1969	.1664	.1118	.1833	.1232	.2118	.1423
6	.2362	.2395	.1609	.2642	.1775	.3049	.2049
7	.2756	.3261	.2191	.3595	.2416	.4152	.2790
8	.3150	.4258	.2861	.4695	.3155	.5422	.3643
9	.3543	.5389	.3621	.5942	.3993	.6862	.4611
10	.3937	.6654	.4471	.7337	.4930	.8471	.5692
11	.4331	.8050	.5409	.8877	.5965	1.0249	.6887
12	.4724	.9581	.6438	1.0563	.7098	1.2199	.8197
13	.5118	1.1243	.7555	1.2398	.8331	1.4316	.9620
14	.5512	1.3040	.8762	1.4378	.9661	1.6602	1.1156
15	.5906	1.4970	1.0059	1.6507	1.1092	1.9059	1.2807
16	.6299	1.7031	1.1444	1.8780	1.2619	2.1686	1.4572
17	.6693	1.9228	1.2920	2.1201	1.4266	2.4481	1.6450
18	.7087	2.1555	1.4484	2.3748	1.5971	2.7445	1.8442
19	.7480	2.4018	1.6139	2.6483	1.7795	3.0580	2.0548
20	.7874	2.6612	1.7882	2.9343	1.9717	3.3883	2.2768
21	.8268	2.9340	1.9715	3.2352	2.1739	3.7357	2.5102
22	.8661	3.2200	2.1637	3.5507	2.3859	4.0998	2.7549
23	.9055	3.5194	2.3649	3.8808	2.6077	4.4811	3.0111
24	.9449	3.8321	2.5750	4.2254	2.8393	4.8792	3.2786
25	.9843	4.1582	2.7941	4.5850	3.0809	5.2943	3.5575
26	1.0236	4.4975	3.0221	4.9591	3.3323	5.7263	3.8478
27	1.0630	4.8500	3.2590	5.3480	3.5936	6.1753	4.1495
28	1.1024	5.2160	3.5049	5.7514	3.8647	6.6411	4.4625
29	1.1417	5.5952	3.7597	6.1696	4.1457	7.1240	4.7870
30	1.1811	5.9878	4.0235	6.6023	4.4364	7.6239	5.1229
31	1.2205	6.3935	4.2961	7.0498	4.7371	8.1405	5.4700
32	1.2598	6.8127	4.5778	7.5120	5.0477	8.6741	5.8286
33	1.2992	7.2452	4.8684	7.9890	5.3682	9.2248	6.1986
34	1.3386	7.6909	5.1679	8.4805	5.6985	9.7922	6.5799
35	1.3780	8.1500	5.4764	8.9866	6.0386	10.3768	6.9727
36	1.4173	8.6223	5.7938	9.5075	6.3886	10.9783	7.3769
37	1.4567	9.1079	6.1201	10.0430	6.7484	11.5966	7.7924
38	1.4961	9.6069	6.4554	10.5932	7.1181	12.2318	8.2192
39	1.5354	10.1192	6.7996	11.1579	7.4976	12.8841	8.6575
40	1.5748	10.6448	7.1528	11.7366	7.8871	13.5533	9.1072
41	1.6142	11.1837	7.5149	12.3318	8.2864	14.2395	9.5683
42	1.6535	11.7359	7.8860	12.9406	8.6955	14.9426	10.0407

*STEEL ROD This is of the order of 8% lighter than brass so for many practical purposes can be taken as the same

Diameter or width across flats (millimetres)	Decimal equivalent inches	Weight kg/m	Weight lb/ft	Weight kg/m	Weight lb/ft	Weight kg/m	Weight lb/ft
43	1.6929	12.3015	8.2660	13.5643	9.1146	15.6627	10.5246
44	1.7323	12.8802	8.6549	14.2025	9.5434	16.3997	11.0198
45	1.7717	13.4724	9.0528	14.8554	9.9821	17.1536	11.5264
46	1.8110	14.0778	9.4596	15.5230	10.4307	17.9243	12.0443
47	1.8504	14.6964	9.8753	16.2053	10.8892	18.7122	12.5737
48	1.8898	15.3285	10.3000	16.9021	11.3574	19.5169	13.1144
49	1.9291	15.9739	10.7337	17.6137	11.8356	20.3385	13.6665
50	1.9685	16.6326	11.1763	18.3400	12.3236	21.1772	14.2301
51	2.0079	17.3045	11.6278	19.0810	12.8215	22.0862	14.8409
52	2.0472	17.9897	12.0882	19.8367	13.3293	22.9052	15.3912
53	2.0866	18.6882	12.5576	20.6068	13.8468	23.7947	15.9889
54	2.1260	19.4002	13.0360	21.3917	14.3742	24.7010	16.5979
55	2.1654	20.1254	13.5233	22.1914	14.9116	25.6243	17.2183
56	2.2047	20.8638	14.0195	23.0056	15.4587	26.5647	17.8502
57	2.2441	21.6157	14.5247	23.8346	16.0157	27.5219	18.4934
58	2.2835	22.3807	15.0388	24.6782	16.5826	28.4959	19.1479
59	2.3228	23.1591	15.5618	25.5366	17.1594	29.4870	19.8139
60	2.3622	23.9508	16.0938	26.4096	17.7460	30.4952	20.4913
61	2.4016	24.7558	16.6347	27.2973	18.3425	31.5201	21.1800
62	2.4409	25.5741	17.1846	28.1996	18.9488	32.5620	21.8801
63	2.4803	26.4057	17.7434	29.1166	19.5650	33.6210	22.5917
64	2.5197	27.2507	18.3112	30.0482	20.1910	34.6966	23.3145
65	2.5591	28.1088	18.8878	30.9944	20.8268	35.7893	24.0487
66	2.5984	28.9805	19.4735	31.9555	21.4726	36.8992	24.7945
67	2.6378	29.8652	20.0680	32.9312	22.1282	38.0256	25.5514
68	2.6772	30.7635	20.6716	33.9216	22.7937	39.1693	26.3199
69	2.7165	31.6748	21.2840	34.9266	23.4690	40.3296	27.0996
70	2.7559	32.5996	21.9054	35.9464	24.1543	41.5072	27.8909
71	2.7953	33.5376	22.5357	36.9806	24.8492	42.7015	28.6934
72	2.8347	34.4892	23.1751	38.0299	25.5543	43.9131	29.5075
73	2.8740	35.4537	23.8232	39.0934	26.2689	45.1411	30.3327
74	2.9134	36.4317	24.4804	40.1719	26.9936	46.3864	31.1695
75	2.9528	37.4230	25.1465	41.2650	27.7281	47.6484	32.0175
76	2.9921	38.4277	25.8216	42.3726	28.4724	48.9277	32.8771
77	3.0315	39.4455	26.5055	43.4949	29.2265	50.2236	33.7479
78	3.0709	40.4768	27.1985	44.6322	29.9907	51.5367	34.6302
79	3.1102	41.5212	27.9003	45.7837	30.7645	52.8665	35.5238
80	3.1496	42.5792	28.6112	46.9503	31.5484	54.2136	36.4290
81	3.1890	43.6502	29.3309	48.1315	32.3421	55.5771	37.3452
82	3.2284	44.7347	30.0596	49.3271	33.1455	56.9580	38.2731
83	3.2677	45.8324	30.7942	50.5376	33.9589	58.3556	39.2122
84	3.3071	46.9435	31.5438	51.7629	34.7822	59.7704	40.1629
85	3.3465	48.0678	32.2993	53.0024	35.6151	61.2019	41.1248
86	3.3858	49.2055	33.0638	54.2569	36.4581	62.6504	42.0981
87	3.4252	50.3565	33.8372	55.5261	37.3109	64.1158	43.0828
88	3.4646	51.5207	34.6195	56.8100	38.1736	65.5984	44.0790
89	3.5039	52.6984	35.4108	58.1083	39.0460	67.0976	45.0864
90	3.5433	53.8892	36.2110	59.4214	39.9284	68.6141	46.1054
91	3.5827	55.0935	37.0202	60.7492	40.8206	70.1472	47.1356
92	3.6221	56.3110	37.8383	62.0919	41.7228	71.6975	48.1773
93	3.6614	57.5417	38.6653	63.4488	42.6366	73.2645	49.2303
94	3.7008	58.7858	39.5013	64.8208	43.5565	74.8486	50.2947
95	3.7402	60.0432	40.3462	66.2072	44.4881	76.4494	51.3704
96	3.7795	61.3140	41.2001	67.6085	45.4297	78.0675	52.4577
97	3.8189	62.5980	42.0629	69.0242	46.3810	79.7022	53.5561

STEEL ROD This is of the order of 8% lighter than brass so for many practical purposes can be taken as the same

43

Brass and steel rod (metric measure) – weights (continued)

Diameter or width across flats (millimetres)	Decimal equivalent inches	Weight kg/m	Weight lb/ft	Weight kg/m	Weight lb/ft	Weight kg/m	Weight lb/ft
98	3.8583	63.8954	42.9347	70.4550	47.3424	81.3541	54.6661
99	3.8976	65.2059	43.8153	71.9000	48.3134	83.0228	55.7874
100	3.9370	66.5300	44.7050	73.3599	49.2944	84.7086	56.9202
101	3.9764	67.8671	45.6035	74.8343	50.2851	86.4111	58.0642
102	4.0158	69.2178	46.5111	76.3237	51.2859	88.1309	59.2198
103	4.0551	70.5816	47.4275	77.8275	52.2964	89.8673	60.3866
104	4.0945	71.9588	48.3529	79.3461	53.3168	91.6209	61.5649
105	4.1339	73.3492	49.2872	80.8792	54.3470	93.3911	62.7544
106	4.1732	74.7530	50.2305	82.4272	55.3872	95.1787	63.9556
107	4.2126	76.1701	51.1827	83.9897	56.4371	96.9827	65.1678
108	4.2520	77.6006	52.1439	85.5672	57.4971	98.8040	66.3916
109	4.2913	79.0443	53.1140	87.1590	58.5667	100.6422	67.6268
110	4.3307	80.5012	54.0930	88.7658	59.6464	102.4972	68.8733
111	4.3701	81.9715	55.0810	90.3969	60.7357	104.3693	70.1312
112	4.4095	83.4551	56.0779	92.0228	61.8350	106.2584	71.4006
113	4.4488	84.9521	57.0838	93.6733	62.9440	108.1642	72.6812
114	4.4882	86.4623	58.0986	95.3387	64.0631	110.0871	73.9733
115	4.5276	87.9858	59.1223	97.0186	65.1919	112.0269	75.2768
116	4.5669	89.5227	60.1550	98.7132	66.3306	113.9838	76.5917
117	4.6063	91.0728	61.1966	100.4224	67.4791	115.9574	77.9179
118	4.6457	92.6363	62.2472	102.1465	68.6376	117.9480	79.2555
119	4.6850	94.2130	63.3067	103.8851	69.8059	119.9556	80.6045
120	4.7244	95.8032	64.3752	105.6385	70.9841	121.9802	81.9649
121	4.7638	97.4064	65.4525	107.4062	72.1719	124.0217	83.3367
122	4.8032	99.0232	66.5389	109.1891	73.3699	126.0802	84.7199
123	4.8425	100.6531	67.6341	110.9862	74.5775	128.1553	86.1143
124	4.8819	102.2965	68.7384	112.7983	75.7951	130.2479	87.5204
125	4.9213	103.9530	69.8515	114.6249	77.0225	132.3569	88.9376
126	4.9606	105.6229	70.9736	116.4662	78.2598	134.4831	90.3663
127	5.0000	107.3061	72.1046	118.3222	79.5069	136.6263	91.8064
128	5.0394	109.0028	73.2447	120.1931	80.7641	138.7866	93.2580
129	5.0787	110.7124	74.3935	122.0784	82.0309	140.9635	94.7208
130	5.1181	112.4356	75.5514	123.9785	83.3077	143.1574	96.1950
131	5.1575	114.1720	76.7182	125.8931	84.5942	145.3685	97.6806
132	5.1969	115.9219	77.8940	127.8224	85.8906	147.5961	99.1776
133	5.2362	117.6848	79.0786	129.7666	87.1970	149.8409	100.6860
134	5.2756	119.4612	80.2723	131.7252	88.5131	152.1027	102.2058
135	5.3150	121.2508	81.4748	133.6985	89.8391	154.3811	103.7368
136	5.3543	123.0539	82.6864	135.6866	91.1750	156.6770	105.2795
137	5.3937	124.8701	83.9068	137.6893	92.5207	158.9893	106.8333
138	5.4331	126.6997	85.1362	139.7067	93.8763	161.3189	108.3987
139	5.4724	128.5425	86.3745	141.7388	95.2418	163.6652	109.9753
140	5.5118	130.3988	87.6218	143.7856	96.6171	166.0288	111.5635
141	5.5512	132.2682	88.8780	145.8470	98.0023	168.4089	113.1628
142	5.5906	134.1511	90.1432	147.9231	99.3973	170.8062	114.7737
143	5.6299	136.0471	91.4172	150.0138	100.8022	173.2204	116.3959
144	5.6693	137.9566	92.7003	152.1192	102.2169	175.6517	118.0296
145	5.7087	139.8792	93.9922	154.2393	103.6415	178.0997	119.6746
146	5.7480	141.8153	95.2932	156.3743	105.0761	180.5646	121.3309
147	5.7874	143.7646	96.6030	158.5237	106.5204	183.0465	122.9986
148	5.8268	145.7272	97.9218	160.6877	107.9745	185.5454	124.6777
149	5.8661	147.7031	99.2495	162.8664	109.4385	188.0613	126.3683
150	5.9055	149.6924	100.5862	165.0600	110.9125	190.5945	128.0705

STEEL ROD This is of the order of 8% lighter than brass so for many practical purposes can be taken as the same

Brass and steel rod – standard hexagons for bolts, screws and nuts

Nominal sizes			
Unified			
BS 1083 Whitworth and fine inches	BS 1768 Normal series inches	BS 1769 Heavy series inches	Widths across flats inches
	$\frac{1}{4}$		.4375
			.445
	$\frac{5}{16}$		.500
$\frac{5}{16}$			.525
			.5625
	$\frac{3}{8}$		.600
$\frac{3}{8}$			.625
	$\frac{7}{16}$ Bolts & Screws $\frac{7}{16}$ Nuts		.6875
$\frac{7}{16}$			.710
	$\frac{1}{2}$		.750
	$\frac{9}{16}$ Bolts & Screws†		.8125
$\frac{1}{2}$			.820
$\frac{9}{16}$	$\frac{9}{16}$ Nuts†	$\frac{1}{2}$	.875
			.920
	$\frac{5}{8}$		.9375
$\frac{5}{8}$			1.010
		$\frac{5}{8}$	1.0625
	$\frac{3}{4}$		1.125
$\frac{3}{4}$			1.200
		$\frac{3}{4}$	1.250
$\frac{7}{8}$			1.300
	$\frac{7}{8}$		1.3125
		$\frac{7}{8}$	1.4375
1			1.480
	1		1.500
		1	1.625
$1\frac{1}{8}$			1.670
	$1\frac{1}{8}$		1.6875
		$1\frac{1}{8}$	1.8125
$1\frac{1}{4}$			1.860
	$1\frac{1}{4}$		1.875
		$1\frac{1}{4}$	2.000
$1\frac{3}{8}$*			2.050
	$1\frac{3}{8}$†		2.0625
		$1\frac{3}{8}$†	2.1875
$1\frac{1}{2}$			2.220
	$1\frac{1}{2}$		2.250
		$1\frac{1}{2}$	2.375
$1\frac{3}{4}$			2.580
	$1\frac{3}{4}$		2.625
		$1\frac{3}{4}$	2.750
2			2.760
	2		3.000
		2	3.125

Note: To avoid confusion with standards now obsolete, purchasers of hexagon rods are advised to specify the decimal sizes across flats.
STEEL ROD This is of the order of 8% lighter than brass so for many practical purposes can be taken as the same
*Not standard with BSW thread
†Avoid if possible

Brass and steel rod (Imperial measure) – weight in lb/ft

Diameter or width across flats in inches	Decimal equivalent	Millimetre equivalent	Weight (lb) per foot — Round	Weight (lb) per foot — Hexagon	Weight (lb) per foot — Square
1/16	.0625	1.588	.0113	.0124	.0144
5/64	.0781	1.984	.0176	.0194	.0224
3/32	.0938	2.381	.0254	.0280	.0323
7/64	.1094	2.778	.0345	.0380	.0439
1/8	.1250	3.175	.0450	.0497	.0574
9/64	.1406	3.572	.0570	.0629	.0726
5/32	.1563	3.969	.0704	.0776	.0896
11/64	.1719	4.366	.0852	.0939	.1085
3/16	.1875	4.763	.1014	.1118	.1291
13/64	.2031	5.159	.1190	.1312	.1515
7/32	.2188	5.556	.1380	.1522	.1757
15/64	.2344	5.953	.1584	.1747	.2017
1/4	.2500	6.350	.1803	.1988	.2295
17/64	.2656	6.747	.2035	.2244	.2591
9/32	.2813	7.144	.2281	.2515	.2905
19/64	.2969	7.541	.2542	.2803	.3236
5/16	.3125	7.938	.2817	.3106	.3586
21/64	.3281	8.334	.3105	.3424	.3954
11/32	.3438	8.731	.3408	.3757	.4339
23/64	.3594	9.128	.3725	.4107	.4742
3/8	.3750	9.525	.4055	.4472	.5164
25/64	.3906	9.922	.4401	.4852	.5603
13/32	.4063	10.319	.4760	.5248	.6060
27/64	.4219	10.716	.5133	.5660	.6535
7/16	.4375	11.113	.5520	.6087	.7029
29/64	.4531	11.509	.5921	.6529	.7539
15/32	.4688	11.906	.6337	.6987	.8068
31/64	.4844	12.303	.6766	.7461	.8615
1/2	.5000	12.700	.7210	.7950	.9180
33/64	.5156	13.097	.7668	.8455	.9763
17/32	.5313	13.494	.8140	.8975	1.0363
35/64	.5469	13.891	.8625	.9510	1.0982
9/16	.5625	14.288	.9125	1.0062	1.1619
37/64	.5781	14.684	.9639	1.0629	1.2273
19/32	.5938	15.081	1.0167	1.1211	1.2945
39/64	.6094	15.478	1.0709	1.1809	1.3636
5/8	.6250	15.875	1.1265	1.2422	1.4344
41/64	.6406	16.272	1.1836	1.3051	1.5070
21/32	.6563	16.669	1.2420	1.3695	1.5814
43/64	.6719	17.066	1.3019	1.4355	1.6576
11/16	.6875	17.463	1.3632	1.5031	1.7356
45/64	.7031	17.859	1.4258	1.5721	1.8154
23/32	.7188	18.256	1.4899	1.6428	1.8970
47/64	.7344	18.653	1.5554	1.7150	1.9803
3/4	.7500	19.050	1.6223	1.7888	2.0655
49/64	.7656	19.447	1.6905	1.8641	2.1525
25/32	.7813	19.844	1.7602	1.9409	2.2412
51/64	.7969	20.241	1.8314	2.0193	2.3318
13/16	.8125	20.638	1.9039	2.0993	2.4241
53/64	.8281	21.034	1.9778	2.1808	2.5182
27/32	.8438	21.431	2.0531	2.2639	2.6141
55/64	.8594	21.828	2.1299	2.3485	2.7119
7/8	.8750	22.225	2.2080	2.4347	2.8114
57/64	.8906	22.622	2.2876	2.5224	2.9127
29/32	.9063	23.019	2.3686	2.6117	3.0158
59/64	.9219	23.416	2.4510	2.7025	3.1206
15/16	.9375	23.813	2.5348	2.7949	3.2274
61/64	.9531	24.209	2.6200	2.8889	3.3358
31/32	.9688	24.606	2.7066	2.9844	3.4461
63/64	.9844	25.003	2.7946	3.0814	3.5581
1	1.0000	25.400	2.8840	3.1800	3.6720

STEEL ROD This is of the order of 8% lighter than brass so for many practical purposes can be taken as the same

Diameter or width across flats in inches	Decimal equivalent	Millimetre equivalent	Weight (lb) per foot — Round ↑d○	Weight (lb) per foot — Hexagon ↑d⬡	Weight (lb) per foot — Square ↑d▢
1 1/64	1.0156	25.797	2.9748	3.2801	3.7876
1 1/32	1.0313	26.194	3.0671	3.3819	3.9051
1 3/64	1.0469	26.591	3.1607	3.4851	4.0243
1 1/16	1.0625	26.988	3.2558	3.5899	4.1454
1 5/64	1.0781	27.384	3.3522	3.6963	4.2681
1 3/32	1.0938	27.781	3.4501	3.8042	4.3928
1 7/64	1.1094	28.178	3.5494	3.9137	4.5192
1 1/8	1.1250	28.575	3.6500	4.0247	4.6474
1 9/64	1.1406	28.972	3.7522	4.1373	4.7774
1 5/32	1.1562	29.369	3.8556	4.2514	4.9091
1 11/64	1.1719	29.766	3.9606	4.3671	5.0427
1 3/16	1.1875	30.163	4.0669	4.4843	5.1781
1 13/64	1.2031	30.559	4.1746	4.6031	5.3153
1 7/32	1.2188	30.956	4.2037	4.7234	5.4542
1 15/64	1.2344	31.353	4.3943	4.8453	5.5950
1 1/4	1.2500	31.750	4.5063	4.9688	5.7375
1 17/64	1.2656	32.147	4.6196	5.0938	5.8818
1 9/32	1.2813	32.544	4.7344	5.2203	6.0280
1 19/64	1.2969	32.941	4.8505	5.3484	6.1759
1 5/16	1.3125	33.338	4.9681	5.4781	6.3256
1 21/64	1.3281	33.734	5.0871	5.6093	6.4771
1 11/32	1.3438	34.131	5.2075	5.7420	6.6304
1 23/64	1.3594	34.528	5.3293	5.8763	6.7855
1 3/8	1.3750	34.925	5.4525	6.0122	6.9424
1 25/64	1.3906	35.322	5.5772	6.1496	7.1011
1 13/32	1.4063	35.719	5.7032	6.2886	7.2615
1 27/64	1.4219	36.116	5.8307	6.4291	7.4238
1 7/16	1.4375	36.513	5.9595	6.5712	7.5879
1 29/64	1.4531	36.909	6.0898	6.7148	7.7537
1 15/32	1.4688	37.306	6.2215	6.8600	7.9213
1 31/64	1.4844	37.703	6.3545	7.0067	8.0908
1 1/2	1.5000	38.100	6.4890	7.1550	8.2620
1 33/64	1.5156	38.497	6.6249	7.3048	8.4350
1 17/32	1.5313	38.894	6.7622	7.4562	8.6098
1 35/64	1.5469	39.291	6.9009	7.6092	8.7864
1 9/16	1.5625	39.688	7.0410	7.7637	8.9649
1 37/64	1.5781	40.084	7.1825	7.9197	9.1450
1 19/32	1.5938	40.481	7.3255	8.0773	9.3270
1 39/64	1.6094	40.878	7.4698	8.2365	9.5108
1 5/8	1.6250	41.275	7.6155	8.3972	9.6964
1 41/64	1.6406	41.672	7.7627	8.5594	9.8837
1 21/32	1.6563	42.069	7.9113	8.7232	10.0729
1 43/64	1.6719	42.466	8.0613	8.8886	10.2639
1 11/16	1.6875	42.863	8.2127	9.0556	10.4566
1 45/64	1.7031	43.259	8.3654	9.2240	10.6511
1 23/32	1.7188	43.656	8.5196	9.3940	10.8475
1 47/64	1.7344	44.053	8.6752	9.5656	11.0456
1 3/4	1.7500	44.450	8.8323	9.7388	11.2455
1 49/64	1.7656	44.847	8.9907	9.9134	11.4472
1 25/32	1.7813	45.244	9.1505	10.0897	11.6507
1 51/64	1.7969	45.641	9.3117	10.2675	11.8560
1 13/16	1.8125	46.038	9.4744	10.4468	12.0631
1 53/64	1.8281	46.434	9.6384	10.6277	12.2720
1 27/32	1.8438	46.831	9.8039	10.8101	12.4826
1 55/64	1.8594	47.228	9.9708	10.9942	12.6951
1 7/8	1.8750	47.625	10.1390	11.1797	12.9094
1 57/64	1.8906	48.022	10.3087	11.3668	13.1254
1 29/32	1.9063	48.419	10.4799	11.5555	13.3433
1 59/64	1.9219	48.816	10.6523	11.7456	13.5629
1 15/16	1.9375	49.213	10.8263	11.9374	13.7844
1 61/64	1.9531	49.609	11.0016	12.1307	14.0076
1 31/32	1.9688	50.006	11.1783	12.3256	14.2326
1 63/64	1.9844	50.403	11.3564	12.5220	14.4594
2	2.0000	50.800	11.5360	12.7200	14.6880

STEEL ROD This is of the order of 8% lighter than brass so for many practical purposes can be taken as the same

Brass and steel rod (Imperial measure) – weight in lb/ft (continued)

Diameter or width across flats in inches	Decimal equivalent	Millimetre equivalent	Weight (lb) per foot		
			d ○	d ⬡	d ▢
2 1/32	2.0313	51.594	11.8993	13.1206	15.1506
2 1/16	2.0625	52.388	12.2683	13.5274	15.6204
2 3/32	2.0938	53.181	12.6429	13.9405	16.0973
2 1/8	2.1250	53.975	13.0230	14.3597	16.5814
2 5/32	2.1562	54.769	13.4089	14.7851	17.0726
2 3/16	2.1875	55.563	13.8004	15.2168	17.5711
2 7/32	2.2188	56.356	14.1975	15.6547	18.0767
2 1/4	2.2500	57.150	14.6003	16.0988	18.5895
2 9/32	2.2813	57.944	15.0086	16.5490	19.1095
2 5/16	2.3125	58.738	15.4227	17.0056	19.6366
2 11/32	2.3438	59.531	15.8423	17.4682	20.1709
2 3/8	2.3750	60.325	16.2675	17.9372	20.7124
2 13/32	2.4063	61.119	16.6985	18.4123	21.2610
2 7/16	2.4375	61.913	17.1350	18.8937	21.8169
2 15/32	2.4688	62.706	17.5772	19.3812	22.3798
2 1/2	2.5000	63.500	18.0250	19.8750	22.9500
2 17/32	2.5313	64.294	18.4785	20.3750	23.5273
2 9/16	2.5625	65.088	18.9375	20.8812	24.1119
2 19/32	2.5938	65.881	19.4022	21.3936	24.7035
2 5/8	2.6250	66.675	19.8725	21.9122	25.3024
2 21/32	2.6563	67.469	20.3485	22.4370	25.9084
2 11/16	2.6875	68.263	20.8302	22.9681	26.5216
2 23/32	2.7188	69.056	21.3174	23.5053	27.1420
2 3/4	2.7500	69.850	21.8103	24.0488	27.7695
2 25/32	2.7813	70.644	22.3087	24.5984	28.4042
2 13/16	2.8125	71.438	22.8129	25.1543	29.0461
2 27/32	2.8438	72.231	23.3226	25.7164	29.6951
2 7/8	2.8750	73.025	23.8380	26.2847	30.3514
2 29/32	2.9063	73.819	24.3591	26.8592	31.0148
2 15/16	2.9375	74.613	24.8858	27.4399	31.6854
2 31/32	2.9688	75.406	25.4181	28.0269	32.3631
3	3.0000	76.200	25.9560	28.6200	33.0480

STEEL ROD This is of the order of 8% lighter than brass so for many practical purposes can be taken as the same

Diameter or width across flats in inches	Decimal equivalent	Millimetre equivalent	Weight (lb) per foot d ◯	Weight (lb) per foot d ⬡	Weight (lb) per foot d ▢
3 1/16	3.0625	77.788	27.0488	29.8249	34.4394
3 1/8	3.1250	79.375	28.1640	31.0547	35.8594
3 3/16	3.1875	80.963	29.3019	32.3093	37.3081
3 1/4	3.2500	82.550	30.4623	33.5888	38.7855
3 5/16	3.3125	84.138	31.6452	34.8931	40.2916
3 3/8	3.3750	85.725	32.8505	36.2222	41.8264
3 7/16	3.4375	87.313	34.0785	37.5762	43.3899
3 1/2	3.5000	88.900	35.2900	38.9550	44.9820
3 9/16	3.5625	90.488	36.6020	40.3587	46.6029
3 5/8	3.6250	92.075	37.8975	41.7872	48.2524
3 11/16	3.6875	93.663	39.2157	43.2406	49.9306
3 3/4	3.7500	95.250	40.5563	44.7188	51.6375
3 13/16	3.8125	96.838	41.9194	46.2218	53.3701
3 7/8	3.8750	98.425	43.3050	47.7497	55.1374
3 15/16	3.9375	100.013	44.7133	49.3024	56.9304
4	4.0000	101.600	46.1440	50.8800	58.7520
4 1/8	4.1250	104.775	49.0730	54.1097	62.4814
4 1/4	4.2500	107.950	52.0923	57.4388	66.3255
4 3/8	4.3750	111.125	55.2015	60.8672	70.2844
4 1/2	4.5000	114.300	58.4010	64.3950	74.3580
4 5/8	4.6250	117.475	61.6905	68.0222	78.5464
4 3/4	4.7500	120.650	65.0703	71.7488	82.8495
4 7/8	4.8750	123.825	68.5400	75.5747	87.2674
5	5.0000	127.000	72.1000	79.5000	91.8000
5 1/8	5.1250	130.175	75.7500	83.5247	96.4474
5 1/4	5.2500	133.350	79.4903	87.6488	101.2095
5 3/8	5.3750	136.525	83.3205	91.8722	106.0864
5 1/2	5.5000	139.700	87.2410	96.1950	111.0780
5 5/8	5.6250	142.875	91.2515	100.6172	116.1844
5 3/4	5.7500	146.050	95.3522	105.1388	121.4055
5 7/8	5.8750	149.225	99.5430	109.7597	126.7414
6	6.0000	152.400	103.8240	114.4800	132.1920

STEEL ROD This is of the order of 8% lighter than brass so for many practical purposes can be taken as the same

Brass and steel rod (decimals of an inch) – weight in lb/ft

Inches	Wt (lb) per foot	Add this for each ·001 increase in d	Wt (lb) per foot	Add this for each ·001 increase in d	Wt (lb) per foot	Add this for each ·001 increase in d	Inches	Wt (lb) per foot	Add this for each ·001 increase in d	Wt (lb) per foot	Add this for each ·001 increase in d	Wt (lb) per foot	Add this for each ·001 increase in d
.06	.0104	.00037	.0114	.00041	.0132	.00048	.54	.8410	.00314	.9273	.00347	1.0708	.00400
.07	.0141	.00044	.0156	.00048	.0180	.00055	.55	.8724	.00320	.9620	.00353	1.1108	.00408
.08	.0185	.00049	.0204	.00054	.0235	.00062	.56	.9044	.00326	.9973	.00359	1.1515	.00415
.09	.0234	.00054	.0258	.00060	.0297	.00070	.57	.9370	.00332	1.0332	.00366	1.1930	.00422
.10	.0288	.00061	.0318	.00067	.0367	.00077	.58	.9702	.00337	1.0698	.00372	1.2353	.00430
.11	.0349	.00066	.0385	.00073	.0444	.00084	.59	1.0039	.00343	1.1070	.00378	1.2782	.00437
.12	.0415	.00072	.0458	.00080	.0529	.00092	.60	1.0382	.00349	1.1448	.00385	1.3219	.00444
.13	.0487	.00078	.0537	.00086	.0621	.00099	.61	1.0731	.00355	1.1833	.00391	1.3664	.00452
.14	.0565	.00084	.0623	.00092	.0720	.00107	.62	1.1086	.00361	1.2224	.00398	1.4115	.00459
.15	.0649	.00089	.0716	.00099	.0826	.00114	.63	1.1447	.00366	1.2622	.00404	1.4574	.00466
.16	.0738	.00095	.0814	.00105	.0940	.00121	.64	1.1813	.00372	1.3025	.00410	1.5041	.00474
.17	.0833	.00101	.0919	.00111	.1061	.00129	.65	1.2185	.00378	1.3436	.00417	1.5514	.00481
.18	.0934	.00107	.1030	.00118	.1190	.00136	.66	1.2563	.00383	1.3852	.00423	1.5995	.00488
.19	.1041	.00113	.1148	.00124	.1326	.00143	.67	1.2946	.00390	1.4275	.00429	1.6484	.00496
.20	.1154	.00118	.1272	.00130	.1469	.00151	.68	1.3336	.00395	1.4705	.00436	1.6979	.00503
.21	.1272	.00124	.1402	.00137	.1619	.00158	.69	1.3731	.00401	1.5140	.00442	1.7482	.00510
.22	.1396	.00130	.1539	.00143	.1777	.00165	.70	1.4132	.00406	1.5582	.00448	1.7993	.00518
.23	.1526	.00135	.1682	.00149	.1942	.00173	.71	1.4538	.00412	1.6031	.00455	1.8511	.00525
.24	.1661	.00142	.1832	.00156	.2115	.00180	.72	1.4951	.00418	1.6485	.00461	1.9036	.00532
.25	.1803	.00147	.1988	.00162	.2295	.00187	.73	1.5369	.00424	1.6946	.00468	1.9568	.00540
.26	.1950	.00152	.2150	.00168	.2482	.00195	.74	1.5793	.00430	1.7414	.00474	2.0108	.00547
.27	.2102	.00159	.2318	.00175	.2677	.00202	.75	1.6223	.00435	1.7888	.00480	2.0655	.00554
.28	.2261	.00164	.2493	.00181	.2879	.00209	.76	1.6658	.00441	1.8368	.00487	2.1209	.00562
.29	.2425	.00171	.2674	.00188	.3088	.00217	.77	1.7099	.00447	1.8854	.00493	2.1771	.00569
.30	.2596	.00176	.2862	.00194	.3305	.00224	.78	1.7546	.00453	1.9347	.00499	2.2340	.00577
.31	.2772	.00181	.3056	.00200	.3529	.00231	.79	1.7999	.00459	1.9847	.00506	2.2917	.00584
.32	.2953	.00188	.3256	.00207	.3760	.00239	.80	1.8458	.00464	2.0352	.00512	2.3501	.00591
.33	.3141	.00193	.3463	.00213	.3999	.00246	.81	1.8922	.00470	2.0864	.00518	2.4092	.00599
.34	.3334	.00199	.3676	.00219	.4245	.00253	.82	1.9392	.00476	2.1383	.00525	2.4691	.00606
.35	.3533	.00205	.3896	.00226	.4498	.00261	.83	1.9868	.00482	2.1907	.00531	2.5296	.00613
.36	.3738	.00210	.4121	.00232	.4759	.00268	.84	2.0350	.00487	2.2438	.00537	2.5910	.00621
.37	.3948	.00216	.4353	.00239	.5027	.00275	.85	2.0837	.00493	2.2976	.00544	2.6530	.00628
.38	.4164	.00223	.4592	.00245	.5302	.00283	.86	2.1330	.00499	2.3520	.00550	2.7158	.00635
.39	.4387	.00227	.4837	.00251	.5585	.00290	.87	2.1829	.00505	2.4070	.00557	2.7793	.00643
.40	.4614	.00234	.5088	.00258	.5875	.00297	.88	2.2334	.00510	2.4626	.00563	2.8436	.00650
.41	.4848	.00239	.5346	.00264	.6173	.00305	.89	2.2844	.00516	2.5189	.00569	2.9086	.00657
.42	.5087	.00246	.5610	.00270	.6477	.00312	.90	2.3360	.00522	2.5758	.00576	2.9743	.00665
.43	.5333	.00250	.5880	.00277	.6790	.00319	.91	2.3882	.00528	2.6334	.00582	3.0408	.00672
.44	.5583	.00257	.6157	.00283	.7109	.00327	.92	2.4410	.00534	2.6916	.00588	3.1080	.00679
.45	.5840	.00263	.6440	.00289	.7436	.00334	.93	2.4944	.00539	2.7504	.00595	3.1759	.00687
.46	.6103	.00268	.6729	.00296	.7770	.00341	.94	2.5483	.00545	2.8099	.00601	3.2446	.00694
.47	.6371	.00274	.7025	.00302	.8111	.00349	.95	2.6028	.00551	2.8700	.00607	3.3140	.00701
.48	.6645	.00279	.7329	.00308	.8460	.00356	.96	2.6579	.00557	2.9307	.00614	3.3841	.00709
.49	.6924	.00286	.7635	.00315	.8816	.00364	.97	2.7136	.00562	2.9921	.00620	3.4550	.00716
.50	.7210	.00291	.7950	.00321	.9180	.00371	.98	2.7698	.00568	3.0541	.00626	3.5266	.00723
.51	.7501	.00297	.8271	.00328	.9551	.00378	.99	2.8266	.00574	3.1168	.00633	3.5989	.00731
.52	.7798	.00303	.8599	.00334	.9929	.00386	1.00	2.8840	.00580	3.1800	.00639	3.6720	.00738
.53	.8101	.00309	.8933	.00340	1.0315	.00393							

STEEL ROD This is of the order of 8% lighter than brass so for many practical purposes can be taken as the same

Aluminium rod (Imperial measure) – weight in lb/ft

Diameter or width across flats in inches	Decimal equivalent	Millimetre equivalent	Weight (lb) per foot — round (d)	Weight (lb) per foot — hexagon (d)	Weight (lb) per foot — square (d)
1/8	.1250	3.175	.014	.016	.018
5/32	.1563	3.969	.023	.025	.029
3/16	.1875	4.763	.032	.036	.041
7/32	.2188	5.556	.044	.049	.056
1/4	.2500	6.350	.058	.064	.074
9/32	.2813	7.144	.073	.081	.093
5/16	.3125	7.938	.090	.099	.115
11/32	.3438	8.731	.109	.120	.139
3/8	.3750	9.525	.130	.143	.165
13/32	.4063	10.319	.152	.168	.194
7/16	.4375	11.113	.177	.195	.225
15/32	.4688	11.906	.203	.224	.258
1/2	.5000	12.700	.231	.255	.294
17/32	.5313	13.494	.261	.287	.332
9/16	.5625	14.288	.292	.322	.372
19/32	.5938	15.081	.326	.359	.415
5/8	.6250	15.875	.361	.398	.459
21/32	.6563	16.669	.398	.438	.507
11/16	.6875	17.463	.437	.481	.556
23/32	.7188	18.256	.477	.526	.608
3/4	.7500	19.050	.520	.573	.662
25/32	.7813	19.844	.564	.621	.718
13/16	.8125	20.638	.610	.672	.776
27/32	.8438	21.431	.658	.725	.837
7/8	.8750	22.225	.707	.779	.900
29/32	.9063	23.019	.759	.836	.966
15/16	.9375	23.813	.812	.895	1.034
31/32	.9688	24.606	.867	.955	1.104
1	1.0000	25.400	.924	1.018	1.176
1 1/16	1.0625	26.988	1.043	1.149	1.328
1 1/8	1.1250	28.575	1.160	1.288	1.488
1 3/16	1.1875	30.163	1.303	1.435	1.658
1 1/4	1.2500	31.750	1.444	1.591	1.838
1 5/16	1.3125	33.338	1.592	1.754	2.026
1 3/8	1.3750	34.925	1.747	1.925	2.223
1 7/16	1.4375	36.513	1.909	2.104	2.430
1 1/2	1.5000	38.100	2.079	2.291	2.646
1 9/16	1.5625	39.688	2.256	2.485	2.871
1 5/8	1.6250	41.275	2.440	2.688	3.105
1 11/16	1.6875	42.863	2.631	2.899	3.349
1 3/4	1.7500	44.450	2.830	3.118	3.602
1 13/16	1.8125	46.038	3.035	3.344	3.863
1 7/8	1.8750	47.625	3.248	3.579	4.134
1 15/16	1.9375	49.213	3.469	3.821	4.415
2	2.0000	50.800	3.696	4.072	4.704
2 1/16	2.0625	52.388	3.931	4.330	5.003
2 1/8	2.1250	53.975	4.172	4.597	5.310
2 3/16	2.1875	55.563	4.421	4.871	5.627
2 1/4	2.2500	57.150	4.678	5.154	5.954
2 5/16	2.3125	58.738	4.941	5.444	6.289
2 3/8	2.3750	60.325	5.212	5.742	6.633
2 7/16	2.4375	61.913	5.490	6.048	6.987
2 1/2	2.5000	63.500	5.775	6.363	7.350
2 5/8	2.6250	66.675	6.367	7.015	8.103
2 3/4	2.7500	69.850	6.988	7.699	8.894
2 7/8	2.8750	73.025	7.637	8.414	9.720
3	3.0000	76.200	8.316	9.162	10.584
3 1/8	3.1250	79.375	9.023	9.941	11.484
3 1/4	3.2500	82.550	9.760	10.753	12.422
3 3/8	3.3750	85.725	10.525	11.596	13.395
3 1/2	3.5000	88.900	11.319	12.471	14.406
3 5/8	3.6250	92.075	12.142	13.377	15.453
3 3/4	3.7500	95.250	12.994	14.316	16.538
3 7/8	3.8750	98.425	13.874	15.286	17.658
4	4.0000	101.600	14.784	16.288	18.816

Brass and steel rectangular bars (Imperial measure) – weight in lb/ft

THICKNESS

WIDTH INS.	1/16	3/32	1/8	5/32	3/16	7/32	1/4	9/32	5/16	11/32	3/8	13/32	7/16	15/32	1/2	17/32	9/16	19/32	5/8
3/32	.0215																		
1/8	.0287	.0431																	
5/32	.0359	.0538	.0717																
3/16	.0430	.0646	.0861	.1076															
7/32	.0502	.0754	.1004	.1256	.1506														
1/4	.0574	.0861	.1148	.1435	.1721	.2009													
9/32	.0646	.0964	.1291	.1614	.1937	.2260	.2582												
5/16	.0717	.1076	.1434	.1794	.2151	.2512	.2869	.3228											
11/32	.0789	.1184	.1578	.1973	.2367	.2762	.3156	.3551	.3945										
3/8	.0861	.1292	.1721	.2152	.2582	.3013	.3443	.3874	.4303	.4734									
13/32	.0932	.1399	.1865	.2332	.2797	.3264	.3730	.4197	.4662	.5129	.5595								
7/16	.1004	.1507	.2008	.2511	.3012	.3515	.4016	.4519	.5020	.5523	.6024	.6527							
15/32	.1076	.1615	.2152	.2691	.3228	.3766	.4304	.4842	.5379	.5918	.6455	.6994	.7531						
1/2	.1148	.1722	.2295	.2870	.3443	.4017	.4590	.5165	.5738	.6312	.6885	.7460	.8033	.8607					
17/32	.1219	.1830	.2439	.3049	.3658	.4269	.4877	.5488	.6097	.6707	.7316	.7927	.8535	.9146	.9755				
9/16	.1291	.1937	.2582	.3228	.3873	.4519	.5164	.5810	.6455	.7101	.7746	.8392	.9037	.9683	1.033	1.097			
19/32	.1363	.2045	.2726	.3408	.4088	.4771	.5451	.6133	.6814	.7496	.8177	.8859	.9539	1.022	1.090	1.158	1.226		
5/8	.1434	.2153	.2869	.3587	.4303	.5021	.5738	.6456	.7172	.7890	.8606	.9325	1.004	1.076	1.148	1.219	1.291	1.363	
21/32	.1506	.2260	.3012	.3767	.4519	.5273	.6025	.6778	.7531	.8285	.9037	.9791	1.054	1.130	1.205	1.280	1.356	1.431	1.506
11/16	.1578	.2368	.3156	.3946	.4733	.5524	.6311	.7101	.7889	.8679	.9467	1.026	1.104	1.183	1.262	1.341	1.420	1.499	1.578
23/32	.1650	.2476	.3299	.4125	.4949	.5775	.6599	.7425	.8248	.9074	.9898	1.072	1.155	1.237	1.320	1.402	1.485	1.567	1.650
3/4	.1721	.2583	.3443	.4305	.5164	.6026	.6885	.7747	.8606	.9468	1.033	1.119	1.205	1.291	1.377	1.463	1.549	1.635	1.721
25/32	.1793	.2691	.3586	.4484	.5379	.6277	.7172	.8070	.8965	.9863	1.076	1.166	1.255	1.345	1.434	1.524	1.614	1.704	1.793
13/16	.1865	.2799	.3729	.4663	.5594	.6528	.7459	.8393	.9323	1.026	1.119	1.212	1.305	1.399	1.492	1.585	1.678	1.772	1.865
27/32	.1937	.2906	.3873	.4843	.5810	.6779	.7746	.8716	.9683	1.065	1.162	1.259	1.356	1.453	1.549	1.646	1.743	1.840	1.937
7/8	.2008	.3014	.4016	.5022	.6024	.7030	.8033	.9038	1.004	1.105	1.205	1.305	1.406	1.506	1.607	1.707	1.807	1.908	2.008
29/32	.2080	.3122	.4160	.5202	.6240	.7281	.8320	.9361	1.040	1.144	1.248	1.352	1.456	1.560	1.664	1.768	1.872	1.976	2.080
15/16	.2152	.3229	.4303	.5381	.6455	.7532	.8606	.9684	1.076	1.184	1.291	1.399	1.506	1.614	1.721	1.829	1.936	2.044	2.152
31/32	.2223	.3337	.4447	.5560	.6670	.7784	.8894	1.001	1.112	1.223	1.334	1.445	1.556	1.668	1.779	1.890	2.001	2.112	2.223
1	.2295	.3444	.4590	.5739	.6885	.8034	.9180	1.033	1.148	1.262	1.377	1.492	1.607	1.721	1.836	1.950	2.066	2.180	2.295
1 1/8	.2582	.3875	.5164	.6457	.7746	.9039	1.033	1.162	1.291	1.420	1.549	1.678	1.807	1.937	2.066	2.195	2.324	2.453	2.582
1 1/4	.2869	.4305	.5738	.7174	.8606	1.004	1.148	1.291	1.434	1.578	1.721	1.865	2.008	2.152	2.295	2.439	2.582	2.726	2.869
1 3/8	.3156	.4736	.6311	.7892	.9467	1.105	1.262	1.429	1.578	1.736	1.893	2.051	2.209	2.367	2.525	2.683	2.840	2.998	3.156
1 1/2	.3443	.5167	.6885	.8609	1.033	1.205	1.377	1.549	1.721	1.894	2.066	2.238	2.410	2.582	2.754	2.926	3.098	3.271	3.443
1 5/8	.3729	.5597	.7459	.9326	1.119	1.306	1.492	1.679	1.865	2.051	2.238	2.424	2.611	2.797	2.984	3.170	3.356	3.543	3.729
1 3/4	.4016	.6028	.8033	1.004	1.205	1.406	1.607	1.808	2.008	2.209	2.410	2.611	2.811	3.013	3.213	3.414	3.615	3.816	4.016
1 7/8	.4303	.6458	.8606	1.076	1.291	1.506	1.721	1.937	2.152	2.367	2.582	2.797	3.012	3.228	3.443	3.658	3.873	4.088	4.303
2	.4590	.6889	.9180	1.148	1.377	1.607	1.836	2.066	2.295	2.525	2.754	2.984	3.213	3.443	3.672	3.902	4.131	4.361	4.590
2 1/4	.5164	.7750	1.033	1.291	1.549	1.808	2.066	2.324	2.582	2.840	3.098	3.357	3.615	3.873	4.131	4.390	4.647	4.906	5.164
2 1/2	.5738	.8611	1.148	1.435	1.721	2.009	2.295	2.582	2.869	3.156	3.443	3.730	4.016	4.304	4.590	4.877	5.164	5.451	5.738
2 3/4	.6311	.9472	1.262	1.578	1.893	2.209	2.525	2.841	3.156	3.472	3.787	4.103	4.418	4.734	5.049	5.365	5.680	5.996	6.311
3	.6885	1.033	1.377	1.722	2.066	2.410	2.754	3.099	3.443	3.787	4.131	4.476	4.820	5.164	5.508	5.853	6.197	6.541	6.885
3 1/4	.7459	1.119	1.492	1.865	2.238	2.611	2.984	3.357	3.729	4.103	4.475	4.849	5.221	5.595	5.967	6.341	6.713	7.086	7.459
3 1/2	.8033	1.206	1.607	2.009	2.410	2.812	3.213	3.615	4.016	4.419	4.820	5.222	5.623	6.025	6.426	6.828	7.229	7.632	8.033
3 3/4	.8606	1.292	1.721	2.152	2.582	3.013	3.443	3.874	4.303	4.734	5.164	5.595	6.024	6.455	6.885	7.316	7.746	8.177	8.606
4	.9180	1.378	1.836	2.296	2.754	3.214	3.672	4.132	4.590	5.050	5.508	5.968	6.426	6.886	7.344	7.804	8.262	8.722	9.180

THICKNESS

STEEL ROD This is of the order of 8% lighter than brass so for many practical purposes can be taken as the same

THICKNESS (top) — **THICKNESS** (top right)

Left axis = **WIDTH**, top axis = **THICKNESS** (both in inches).

WIDTH	21/32	11/16	23/32	3/4	25/32	13/16	27/32	7/8	29/32	15/16	31/32	1	1 1/8	1 1/4	1 3/8	1 1/2	1 5/8	1 3/4	1 7/8	2	WIDTH
3/32																					3/32
1/8																					1/8
5/32																					5/32
3/16																					3/16
7/32																					7/32
1/4																					1/4
9/32																					9/32
5/16																					5/16
11/32																					11/32
3/8																					3/8
13/32																					13/32
7/16																					7/16
15/32																					15/32
1/2																					1/2
17/32																					17/32
9/16																					9/16
19/32																					19/32
5/8																					5/8
21/32																					21/32
11/16	1.657																				11/16
23/32	1.732	1.815																			23/32
3/4	1.807	1.893	1.980																		3/4
25/32	1.883	1.972	2.062	2.152																	25/32
13/16	1.958	2.051	2.145	2.238	2.331																13/16
27/32	2.033	2.131	2.227	2.324	2.420	2.517															27/32
7/8	2.109	2.209	2.310	2.410	2.510	2.611	2.711														7/8
29/32	2.184	2.288	2.392	2.496	2.600	2.704	2.808	2.912													29/32
15/16	2.259	2.367	2.474	2.582	2.690	2.797	2.905	3.012	3.120												15/16
31/32	2.335	2.446	2.557	2.668	2.779	2.890	3.002	3.113	3.224	3.335											31/32
1	2.410	2.525	2.639	2.754	2.869	2.984	3.098	3.213	3.328	3.443	3.557										1
1 1/8	2.711	2.840	2.969	3.098	3.228	3.356	3.486	3.618	3.744	3.873	4.002	4.131									1 1/8
1 1/4	3.102	3.156	3.299	3.443	3.586	3.729	3.873	4.016	4.160	4.303	4.447	4.590	5.164								1 1/4
1 3/8	3.314	3.472	3.629	3.787	3.945	4.102	4.260	4.418	4.576	4.733	4.891	5.049	5.680	6.311							1 3/8
1 1/2	3.615	3.787	3.959	4.131	4.303	4.475	4.648	4.820	4.992	5.164	5.336	5.508	6.197	6.885	7.574						1 1/2
1 5/8	3.916	4.102	4.289	4.475	4.662	4.848	5.035	5.221	5.408	5.594	5.781	5.967	6.713	7.459	8.205	8.951					1 5/8
1 3/4	4.217	4.418	4.619	4.820	5.021	5.221	5.422	5.623	5.824	6.024	6.226	6.426	7.229	8.033	8.836	9.639	10.442				1 3/4
1 7/8	4.519	4.733	4.949	5.164	5.379	5.594	5.810	6.024	6.240	6.455	6.670	6.885	7.746	8.606	9.467	10.328	11.188	12.049			1 7/8
2	4.820	5.049	5.279	5.508	5.738	5.967	6.197	6.426	6.656	6.885	7.115	7.344	8.262	9.180	10.098	11.016	11.934	12.852	13.770		2
2 1/4	5.422	5.680	5.939	6.197	6.455	6.713	6.970	7.229	7.488	7.746	8.004	8.262	9.295	10.328	11.360	12.393	13.426	14.459	15.491	16.524	2 1/4
2 1/2	6.025	6.311	6.599	6.885	7.172	7.459	7.746	8.033	8.320	8.606	8.894	9.180	10.328	11.475	12.623	13.770	14.918	16.065	17.213	18.360	2 1/2
2 3/4	6.627	6.942	7.258	7.574	7.890	8.205	8.520	8.836	9.152	9.467	9.783	10.098	11.360	12.623	13.885	15.147	16.409	17.672	18.934	20.196	2 3/4
3	7.230	7.574	7.918	8.262	8.607	8.951	9.295	9.639	9.984	10.328	10.672	11.016	12.393	13.770	15.147	16.524	17.901	19.278	20.655	22.032	3
3 1/4	7.832	8.205	8.578	8.951	9.324	9.696	10.070	10.442	10.816	11.188	11.562	11.934	13.426	14.918	16.409	17.901	19.393	20.885	22.376	23.868	3 1/4
3 1/2	8.435	8.836	9.238	9.639	10.041	10.442	10.845	11.246	11.648	12.049	12.451	12.852	14.459	16.065	17.672	19.278	20.885	22.491	24.098	25.704	3 1/2
3 3/4	9.037	9.467	9.898	10.328	10.759	11.188	11.619	12.049	12.480	12.909	13.340	13.770	15.491	17.213	18.934	20.655	22.376	24.098	25.819	27.540	3 3/4
4	9.640	10.098	10.558	11.016	11.476	11.934	12.394	12.852	13.312	13.770	14.230	14.688	16.524	18.360	20.196	22.032	23.868	25.704	27.540	29.376	4
INS.	21/32	11/16	23/32	3/4	25/32	13/16	27/32	7/8	29/32	15/16	31/32	1	1 1/8	1 1/4	1 3/8	1 1/2	1 5/8	1 3/4	1 7/8	2	INS.

THICKNESS (bottom) — **THICKNESS** (bottom right)

STEEL ROD This is of the order of 8% lighter than brass so for many practical purposes can be taken as the same

Brass and steel rod (BA sizes) – weight in lb/ft

BA no*	Round		Hexagon	
	Diameter of head (in)	Weight (lb) per foot	Width across flats (in)	Weight (lb) per foot
0	.413	.4920	.413	.5425
1	.366	.3864	.365	.4237
2	.319	.2935	.324	.3339
3	.283	.2310	.282	.2529
4	.252	.1832	.248	.1957
5	.221	.1409	.220	.1539
6	.194	.1086	.193	.1185
7	.173	.0863	.172	.0941
8	.157	.0711	.152	.0736
9	.128	.0473	.131	.0546
10	.112	.0362	.117	.0436
11	.110	.0349	.103	.0338
12	.095	.0261	.090	.0258
13	.081	.0190	.083	.0220
14	.064	.0119	.069	.0151
15	.064	.0119	.062	.0122
16	.058	.0097	.056	.0100

Brass and steel wire (in swg) – weight in lb/100 ft

Gauge number	Diameter inches	Weight (lb) per 100 feet	Gauge number	Diameter inches	Weight (lb) per 100 feet
7/0	.500	72.34	16	.064	1.190
6/0	.464	62.30	17	.056	0.908
5/0	.432	54.00	18	.048	0.668
4/0	.400	46.29	19	.040	0.464
3/0	.373	40.04	20	.036	0.375
2/0	.348	35.04	21	.032	0.297
0	.324	30.38	22	.028	0.227
1	.300	26.04	23	.024	0.167
2	.276	22.04	24	.022	0.140
3	.252	18.37	25	.020	0.116
4	.232	15.57	26	.018	0.0939
5	.212	13.00	27	.0164	0.0779
6	.192	10.67	28	.0148	0.0635
7	.176	8.96	29	.0136	0.0536
8	.160	7.41	30	.0124	0.0445
9	.144	6.00	31	.0116	0.0389
10	.128	4.74	32	.0108	0.0338
11	.116	3.89	33	.0100	0.0290
12	.104	3.13	34	.0092	0.0245
13	.092	2.45	35	.0084	0.0205
14	.080	1.85	36	.0076	0.0167
15	.072	1.50			

STEEL ROD This is of the order of 8% lighter than brass so for many practical purposes can be taken as the same

Steel and wood pillars – simple approximate formulae

Note: Safety factors should be added

Long, solid, circular section pillars

where L = pillar length in feet;   d = diameter in inches

Maximum loads: Steel $\dfrac{45d^4}{L^2}$

Oak $\dfrac{2d^4}{L^2}$

Pine $\dfrac{2\cdot5d^4}{L^2}$

Long, hollow, circular section pillars

Maximum load: $\dfrac{kt^2}{\left(1 + 6\cdot5\dfrac{L^2t}{d^3}\right)}$

where t = thickness of tube, d = mean diameter
       k = 2300 (steel), 100 (oak), 130 (pine)

Short pillars

Maximum load (tons) = $\dfrac{\text{Sectional area (sq in) x } j}{1 + \dfrac{1}{q}\left(\dfrac{CS}{t} + \dfrac{L^2}{p^2}\right)}$

where j = 36 for steel; 3·2 for wood
       q = 4000 for steel; 750 for wood
       CS = Coefficient of shape
          = 500 for circular pillar; 600 for square; 700 for I-section;
            0 for solid pillar
       t = thickness of material (wall)
       L = length in inches (unsupported both ends)
          = length x $\sqrt{1/2}$ (one end fixed)
          = length x 1/2 (both ends fixed)
       p = least radius of gyration of cross-section in inches

Long pillars

where $\dfrac{L}{p}$ is greater than 140

ie if L is more than about 38 diameters and the pillar is circular.

Maximum load (tons)= $\dfrac{\text{Sectional area (sq in) x } \pi^2 E}{\dfrac{CS.p}{t} + \dfrac{L^2}{p^2}}$

where E = modulus of elasticity

55

Circular hollow sections (mild steel) – dimensions and strength in tension and compression

To save calculating the correct size of the pillar the following tables give the loading that can be carried by different sizes and length of pillar. Where a single pillar is inadequate two or four may be used. Alternatively some sections are available in High Yield Stress steel to BS 968.1962.

Interpolation should be used for intermediate lengths and diameters of pillars. Extrapolation (figures beyond those quoted) should be used with great caution.

Outside	mm	26·9	33·7	42·4
diameter	in	1·062	1·344	1·688
Thickness	mm	3·2	3·2	3·2
	in	0·128	0·128	0·128
Weight	kg/m	1·89	2·42	3·11
	lb/ft	1·27	1·63	2·09
Area	sq cm	2·43	3·15	4·05
	sq in	0·376	0·489	0·627
I	cm⁴	1·75	3·79	7·99
	in⁴	0·042	0·091	0·192
Z	cm³	1·28	2·23	3·72
	in³	0·078	0·136	0·227
S	cm³	1·84	3·11	5·11
	in³	0·112	0·190	0·312
r	cm	0·846	1·10	1·40
	in	0·333	0·432	0·553

Axial tension (tonnef) 3·84   4·98   6·40
Axial compression (tonnef)
for effective lengths (metres)

	1·5 m	0·73 tonnef	1·54 tonnef	2·95 tonnef
	2·0 m	0·42 "	0·91 "	1·82 "
	2·5 m	0·27 "	0·59 "	1·21 "

Axial tension (tonf) 3·77   4·91   6·29
Axial compression (tonf)
for effective lengths (feet)

	5 ft	0·70 tonf	1·47 tonf	2·85 tonf
	7 ft	0·37 "	0·79 "	1·60 "
	9 ft	0·22 "	0·48 "	1·00 "

Tonf means tons force and *tonnef* means metric tonnes force

Outside	mm	48·3	60·3	76·1	88·9	114·3
diameter	in	1·906	2·375	3·0	3·5	4·5
Thickness	mm	4·0	4·0	4·5	4·0	4·5
	in	0·160	0·160	0·176	0·160	0·176
Weight	kg/m	4·41	5·59	7·92	8·43	12·1
	lb/ft	2·96	3·76	5·32	5·00	8·13
Area	sq cm	5·66	7·16	10·1	10·8	15·4
	sq in	0·878	1·11	1·56	1·68	2·39
I	cm⁴	14·0	28·6	64·9	97·8	233·0
	in⁴	0·337	0·686	1·56	2·35	5·60
Z	cm³	5·80	9·47	17·0	22·0	40·8
	in³	0·354	0·578	1·04	1·34	2·49
S	cm³	8·01	12·9	23·1	29·3	53·9
	in³	0·489	0·786	1·41	1·79	3·29
r	cm	1·57	1·99	2·54	3·00	3·89
	in	0·620	0·785	1·00	1·18	1·53

Here I is the second moment of area notation, Z and S are section moduli, r is the radius of gyration.

Axial tension (tonnef) 8·95   11·32   15·96   17·07   24·34
Axial compression (tonnef)
for effective lengths (metres)

	1·5 m	4·87 tonnef	7·97 tonnef	13·01 tonnef	14·68 tonnef	21·92 tonnef
	2·0 m	3·11 "	5·74 "	10·82 "	13·11 "	20·78 "
	2·5 m	2·09 "	4·03 "	8·34 "	10·94 "	19·08 "

Axial tension (tonf) 8·81 tonf   11·14 tonf   15·66 tonf   16·86 tonf   23·99 tonf
Axial compression (tonf)
for effective lengths (feet)

	6 ft	3·58 " .	6·39 "	11·43 "	13·55 "	20·92 "
	8 ft	2·16 "	4·16 "	8·47 "	11·08 "	19·03 "
	10 ft	1·42 "	2·80 "	6·03 "	8·41 "	16·32 "

Tonf means tons force and *tonnef* means metric tonnes force

Rectangular hollow sections (mild steel) – dimensions and strength in tension and compression

Dimensions	mm	50·8 × 25·4		63·5 × 38·1		76·2 × 50·8	
	in	2·0 × 1·0		2·5 × 1·5		3·0 × 2·0	
Thickness	mm	3·2		4·0		4·0	
	in	0·128		0·160		0·160	
Weight	kg/m	3·51		5·89		7·52	
	lb/ft	2·36		3·96		5·05	
Area	sq cm	4·48		7·55		9·61	
	sq in	0·695		1·17		1·49	
Axis		X–X	Y–Y	X–X	Y–Y	X–X	Y–Y
I	cm^4	13·6	4·33	37·8	16·4	73·7	38·5
	in^4	0·327	0·104	0·909	0·394	1·77	0·924
Z	cm^3	5·36	3·39	11·9	8·62	19·3	15·1
	in^3	0·327	0·207	0·727	0·526	1·18	0·924
S	cm^3	6·96	4·15	15·1	10·4	23·9	17·9
	in^3	0·425	0·253	0·924	0·635	1·46	1·09
r	cm	1·74	0·980	2·24	1·48	2·77	2·00
	in	0·687	0·386	0·883	0·582	1·09	0·789
Axial tension (tonnef)		7·08		11·93		15·19	
Axial compression (tonnef) for effective lengths (metres)							
	1·5 m	4·37	1·78	9·14	5·98	12·77	10·74
	2·0 m	2·93	1·03	7·08	3·75	11·06	7·76
	2·5 m	1·99	0·67	5·17	2·49	8·89	5·46
Axial tension (tonf)		6·98		11·74		14·95	
Axial compression (tonf) for effective lengths (feet)							
	6ft	3·33	1·21	7·70	4·30	11·54	8·64
	8ft	2·06	0·69	5·30	2·57	9·01	5·63
	10ft	1·37	0·45	3·65	1·68	6·62	3·80

Tonf means tons force and *tonnef* means metric tonnes force.

Square hollow sections (mild steel)

127·0 × 76·2	25·4 × 25·4	38·1 × 38·1	50·8 × 50·8	63·5 × 63·5	76·2 × 76·3
5·0 × 3·0	1·0 × 1·0	1·5 × 1·5	2·0 × 2·0	2·5 × 2·5	3·0 × 3·0
6·3	2·0	3·2	4·0	4·0	4·0
0·250	0·104	0·128	0·160	0·160	0·160
18·6	1·86	3·51	5·89	7·52	9·14
12·6	1·25	2·36	3·96	5·05	6·14
24·0	2·37	4·48	7·55	9·61	11·7
3·72	0·368	0·695	1·17	1·49	1·81
X–X Y–Y					
499 221	2·04	8·99	27·1	56·2	101
12·0 5·30	0·049	0·216	0·652	1·35	2·42
78·8 57·8	1·59	4·72	10·7	17·7	26·4
4·81 3·53	0·097	0·288	0·652	1·08	1·61
98·5 68·2	2·00	5·82	13·1	21·3	31·5
6·01 4·16	0·122	0·355	0·799	1·3	1·92
4·57 3·02	0·952	1·42	1·90	2·42	2·95
1·80 1·19	0·364	0·558	0·748	0·953	1·16
37·93	3·75	7·08	11·93	15·19	18·49
34·71 32·68	0·84	3·34	8·07	12·12	15·84
33·53 29·24	0·49	2·07	5·66	9·82	14·06
31·80 24·49	0·32	1·37	3·93	7·41	11·64
37·33	3·69	6·98	11·74	14·95	18·17
33·46 30·12	0·81	3·20	7·82	10·51	14·49
31·55 24·73	0·43	1·80	5·04	7·56	11·73
28·67 18·85	0·26	1·13	3·28	5·31	8·84

Pitch pine pillars – safe working loads

The approximate safe working load is given in tons or tonnes which are almost the same for the purpose of this table. One tonne equals 0·9842 tons. The safety factor is five times.

- For rectangular columns having sides X and Y, where X is the smaller, the safe load equals (load for X) x $\frac{Y}{X}$. For example, a column of 1·8 metres, 100 millimetres by 150 millimetres has a safe load of 5·3 x $\frac{150}{100}$ =7·5 tonnes.
- For round columns take the side as equal to the diameter and multiply by 0·75. For example, a round column ten feet long and six inches diameter has a safe load of 11·5 x 0·75 = 8·6 tons.

- For oak take 90% of the load, for spruce take 80% of the load.

Length		Dimensions of sides								
Metres	Feet	100 mm (4 ins)	130 mm (5 ins)	150 mm (6 ins)	180 mm (7 ins)	200 mm (8 ins)	230 mm (9 ins)	250 mm (10 ins)	280 mm (11 ins)	300mm (12 ins)
0·6	2	6·8	10·9	15·8	21·6	28·3				
1·2	4	6·2	10·0	14·9	20·8	27·3	34·1	43·4	52·6	63·0
1·8	6	5·3	9·1	13·8	19·5	26·1	33·5	42·0	51·3	61·5
2·4	8	4·6	8·2	12·5	18·1	24·6	31·9	40·2	49·3	59·7
3·1	10	4·0	7·2	11·5	16·8	23·0	30·3	38·4	47·5	57·6
3·7	12	3·5	6·6	10·4	15·4	21·3	28·4	36·5	45·3	55·3
4·3	14	3·1	5·8	9·4	14·1	19·9	26·5	34·6	44·0	53·0
4·9	16	2·7	5·2	8·6	13·0	18·4	25·2	32·7	41·1	50·5
5·5	18		4·8	7·9	12·3	17·2	23·4	30·7	38·9	47·7
6·1	20		4·2	7·2	11·0	16·0	22·0	28·8	36·8	45·9
6·7	22			6·6	10·5	15·0	20·9	27·3	34·9	43·7
7·3	24			6·1	9·6	13·9	19·4	25·8	33·1	41·6
7·9	26				8·9	13·0	18·2	24·4	31·5	39·6
8·5	28				8·3	12·2	17·3	23·1	30·1	37·8
9·1	30					11·5	16·2	21·8	28·3	36·2

Paint – container sizes and covering properties

Paint is sold in the following size containers in Europe and many other countries

Metric paint container sizes							
100	ml	=	0·022 gal	2·5	litres	=	0·55 gal
250	ml	=	0·055 gal	5	litres	=	1·1 gal
500	ml	=	0·11 gal	10	litres	=	2·2 gal
750	ml	=	0·17 gal	20	litres	=	4·4 gal
1	litre	=	0·22 gal				

Paint conversion table – covering properties

sq ft/gallon	sq yds/gallon	sq m/litre
90	10	1·84
100	11·1	2·04
150	16·7	3·07
200	22·2	4·09
250	27·8	5·11
300	33·4	6·13
350	38·9	7·15
400	44·4	8·17
450	50	9·19
500	55·6	10·2
550	61·2	11·2
600	66·7	12·3
650	72·3	13·3
700	77·8	14·3
750	83·3	15·3
800	89	16·3
850	94·5	17·4
900	100	18·4
1000	111	20·1

Antifouling paint requirements

To ensure a clean hull for a full season it is normally essential to apply two coats of antifouling paint. The data below gives the amount of antifouling needed for *two full coats*.

It is always best to order a little extra paint. If the antifouling is the sort which works by eroding away under water, a third and even a fourth coat should be applied to areas which erode extra fast, such as at the waterline and by sharp leading edges, especially on the keel and rudder.

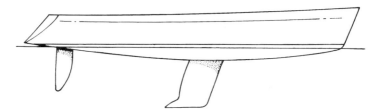

Hull shape of a typical modern sailing yacht, with short fin and separate rudder.

Waterline length	In feet	20	25	30	35	40	45	50
	In metres	6·1	7·6	9·1	10·7	12·2	13·6	15
Litres required for two full coats			2·5	3·5	5	7	9·5	11	14

Basic formula (see note below) LWL × [B+D] × 0·5 = area of bottom

Note on the basic hull shape

The LWL is the length along the actual flotation waterline and not, for instance, along the top of the boot top. B stands for the waterline beam which may be much less than the beam at deck level. D is the draft of the hull. If there is a centreplate, then the draft is with centreplate up. These formulae may be used to discover the area under water if it is considered that the above tables are not sufficiently accurate. It has to be remembered that normally *two coats of antifouling* are needed, so the calculated bottom area has to be multiplied by two to give the *total* area to be covered. Divide the resulting area by the covering ability of the paint, shown on page 64.

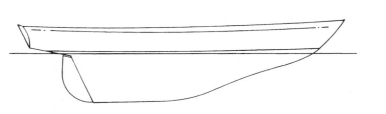

Hull shape of a traditional sailing yacht, with moderate length of keel and rudder attached.

Waterline length	In feet	20	25	30	35	40	45	50
	In metres	6·1	7·6	9·1	10·7	12·2	13·6	15
Litres required for two full coats			3	4	5·5	7	9·	12	14·5

Basic formula (see note on page 60) LWL × [B+D] × 0·75 = area of bottom

Hull shape of a shallow draft long keel sailing yacht, or full bodied powerboat.

Waterline length	In feet	20	25	30	35	40	45	50
	In metres	6·1	7·6	9·1	10·7	12·2	13·6	15
Litres required for two full coats			4	5	7	9·5	12	16·5	19·5

Basic formula (see note on page 60) LWL × [B+D] = area of bottom

Paint – covering properties (continued)

These figures are a rough guide. The covering ability of paint varies from one brand to another and with different methods of application. It also depends on the skill of the painter. The temperature and the surface being painted also have different effects.

	sq m /litre	sq yds /gallon		sq m /litre	sq yds /gallon
Primers			**Varnish**		
Pink priming	10·2	55	Polyurethane varnish	10	55
Metallic pink wood			Marine varnish	13	70
primer	11	60			
Bare plate primer	7	35			
Glassfibre primer	18·5	100	**Underwater paint**		
Metal primer	12	66	Underwater undercoat	10	55
Light alloy primer	10·2	55	Antifouling – normal	10	55
Self etch primer for			– heavy	7	35
light alloy and			boot-top	8·5	45
galvanized steel	13	70			
Primer for ferro-cement	8·2	44			
Primer for polystyrene	13	70	**Miscellaneous materials**		
			Anti-condensation paint		
Undercoats & enamels			(contains granulated		
Undercoating	10	55	cork)	7·0	35
Enamel	10	55	Non-slip deck paint	7·2	38
One-pot polyurethane	10	55	Ordinary deck paint	8·2	44
Two-pot polyurethane	11	60			

Paint – efficiency in preventing moisture absorption

	28-day efficiency
Enamel (two applications of commercial undercoat, one top coat of enamel)	58%
Oil paint (three coats as for lead paint)	44 to 56%
Lead paint (one coat pink primer, second coat of mixed primer and finishing, third coat exterior lead paint)	45%
Shellac (two coats)	31%
Copal varnish (two coats)	20%
Spar varnish (two coats)	17%
Pink primer (one coat)	14%
Wax polish (two coats of beeswax and turps over cellulose grain sealer)	3%
Boiled oil and turps (two brushed coats)	Low efficiency
Raw linseed oil (one rubbed coat)	Low efficiency

Galvanic corrosion

	CORRODED END	Approx.
	Metal	voltage
	Magnesium	-1·6
	Galvanised iron	-1·05
	Zinc	-1·03
	Aluminium alloys	-0·76 to -1·0
	Cadmium	-0·72
INCREASING NOBILITY	Mild steel & cast iron	-0·6 to -0·72
	Low alloy steel	-0·6
	Nickel cast iron	-0·49
	Aluminium bronze	-0·37
	Brasses	-0·35
	Copper	-0·34
	Tin	-0·32
	Stainless steel 400 series	- 0·31
	Aluminium brass & manganese bronze	- 0·31
	Gunmetal (tin bronzes)	- 0·28
	Lead	- 0·26
	Stainless steel 430	- 0·23
	70–30 copper-nickel	- 0·21
	Nickel-aluminium bronze	- 0·19
	Monel	- 0·08
	Stainless steel types 302, 304, 321 & 347	- 0·08
	Stainless steel types 316 & 317	- 0·05
	Titanium	+ 0·01
	PROTECTED END	

To prevent corrosion in the presence of seawater the voltage difference between two dissimilar metals should not exceed 0·20 volts. The less noble metal corrodes away fastest.

The stainless steels are normally passive in atmospheric conditions because they are protected by a layer of oxide. However this is liable to penetration and stainless steels are not recommended for use below or near the waterline.

This series is based on comparisons with a saturated calomel half cell, but the voltages can vary with temperature, adjacent flow and other factors. Where dissimilar metals must be used, make sure the less noble one has a much larger area and volume than the noble one so that corrosion will be negligible. If the volume alone is large but the exposed area is small there will be intense corrosion on the small area open to attack.

Stock timber sizes

See table opposite

When ordering timber it is almost always better to buy stock sections both for quick delivery and economy. Not every timber merchant will stock all these sizes. 40 mm thickness in particular might be described as 'semi non-standard'.

Allowance will have to be made for planing when ordering timber. By its nature the material expands with varying moisture content, so these dimensions are no more than a valuable buyer's guide and are not an engineer's exact specification.

It is always advisable to check stocks before designing and certainly before ordering.

Mechanical properties of wood

WOOD	WEIGHT			TEARING FORCE	
	Specific gravity	*kg per cu m*	*lb per cu ft*	*kg per sq cm*	*lb per sq in*
Ash	0·75	750	47·0	1 190	17 000
Beech	0·70	700	43·8	800	11 500
Birch	0·75	750	46·9	1 050	15 000
Cedar	0·49	492	30·8	800	11 400
Elm	0·54	540	33·8	945	13 490
Greenheart	1·00	999	62·5		
Larch	0·50	496	31·0	720	10 200
Lignum Vitae	1·33	1 330	83·2	835	11 800
Mahogany (Honduras)	0·56	559	35·0		
Mahogany (Spanish)	0·85	848	53·2	1 530	21 800
Oak (British)	0·93	929	58·3	700	10 000
Oak (Riga)	0·68	687	43·0		
Oak (Red)	1·02	1 021	64·4	720	10 250
Pine (Red)	0·58	576	36·1	1 010	14 300
Pine (Pitch)	0·66	658	41·2	550	7 820
Pine (Yellow)	0·46	460	28·8		
Spruce	0·51	511	32·0	700	10 000
Teak (Indian)	0·88	879	55·0	1 050	15 000
Teak (African)	0·93	934	61·3	1 470	21 000
Walnut	0·67	667	41·8	570	8 130

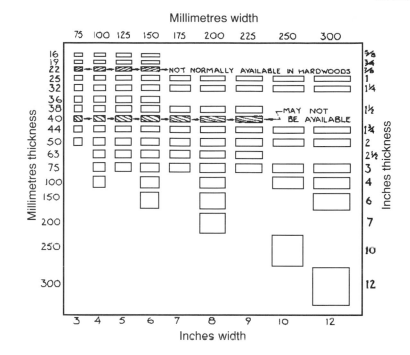

Millimetres width

Inches width

CRUSHING FORCE		BREAKING FORCE		MODULUS OF ELASTICITY	
kg per sq cm	*lb per sq in*	*kg per sq cm*	*lb per sq in*	*kg per sq cm*	*lb per sq in*
632	9 000	855	12 200	115 500	1 645 000
658	9 360	657	9 340	95 000	1 354 000
450	6 400	820	11 670	115 500	1 645 000
412	5 860	522	7 420	34 200	486 000
725	10 330	427	6 080	49 200	700 000
		1 160	16 550	186 000	2 656 000
392	5 570	417	5 940	95 700	1 363 000
647	9 920	800	11 400	39 000	558 000
		810	11 480	110 000	1 593 000
576	8 200	531	7 560	88 200	1 255 000
700	10 000	700	10 000	102 000	1 451 000
		905	12 890	113 000	1 610 000
421	5 990	745	10 600	142 500	2 149 000
378	5 380	621	8 840	102 500	1 458 000
		688	9 790	86 100	1 226 000
383	5 450			112 300	1 600 000
457	6 500	865	12 350	126 500	1 804 000
		1 030	14 600	197 000	2 800 000
656	9 320	1 050	14 980	161 500	2 305 000
467	6 650	562	8 000		

Bending marine plywood

Thickness (mm)	4	5	6	6*	8	9	12	15	18
Radius of curvature along the grain (metres)	0·38	0·455	0·61	0·685	0·76	0·99	1·52	1·83	2·74
(inches)	15	18	24	27	30	39	60	72	108
Radius of curvature across the grain (metres)	0·23	0·305	0·51	0·61	0·76	0·99	1·14	1·52	2·74
(inches)	9	12	20	24	30	39	45	60	108

three equal thickness plies

Moisture content of timber

The figures above are approximate minimum radii to which marine
ply can be bent with a standard moisture content of about 10%. In

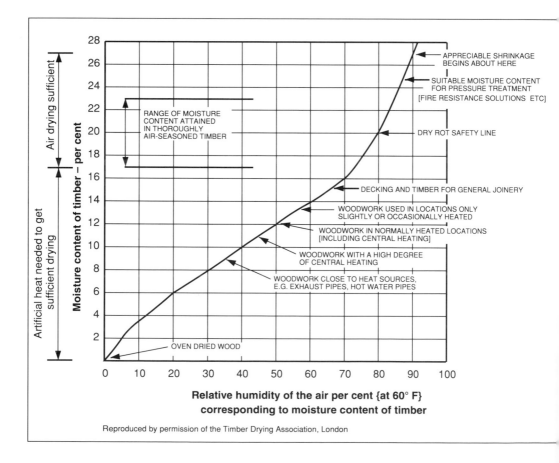

Reproduced by permission of the Timber Drying Association, London

general the radii listed should be considered the 'optimistic achievable' best. Some plywood can be bent more if it is of low grade. When wet, plywood boards can sometimes be bent to tighter curves than given opposite.

Bending should be done slowly while reducing the radius of curvature evenly. Straps on the convex side of the curve will help to keep the curvature even which will also reduce breakages. A creaking sound from the ply is an indication that it is about to fail.

To form tight bends it is often advisable to make a former and build up a lamination of layers of thin ply glued together. This technique is especially recommended where the final thickness is considerable because ply over about 12 mm needs considerable force to coax it into a curve.

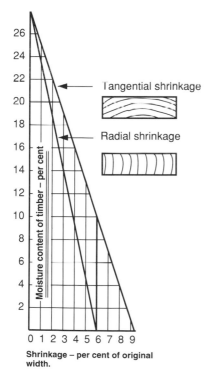

Shrinkage – per cent of original width.
Average values – figures vary with different woods.

Any wood used in boat or ship construction should have the correct moisture content to allow paint or polish to go on, and stay on, efficiently. Moisture content is also important to reduce the movement of timber, and ensure that rot preservative fluids work in as deeply as possible.

Particular note should be taken of timber components which are to be used in heated cabins, or near warm, or even hot, components like exhaust pipes.

It is important to select the right timber for a given job and then get it down to the right moisture content before working it. Just as vital, the timber should be kept at the correct moisture content by protecting it properly, both from the weather, from rain, and from variations in temperature.

Wood should be used so that the smallest movement occurs in the most important direction. An obvious example of this is decking, which should always be radial sawn, sometimes called rift sawn, so that the grain is vertical. This is not only to minimise shrinkage athwartships but also to give the best wear.

Natural seasoning of timber

Thickness	mm	12	18	25	50	75	l00
Thickness	inches	1/2	3/4	1	2	3	4
Time needed to season	months	13	16	24	36	46	52

Lightweight materials – mechanical properties

Material	Weight at 12% moisture content kg/m³	lbs /cu ft	Specific gravity	Crushing strength Max – parallel to grain kN/m³	psi	Stress at proportional limit perpendicular to grain kN/m³	psi	Compressive Modulus of elasticity parallel to grain kN/m²	psi
Lightweight balsa	96	6	0·0962	5160	750	344–580	50–84	2 270 000	330 000
Medium weight balsa	176	11	0·176	13 400	1910	690–990	100–144	5 280 000	768 000
Heavy type balsa	248	15½	0·248	20 300	2950	1 000	145–198	8 020 000	1 164 000
CCA foam	64–144	4–9	0·064–0·144	520–2070	75–300	510–2070	75–300	9300–24 100	1350–3500
Styrene foam	16–32	1–2	0·016–0·032	138–276	20–40	138–276	20–40	5850	850
Extra dense styrene foam	80–112	5–7	0·080–0·112	760–1380	110–200	760–1380	110–200	48200–68 950	7000–10 000
Polyurethane foam	16	2	0·032	110300	16–43			8900	1300
Extra dense polyurethane foam	96	6	0·096	1030	150			38 600	5600
Aspen (populus tremuloides)	416	26	0·380	29 200	4250	3160	460	8 930 000	1 298 000
Western red cedar (Thuja plicata)	368	23	0·330	34 600	5020	4200	610	8 490 000	1 232 000

Strength		Tensile strength				Bending strength			
Modulus of elasticity perpendicular to grain		Maximum parallel to grain		Maximum perpendicular to grain		Modulus of rupture		Modulus of elasticity	
kN/m²	psi	kN/m²	psi	kN/m²	psi	kN/m²	psi	kN/m²	psi
35100–110000	5100–16000	9460	1375	496–770	72–112	9460	1375	1925000	280000
89500–255000	13000–37000	21000	3050	815–1170	118–170	21000	3050	4300000	625000
137000–379000	19000–55000	31100	4525	1070–1530	156–223	31400	4525	6360000	925000
9300–24100	1350–3500	2140	310	2140	310				
5850	850	276–552	40–80	276–552	40–80				
48200–68950	7000–10000	1380–2400	200–350	1380–2400	200–350				
4130	600	250	36	200	29			4130–8950	600–1300
		1310	190					38500	5600
447000–893000	64900–129800	57900	8400	1790	260	57814	8400	8120000	1180000
425000–847000	61600–123200	53000	7700	1510	220	53000	7700	7710000	1200000

Typical marine laminates (glassfibre) – physical properties

From T & R Bulletin 2–12 to which acknowledgement is made.

Note: These properties are from short term loading tests – wet conditions. Composite and woven roving values are for the warp direction. The physical properties were tested in accordance with

Physical properties				Chopped strand mat laminate Low glass content	
Percentage Glass by weight				25–30	
Specific gravity				1·40–1·50	
Flexural strength	$kN/m^2 \times 10^3$	and	$psi \times 10^3$	124–172	18–25
Flexural modulus	$kN/m^2 \times 10^6$	and	$psi \times 10^6$	5·5–8·3	0·8–1·2
Tensile strength	$kN/m^2 \times 10^3$	and	$psi \times 10^3$	76–103	11–15
Tensile modulus	$kN/m^2 \times 10^6$	and	$psi \times 10^6$	6·2–8·3	0·9–1·2
Compressive strength	$kN/m^2 \times 10^3$	and	$psi \times 10^3$	117–145	17–21
Compressive modulus	$kN/m^2 \times 10^6$	and	$psi \times 10^6$	6·2–9·0	0·9–1·3
Shear strength perpendicular	$kN/m^2 \times 10^3$	and	$psi \times 10^3$	69–90	10–13
Shear strength parallel	$kN/m^2 \times 10^3$	and	$psi \times 10^3$	69–83	10–12
Shear modulus parallel	$kN/m^2 \times 10^6$	and	$psi \times 10^6$	2·75	0·4

Comparison of typical mechanical properties

Product type		Glass content % by weight	Ultimate tensile strength		Tensile modulus PSI $KN/mm^2 \times 10^6$	
			$N/mm^2 \times 10^3$	$PSI \times 10^3$		
C.S.M	$450g/m^2$	30	90	13.1	6.9	1.0
C.S.M.	$600g/M^2$	30	90	13·1	6·9	1·0
Woven roving	$800g/M^2$	50	250	36·3	13·2	1·91
Fabmat	600:300	47	210	30·5	13·0	1·89
Fabmat	600:450	43	186	27·0	11·5	1·67
Fabmat	800:300	44	190	27·6	12·0	1·74
H.P. Fabmat	800:150	44	250	36·3	15·0	2·18
H.P. Fabmat	800:300	45	210	30·0	12·3	1·75
Linrovmat	600:150	46	460	66·7	21·0	3·05
Linrovmat	600:300	45	430	62·4	19·0	2·76

ASTM Standard Specification or equivalent Federal Standard LP-406b.

The composite laminate is based on typical alternate plies of 610 g/m² (2 oz/sq ft) mat and 820 g/m² (24 oz/sq yd) woven roving.

Composite laminate Medium glass content		Woven roving laminate High glass content	
30–40		40–45	
1·50–1·65		1·65–1·80	
172–206	25–30	206–240	30–35
7·6–10·3	1·1–1·5	10·3–15·1	1·5–2·2
124–172	18–25	193–220	28–32
6·9–9·7	1·0 1·4	10·3–13·8	1·5–2·0
117–145	17–21	117–145	17–22
6·9–11	1·0–1·6	11·7–16·5	1·7–2·4
76–97	11–14	90–103	13–15
62–83	9–12	55–76	8–11
3·1	0·45	3·44	0·5

Ultimate compressive strength		Ultimate tensile strength per unit width per layer		Extensibility per unit width per layer		Thickness per unit layer in millimetres
N/mm² x 10³	PSI	N/mm	P/l	N/mm	P/l x 10³	
140	20.3	90	514	5715	32.6	1.0
140	30·3	120	685	7620	43·5	1·4
120	17·4	240	1370	12960	74·0	1·0
150	21·8	280	1600	16000	91·4	1·3
145	21·0	300	1714	18000	102·8	1·6
200	29·0	290	1656	19000	108·5	1·7
160	23·2	300	1714	18000	102·8	1·4
203	29·0	350	2000	20000	114·2	1·6
240	34·8	450	2570	20000	114·2	1·0
250	36 3	470	2684	22000	125·6	1·3

Reinforced plastic laminates – thickness (average figures)

	Lay up	
Kilos per sq metre	*oz per sq yd*	*material*
0·039	1·5	mat
0·052	2	mat
0·26	10	cloth
0·42	16	woven roving
0·62	24	woven roving

Mechanical properties of laminates – compared with other materials

	Glass Content		Specific Gravity	Tensile Strength		Tensile Modulus	
	$\frac{\%}{\text{weight}}$	$\frac{\%}{\text{volume}}$		$\frac{N}{mm^2}$	$\frac{lbf}{ins^2}$	$\frac{KN}{mm^2}$	$\frac{lbf}{ins^2}$
Random RP	30	17	1·4	110	16 000	7·6	1 100 000
Uni-directional R P	75	59	2·0	828	120 000	27·6	4 000 000
Mild Steel			7·8	862	125 000	207	30 000 000
Light Alloy			2·8	450	65 000	69	10 000 000

Fresh water–allowance and measurements

Normal allowance per man per day is ½ gallon (2¼ litres)

1 litre	weighs	1 kilogram
1 gallon	weighs	10 lbs
1 cubic metre	weighs	1000 kilograms
1 cubic foot	weighs	62·4 lbs
1 cubic metre	is	1000 litres
1 cubic foot	is	6·23 gallons
1 ton	occupies	35·96 cubic feet
1 ton	is	224 gallons (Imperial)

Number of plies

1		2		3		4		5	
mm	ins	mm	ins	mm	ins	mm	ins	mm	ins
1·1	0·044	2·2	0·081	3·3	0·131	4·5	0·178	5·7	0·224
1·5	0·058	2·9	0·116	4·4	0·175	6·0	0·237	7·6	0·299
0·4	0·016	0·8	0·032	1·2	0·048	1·6	0·064	2·0	0·080
0·6	0·024	1·2	0·048	1·9	0·074	2·4	0·098	3·1	0·123
0·9	0·036	1·8	0·071	2·8	0·109	3·7	0·147	4·7	0·185

Compressive Strength		Impact Strength		Specific Strength		Specific Modulus	
$\frac{N}{mm^2}$	$\frac{lbf}{ins^2}$	N metre	ft lb f	$\frac{N}{mm^2}$	$\frac{lbf}{ins^2}$	$\frac{KN}{mm^2}$	$\frac{lbf}{ins^2}$
138	20 000	20	15	79	11 400	5·5	800 000
345	50 000	68	50	414	60 000	14	2 000 000
193	28 000	13·5	10	110	16 000	25·5	3 700 000
83	12 000	7	5	160	23 000	25	3 600 000

Sailcloth weights – comparative figures

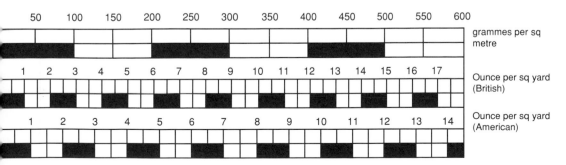

75

Tank materials

Tank material	Uses	Advantages	Treatment
Mild steel	Fuel	Cheap May be built into steel craft	Paint outside
Galvanised steel	Fresh water Sewage	Cheap	Cement wash or treat with 'Water Tank Black' or similar paint inside. Paint outside
Stainless steel	Fresh water Sewage Fuels	Long lasting Easily maintained	
Aluminium alloys	Fresh water Fuels	Long lasting Light weight Sea water resisting	If used for water the inside may need painting
Glass/polyester	Fresh water Sewage	Cheap Long lasting May be built in	Internal treatment to prevent osmosis
Flexible materials such as rubberised cloth	Fresh water Sewage Fuel	Cheap when installation costs are included Light weight Fits irregular and inaccessible spaces	The space containing the tank must be free from sharp projections

All tanks should have at least one access panel and be fully accessible inside. All tanks need cleaning every year.

Modulus of elasticity and density

Material		Elasticity		Density	
		kN/mm²	lb/in²	kg/m³	lbs/ft³
Aluminium – sheet		69	10 000 000	2770	196
– cast		76	11 000 000	2250	160
Brass – common		63	9 170 000	7500	533
– wire annealed		97	14 000 000	8425	600
Steel		207	30 000 000	7850	558
Concrete		13	1 900 000	2400	170
Wood – oak (white)		14·5	2 090 000	700	50
– pine (yellow)		11·0	1 600 000	540	38
Reinforced plastic		10·5	1 500 000	1300	92
Nylon		2·0	300 000	1000	70

3 FASTENINGS

Standard available bolt lengths for given diameters

This table also shows the common diameters for given lengths

Length		Diameter					
Millimetres	Inches Nominal	Millimetres Inches	6 1/4	8 5/16	10 3/8	12 1/2	16 5/8
10	3/8		×				
12	1/2		×	×			
16	⅝		×	×	×		
20	3/4		×	×	×	×	
25	1		×	×	×	×	×
30	1¼		×	×	×	×	×
35			×	×	×	×	×
40	1½		×	×	×	×	×
45	1¾		×	×	×	×	×
50	2		×	×	×	×	×
55	2¼		×	×	×	×	×
60			×	×	×	×	×
65	2½		×	×	×	×	×
70			×	×	×	×	×
75	3		×	×	×	×	×
80			×	×	×	×	×
90	3½			×	×	×	×
100	4			×	×	×	×
110					×	×	×
120	4½				×	×	×
130	5					×	×
140						×	×
150	6					×	×

It is not easy to find standard bolts above 150 mm (6 ins) length off the shelf, so larger lengths have to be ordered specially.

Hexagonal bolts, nuts and screws – ISO metric sizes

Standard diameters mm	Pitch of threads	Max width across flats	Max width across corners	Max height of head	Max thickness of nut
5	0·8	8	9·2	3·88	4·38
6	1	10	11·5	4·38	5·38
8	1·25	13	15·0	5·88	6·88
10	1·5	17	19·6	7·45	8·45
12	1·75	19	21·9	8·45	10·45
16	2	24	27·7	10·45	13·55
20	2·5	30	34·6	13·90	16·55
[22]	2·5	32	36·9	14·90	18·55
24	3	36	41·6	15·90	19·65
[27]	3	41	47·3	17·90	22·65
30	3·5	46	53·1	20·05	24·65
[33]	3·5	50	57·7	22·05	26·65
36	4	55	63·5	24·05	29·65
[39]	4	60	69·3	26·05	31·80
42	4·5	65	75·1	27·05	34·80
45	4·5	70	80·8	29·05	36·80
48	5	75	86·6	31·05	38·80
[52]	5	80	92·4	34·25	42·80
56	5·5	85	98·1	36·25	45·80
[60]	5·5	90	103·9	39·25	48·80
64	6	95	109·7	41·25	51·95
68	6	100	115·5	44·25	54·95

ISO and metric thread equivalents

NOMINAL THREAD SIZE	I.S.O. PITCH		NEAREST ENGLISH EQUIVALENT	NEAREST UNIFIED SIZE	INCH EQUIVALENT
	COARSE	FINE			
M2	0·40	—	9BA	—	—
M2·5	0·45	—	7BA (·098)	4UN (·112)	—
M3	0·50	—	6BA (·110)	5UN (·125)	0·1181
M3·5	0·60	—	4BA (·142)	6UN (·138)	0·1378
M4	0·70	—	3BA (·161)	8UN (·164)	0·1575
M4·5	0·75	—	—	—	0·1772
M 5	0·80	—	2BA (·185)	10UN (·190)	0·1968
M6	1·00	—	0BA (·236)	—	0·2362
M7·0	1·00	—	$\frac{1}{4}$ (·250)	$\frac{1}{4}$UN (·250)	0·2756
M8·0	1·25	1·00	$\frac{5}{16}$ (·312)	$\frac{5}{16}$UN (·312)	0·3150
M10·0	1·50	1·25	$\frac{3}{8}$ (·375)	$\frac{3}{8}$UN (·375)	0·3937
M12·0	1·75	1·25	—	$\frac{1}{2}$UN (·500)	0·4724

Screw threads per inch

Diameter		Threads per inch (25·4 mm)				
mm	in	BSW	BSF	UNC	UNF	BSP
3·2	1/8	40				28
4·8	3/16	24	32			
5·6	7/32		28			
6·4	1/4	20	26	20	28	19
7·1	9/32		26			
7·9	5/16	18	22	18	24	
9·5	3/8	16	20	16	24	19
11·1	7/16	14	18	14	20	
12·7	1/2	12	16	13	20	14
14·3	9/16	12	16	12	18	
15·9	5/8	11	14	11	18	14
17·5	11/16	11	14			
19·1	3/4	10	12	10	16	14
20·6	13/16		12			
22·2	7/8	9	11	9	14	14
25·4	1	8	10	8	12	11
28·6	1 1/8	7	9	7	12	11 for each
31·8	1 1/4	7	9	7	12	size to 6"
34·9	1 3/8	6	8	6	12	
38·1	1 1/2	6	8	6	12	
44·5	1 3/4	5	7	5		
50·8	2	4 1/2	7	4 1/2		

BA No	0	1	2	3	4	5	6	7	8	9	10
Diameter in mm	6·0	5·3	4·7	4·1	3·6	3·2	2·8	2·5	2·2	1·9	1·7
Inches	0·236	0·209	0·185	0·161	0·142	0·126	0·110	0·098	0·087	0·075	0·067
Threads per inch	25·4	28·2	31·4	34·8	38·5	43·1	47·9	52·9	59·1	65·1	72·6

GERMAN D.I.N. PITCH	FRENCH C.N.M. PITCH
—	—
—	0·45
0·50	0·60
0·60	0·60
0·70	0·75
0·75	0·75
0·80	0·90
1·00	1·00
1·00	1·00
1·25	1·25
1·50	1·50
1·75	1·75

Note

These tables are particularly useful for identifying a bolt or nut.

BSW = British Standard Whitworth
BSF = British Standard Fine
UNC = Unified Screw Threads – Coarse
UNF = Unified Screw Threads – Fine
BA = British Association
BSP = British Standard Pipe & Whitworth Pipe

NB for pipes the diameter is the bore diameter

Bolts in wood–failing loads

These curves are for a constant load applied equally at the two
ends of the bolt. For a constant load at one end take half the
figure given on the graph.

The loads given apply to two or more bolts, or one bolt and
several screws. For an isolated bolt take two thirds the given value.

When working in lb/ft² Load   =4500 x diameter x length
Above 16 diameters   Load   =4800 x diameter x length
Note: These are failing loads and a safety factor must be used in
practice.

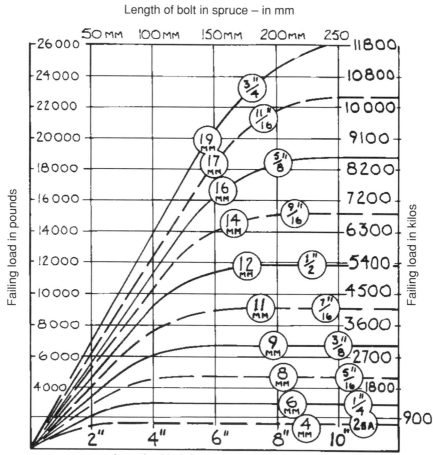

Length of bolt in spruce – in mm

Length of bolt in spruce – in inches

Breaking loads of bolts

To find the strength of a bolt, select from the left hand columns
the size of bolt of the correct thread type. Read across horizontally
to the appropriate curve and then down to the breaking load.

In practice the majority of bolts are 25 tonf/in² (385 MN/m²) and
only the high tensile ones are up to the higher strength standards.
Common brass bolts are about ⅓ or ¼ the strength of 25 tonf/in²
steel and bronze.

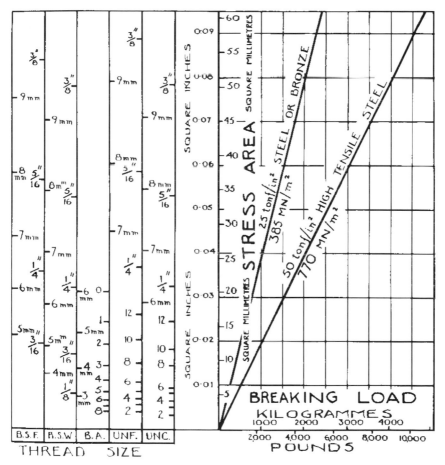

Wood screws – weight in pounds per 1000

Brass, counter-sunk head

Length ins	Screw Gauge										
	0	2	4	6	8	10	12	14	16	18	20
1/4	0·201	0·333	0·688								
3/8	0·299	0·479	0·896	1·50	2·24						
1/2		0·611	1·16	1·92	2·85	4·22					
5/8		0·715	1·41	2·36	3·47	4·88					
3/4		0·819	1·62	2·68	4·10	5·74	7·08				
7/8			1·85	3·13	4·70	6·48	8·33				
1			2·17	3·58	5·29	7·29	9·51	11·94			
1 1/4			2·63	4·40	6·49	8·96	11·67	15·21	18·54		
1 1/2			3·18	5·25	7·71	10·56	13·61	17·85	21·88	27·85	
1 3/4				6·11	8·89	12·08	15·69	20·56			
2				6·94	10·07	13·75	18·19	23·19	28·68	36·81	42·92
2 1/4					11·25	15·49	20·07	25·90			
2 1/2				8·68	12·57	17·15	22·22	28·61	35·42	45·83	
2 3/4					13·68		24·17				
3					14·86	20·28	26·32	33·96	42·22	54·86	63·26
3 1/2						21·81	30·49	39·31	49·03		
4						26·94	34·93	44·72	55·14		83·54

Brass, round head

Length ins	Screw Gauge							
	2	4	6	8	10	12	14	16
1/4	0·486	0·896						
3/8	0·597	1·15	2·13	3·49				
1/2	0·736	1·39	2·55	4·04	6·07	7·92		
5/8	0·896	1·63	2·96	4·59	6·87	9·03		
3/4	1·06	1·87	3·38	5·15	7·64	10·14		
7/8		2·10	3·74	5·69	8·40			
1		2·37	4·19	6·25	9·24	12·01	15·97	
1 1/4		2·81	5·00	7·36	10·76	14·03	18·54	
1 1/2		3·36	5·83	8·40	12·43	16·25	21·04	27·71
1 3/4			6·65	9·51	14·03	18·40		
2			7·43	10·63	15·56	20·49	28·38	
2 1/4						22·5		
2 1/2				12·92	18·75	24·58	31·74	
3				15·07	21·94	28·89	37·15	

Note: The tables are for brass screws. For silicone bronze multiply these weights by 1·062. For aluminium alloy divide these weights by three.
The table also shows the available gauge sizes for different screw lengths.

Barbed ring nails

These nails have barbed rings along the length to give them particularly effective holding power in all types of wood. They have various trade names including 'Gripfast' and 'Anchorfast'. They cost less per fastening than screws both to buy and to fix. They are hammered in, like ordinary nails, which is far quicker than drilling, counter sinking and screwing for a wood screw. However a little of the time and cost advantage is off-set by the need to put in more barbed nails than screws for a given measure of strength.

The makers recommend that the 14 and 16 gauge sizes do not need pilot holes, but some experienced shipwrights make pilot holes for all sizes which should be half the nail diameter. When using very hard woods a hole should always be drilled. These nails are available countersunk or with flat heads. They can easily be punched below the surface or they can be driven flat and varnished over.

Barbed ring nails have good corrosion resistance, being made of such materials as silicon bronze or stainless steel. They can therefore be used to replace the ferrous nails (which rust) fitted in various types of electric cable clip.

Thickness			Available lengths					
mm	swg	inches			mm/inches			
4	8	0·160	34 $1^1/_2$	44·5 $1^3/_4$	51 2	57 $2^1/_4$	63·5 $2^1/_2$	76 3
3·3	10	0·128	25·4 1	32 $1^1/_4$	38 $1^1/_2$	44·5 $1^3/_4$	50·8 2	57 $2^1/_4$
2·6	12	0·104	19 $^3/_4$	22 $^7/_8$	25·4 1	32 $1^1/_4$	38 $1^1/_2$	50·8 2
2	14	0·080	19 $^3/_4$	22 $^7/_8$	25·4 1	32 $1^1/_4$		
1·6	16	0·064	16 $^5/_8$	19 $^3/_4$	22 $^7/_8$	25·4 1		

Pilot hole sizes–wood screws

Screw Gauge	P	Hard Woods				Soft Woods			
		Pilot Hole Dia.	Drill Sizes Fraction	mm		Pilot Hole Dia.	Drill Sizes Fraction	mm	
3	1/8"	·057		1·45		No Pilot Hole necessary for these sizes			
4	1/8"	·066		1·70					
5	5/32"	·073		1·85					
6	5/32"	·082		2·10		·059		1·50	
7	3/16"	·091	3/32"	2·30		·066		1·70	
8	7/32"	·097		2·50		·071		1·80	
9	1/4"	·103		2·65		·078	5/64"	2·00	
10	1/4"	·108	7/64"	2·75		·084		2·15	
12	5/16"	·124	1/8"	3·15		·097		2·50	
14	11/32"	·140	9/64"	3·60		·108	7/64"	2·75	

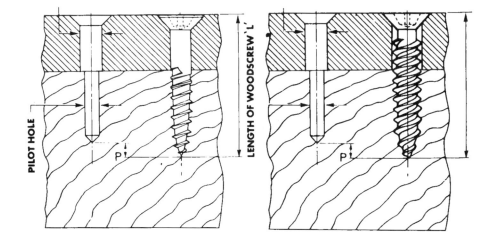

Screw Gauge	P	Hard Woods High Density Boards			Soft Woods Low Density Boards		
		Pilot Hole Dia.	Drill Sizes Fraction	mm	Pilot Hole Dia.	Drill Sizes Fraction	mm
3	·100	·063	1/16"		·035		0·90
4	·125	·070		1·80	·049		1·25
5	·136	·082		2·10	·057		1·45
6	·150	·093	3/32"		·062	1/16"	
7	·166	·106		2·70	·065		1·65
8	·166	·116		2·95	·076		1·95
10	·200	·125	1/8"		·089		2·25
12	·231	·142		3·60	·102		2·60
14	·250	·166		4·20	·116		2·95

Pilot hole sizes – nails and copper clenches

Nail gauge and clench diameter		Drill size hardwood		Drill size softwood		Roove size	
mm	ins	mm	ins	mm	ins	mm	ins
14 g		2	1/16	1	3/64	8	5/16
13 g		2	5/64	2	1/16	10	3/8
12 g		2	5/64	2	1/16	11	7/16
11 g		2·5	3/32	2	5/64	13	1/2
10 g		2·5	3/32	2	5/64	13	1/2
8 g		3	1/8	2·5	3/32	13	1/2
4·88	3/16	4·5	3/16	4	11/64	15	9/16
6·4	1/4	6·4	1/4	6	15/64	16	5/8
7·9	5/16	7·9	5/16	7	9/32	19	3/4
9·5	3/8	9·5	3/8	9	11/32	22	7/8

For hardwood: drill diam $= \dfrac{D}{2}$

For softwood: drill diam $= \dfrac{A}{2}$

Section through copper nail

Pipe clips – sizes

Not all manufacturers use the same scale for their size numbers. For marine use stainless steel pipe clips are recommended, especially in awkward locations. Galvanizing on mild steel clips is sometimes thin and often scratched. As a result, the corrosion rate is high.

On exhaust and toilet pipes the clips should be in pairs at each end. They should also be used in pairs on all important pipes. Extra large sizes, not listed here, are available from mast makers, who use them to secure mast coats.

Inside diameter				Inside diameter			
mm	Inches	Size No	BS 3628 No	mm	Inches	Size No	BS 3628 No
9–13	3/8–1/2	000	050	44–60	1 3/4–2 3/8	2X	237
9–16	3/8–5/8	M00	062	50–70	2–2 3/4	3	275
13–19	1/2–3/4	00	075	60–80	2 3/8–3 1/8	3X	312
16–22	5/8–7/8	0	087	70–90	2 3/4–3 1/2	4	350
19–25	3/4–1	0X	100	82–100	3 1/4–4	4X	400
22–28	7/8–1 1/8	1A	112	95–115	3 3/4–4 1/2	5	450
25–35	1–1 3/8	1	137	105–125	4 1/8–5	6	500
28–41	1 1/8–1 5/8	1X	162	125–146	5–5 3/4	6X	575
32–48	1 1/4–1 7/8	2A	187	133–158	5 1/4–6 1/4	7	625
38–54	1 1/2–2 1/8	2	212				

4 SPARS AND RIGGING

Aluminium alloy masts – general guide

This scale is a rough guide to mast dimensions which is quick and conveniently useful. For long range cruising go up one or two sizes. Except where stated the dimensions do not include mast track.

Acknowledgement is made to Ian Proctor Metal Masts Ltd for assistance

Yacht size (approx waterline length)		Typical mast section		Wall thickness		Approx mast weight	
m	*ft*	*mm*	*ins*	*mm*	*ins*	*kg/m*	*lb/ft*
5·5	18	105 × 75	4·0 × 3·0	integral track		2·15	1·44
5·5	18	115 × 75	4·5 × 3·0	2·0	0·08	1·7	1·15
5·8	19	120 × 80	4·8 × 3·2	2·0	0·08	1·8	1·21
6·4	21	130 × 85	5·2 × 3·9	2·3	0·09	2·25	1·51
6·7	22	140 × 92	5·5 × 3·6	2·6	0·10	2·7	1·81
6·7	22	153 × 92	6·0 × 3·6	2·6	0·10	2·93	1·97
7·3	24	140 × 108	5·5 × 4·25	3·2	0·13	3·44	2·3
7·3	24	125 × 90	4·8 × 3·5	integral track		3·2	2·15
7·9	26	160 × 120	6·3 × 4·8	3·2	0·13	3·68	2·47
8·5	28	205 × 115	8·0 × 4·5	3·2	0·13	4·38	2·94
9·1	30	200 × 140	7·8 × 5·5	4·1	0·16	5·46	3·67
10	33	205 × 170	8·0 × 6·6	4·1	0·16	6·47	4·35
10·7	35	240 × 165	9·5 × 6·5	4·1	0·16	7·29	4·9
13·7	45	270 × 190	10·5 × 7·5	5·4	0·21	9·9	6·7
15·2	50	305 × 205	12·0 × 8·0	6·4	0·25	14·5	9·7
25	80	360 × 250	14·0 × 10·0	6·4	0·25	16·4	11·5

Aluminium alloy masts–size selection graph

(See graphs on opposite page)
To find the diameter and wall thickness of a mast given:
1) The yacht's waterline length
2) The height of the fore-triangle

Items 1) and 2) are first added. If they are in metric units use the top of the graph. If in imperial units use the bottom. The plotting method is shown opposite in the small graph.

Where the sum of items 1) and 2) intercepts the type of rig, read horizontally down for the area of the rectangle which will enclose the mast tube. Read on further across for the mast wall thickness.

When using this type of graph, it is important to make adjustments according to the type of yacht. For long range cruising in severe weather conditions increase the mast size by one or two steps.

Example: An ocean racer having a waterline length plus foretriangle height added together to give a total of 22 m with a single spreader mast head rig. The mast section would be something approaching 27×10^3 sq mm in area. The section might be 190 mm × 145 mm or 180 mm × 150 mm. Its wall thickness would be of the order of 4 mm.

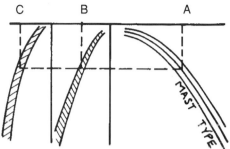

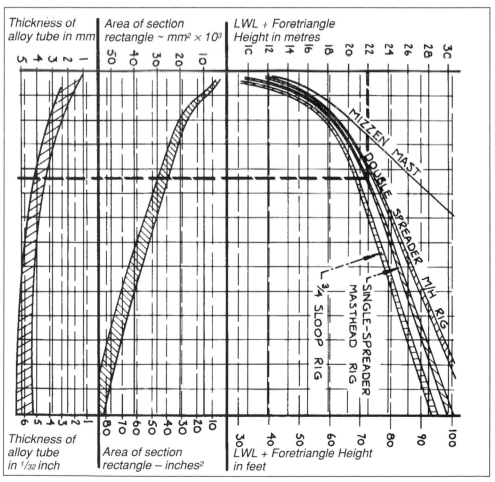

87

Aluminium alloy – boom dimensions

The graph for boom diameter against overall length is drawn in metric figures (left and bottom scales with solid lines) and also in feet and inches (top and right hand scales with dotted lines).

The graph is an approximate guide. For long range cruising an increase of at least 10% would be usual. For inshore racing special considerations apply but the diameter might be reduced.

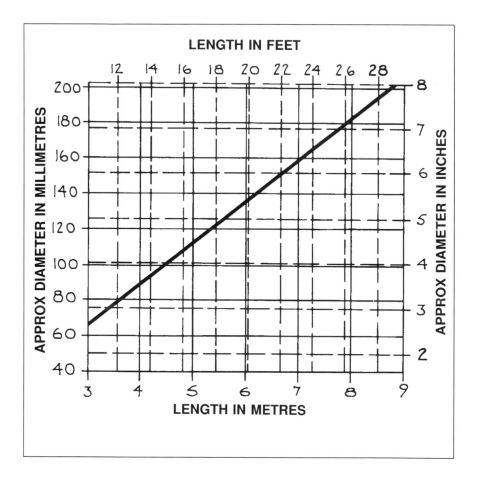

Aluminium alloy – spinnaker boom dimensions

The graph is for the maximum spinnaker boom diameter and is marked in metric figures (left hand side and bottom scales with solid lines) and also in feet and inches (right hand side and upper scale with dotted lines). These booms normally taper considerably at each end, though some of the smaller or cheaper ones are parallel.

The graph is an approximate guide. For extended cruising, particularly when using twin running headsails, these dimensions may well be increased. However, the larger the overall diameter of a boom, the more difficult it is to grasp in the hand. About 75 mm (3 in) is the biggest convenient diameter for most people. This fact may influence a choice towards a thinner maximum section with a thicker wall.

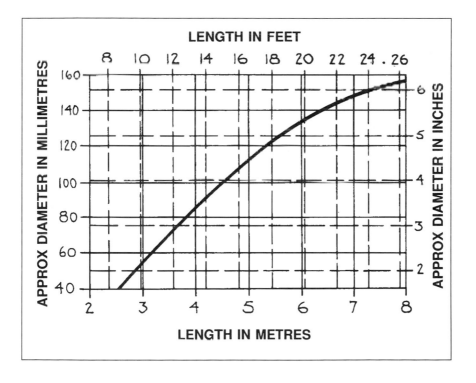

Standing rigging sizes

The thickness of standing rigging on a boat depends on her purpose, her beam, the mast height, sail area, the intended cruising ground and similar factors.

The graph gives a good working average, but for ocean cruising the sizes should be increased at least one step on the scale. For inshore racing the sizes might be reduced by one step.

Since rigging is relatively cheap but a dismasting is expensive, it is better to fit one size too large than one too small. Even when racing it is worth remembering that in order to win it is necessary to finish.

On the left side of the graph are the metric sizes; on the right are imperial. The base is in tonnes or tons, which for the purposes of this graph are closely similar.

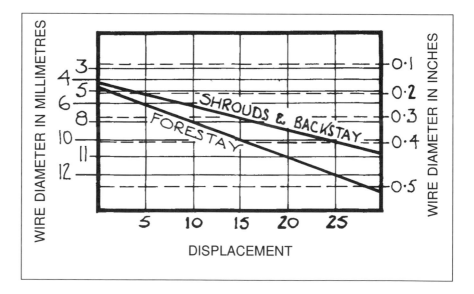

Rigging screw pins, forks and standard ends

Since rigging screws break far more often than the wire, the screw should be $1\frac{1}{2}$ times as strong as the shroud it is connected to. For ocean racing the factor should be 3. However where standard components are used the correct standing rigging screw must be bought to fit the standard rigging terminal, standard chain plate, toggle etc.

Note: Ropes of sizes other than those listed should be associated with the next maximum size above it in the table. The working depth l_1 indicates the limit of parallelism of the facing sides of the fork slot. The threaded length of shaft (l_2) is to be not less than nominal screw thread diameter (d_3).

Where the pin is secured by a screwed nut the thread length is to be not less than the diameter of the screw thread.

Limits of tolerance of ± 0.3 mm are allowable on dimensions d_1 and d_2, plus 1.0 mm on dimension l_1.

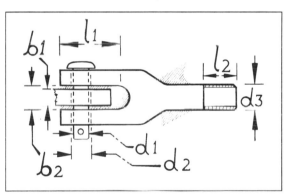

Maximum diameter of wire rope	Size of rigging screw	Designation of screw thread of shank	Diameter of pin	Diameter of eye	Working depth of fork end	Width of fork slot [$d_2 \pm 5\%$] b_2		Thickness of eye b_1	
			d_1	d_2	l_1	*Min*	*Max*	*Min*	*Max*
3	6	6 × 1 × 8 g	5	6·5	10	6·3	6·7	4·5	5·3
4	8	8 × 1·25 × 8 g	7	8	12	7·5	8·5	6·5	7·5
5	10	10 × 1·5 × 8 g	8	10	15	9·5	10·5	7·5	8·5
7	12	12 × 1·75 × 8 g	11	13	20	12·3	13·7	10·5	11·5
10	16	16 × 2 × 8 g	14	16	24	15·2	16·8	13·3	14·7
12	20	20 × 2·5 × 8 g	18	20	30	19·0	21·0	17·0	19·0
16	24	24 × 3 × 8 g	22	25	38	23·7	26·3	21·0	23·0

Nitronic 50 rod rigging

DIAMETER		SIZE	BREAK STRENGTH		WEIGHT	
mm	in		Kg	lb	Kg/m	lb/ft
3.5	0.138	−2	1452	3200	0.076	0.051
4.0	0.157	−3	1860	4100	0.10	0.067
4.5	0.177	−4	2270	5000	0.13	0.087
5.0	0.197	−6	2720	6000	0.15	0.101
5.5	0.217	−8	3220	7100	0.19	0.128
6.0	0.236	−9	3900	8600	0.22	0.148
6.5	0.256	−10	4500	9900	0.26	0.175
7.0	0.276	−12	5350	11800	0.3	0.201
7.5	0.295	−15	6400	14100	0.35	0.235
8.5	0.335	−17	8000	17650	0.45	0.302
9.5	0.375	−22	9750	21500	0.56	0.376
11.1	0.437	−30	13600	30000	0.76	0.515
12.7	0.500	−40	16300	36000	1.00	0.674
14.3	0.563	−48	20900	46000	1.25	0.844
16.75	0.660	−60	26800	59000	1.74	1.174
18.03	0.710	−66	29500	65000	2.02	1.359
20.6	0.811	−75	34000	75000	2.65	1.777
22.23	0.875	−90	40800	90000	3.07	2.064
25.4	1.000	−110	49900	110000	4.02	2.696
28.0	1.102	−140	63500	140000	4.87	3.273
30.2	1.189	−180	81700	180000	5.68	3.811
33.38	1.314	−220	99800	220000	6.93	4.655
36.55	1.439	−260	118000	260000	8.31	5.581
41.22	1.623	−300	136000	300000	1.027	7.099
44.45	1.75	−400	181500	400000	12.29	8.255
50.8	2.000	−500	226800	500000	16.05	10.781

Composition: 22% Ni, 13% Cr, 5% Mo

Ultimate tensile strength: 200–220 Ksi (1380–1520 MPa)

Density: 0·286 lbs/cu in (7920 Kg/m³)

Modulus of elasticity: 28 Msi (193 GPa)

Gamma rod rigging

DIAMETER		SIZE	BREAK STRENGTH		WEIGHT	
mm	in		Kg	lb	Kg/m	lb/ft
17.9	0.705	−76	34500	76000	1.986	1.335
19.5	0.768	−91	40900	90000	2.356	1.584
22.2	0.875	−115	53200	117000	3.060	2.057
25.4	1.000	−150	68200	150000	3.996	2.686
27.1	1.066	−170	77300	170000	4.540	3.052
28.6	1.125	−195	86400	190000	5.058	3.400
30.3	1.191	−220	98600	217000	5.668	3.810
33.4	1.313	−260	118200	260000	6.890	4.631
38.1	1.500	−320	145200	320000	8.991	6.044

Composition: 22% Ni, 13% Cr, 5% Mo

Ultimate tensile strength: 200–220 Ksi (1380–1520 MPa)

Density: 0·286 lbs/cu in (7920 Kg/m³)

Modulus of elasticity: 28 Msi (193 GPa)

Cobalt rod rigging

DIAMETER		STRETCH EQUIV NITRONIC	BREAK STRENGTH		WEIGHT	
mm	in		Kg	lb	Kg/m	lb/ft
4.5	0.177	−6	2684	5916	0.134	0.090
5.2	0.205	−8	3585	7900	0.179	0.120
6.35	0.250	−12	5345	11781	0.266	0.179
7.2	0.283	−15	6872	15146	0.342	0.230
7.92	0.312	−17	8315	18327	0.415	0.279
8.35	0.329		9243	20371	0.416	0.310
8.71	0.343	−22	10057	22165	0.501	0.337
9.5	0.375		12027	26507	0.600	0.403
10.3	0.406	−30	14064	30996	0.701	0.471
11.1	0.437		16333	35998	0.814	0.547
11.58	0.456	−40	17776	39179	0.887	0.596
12.7	0.500	−48	21381	47124	1.066	0.716
13.5	0.531		23618	51960	1.204	0.807
14.3	0.562		27012	59535	1.347	0.905
15.3	0.603	−60	28584	63000	1.551	1.012
16.76	0.660	−66	30853	68000	1.856	1.247
18.8	0.740	−75	39020	86000	2.337	1.570
20.6	0.811	−90	43103	95000	2.805	1.885
22.2	0.874		49909	110000	3.257	2.189
23.2	0.913	−110	71351	157257	3.557	2.390
24.0	0.945		76356	168289	3.807	2.558
25.4	1.000	−140	85524	188496	4.264	2.865

Composition: 35% Co, 35% Ni, 20% Cr, 10% Mo

Ultimate tensile strength: 220–240 Ksi   (1520–1650 MPa)

Density: 0·304 lbs/cu in (8414 Kg/m³)

Modulus of elasticity: 33·6 Msi   (232 GPa)

Carbon rod rigging

DIAMETER		STRETCH EQUIV NITRONIC	BREAK STRENGTH		WEIGHT	
mm	in		Kg	lb	Kg/m	lb/ft
3.20	0.126	−3	1357	2992	0.010	0.006
4.76	0.187	−4	3004	6620	0.021	0.014
5.50	0.217	−8	4010	8838	0.028	0.019
6.35	0.250	−10	5345	11781	0.038	0.025
8.00	0.315	−15	8484	18699	0.060	0.040
9.50	0.374	−22	11964	26368	0.084	0.057
11.1	0.437	−30	16333	35998	0.115	0.077
12.7	0.500	−40	21381	47124	0.151	0.101
14.3	0.562	−48	27012	59525	0.190	0.128
16.7	0.660	−60	37254	82109	0.263	0.177
18.0	0.710	−66	43094	94978	0.304	0.204
20.6	0.811	−75	56254	123985	0.397	0.267
22.2	0.874	−90	65332	143992	0.461	0.310
25.4	1.000	−110	85524	188496	0.603	0.405

Ultimate tensile strength: 217–290 Ksi   (1496–2000 MPa)

Density: 0·043 lbs/cu in (1190 Kg/m³)

Modulus of elasticity: 29 Msi   (200 GPa)

Soft Kevlar rigging

DIAMETER		STRETCH EQUIV NITRONIC	BREAK STRENGTH		WEIGHT	
mm	in		Kg	lb	Kg/m	lb/ft
5.70	0.224	−2	960	2166	0.029	0.019
6.60	0.260	−3	1500	3306	0.038	0.025
7.50	0.295	−4	2304	5078	0.048	0.033
8.60	0.339	−6	3264	7194	0.065	0.044
10.3	0.406	−8	5184	11426	0.089	0.060
11.0	0.433	−12	6144	13541	0.130	0.087
13.3	0.524	−17	9024	19889	0.140	0.094
15.5	0.610	−22	12096	26660	0.185	0.124
16.8	0.662	−30	14784	32584	0.215	0.144
19.0	0.748	−40	20160	44433	0.290	0.194
22.0	0.866	−48	25200	55541	0.390	0.262
25.2	0.992	−60	31500	69426	0.520	0.349
28.6	1.126	−75	42840	94419	0.670	0.449
32.6	1.283	−90	54180	119413	0.870	0.583

Modulus of Elasticity:
18 Msi (120 GPa)

Polyurethane coating

Kevlar fibres

Pultruded Kevlar rod rigging

DIAMETER		STRETCH EQUIV NITRONIC	BREAK STRENGTH		WEIGHT	
mm	in		Kg	lb	Kg/m	lb/ft
3.18	0.125		1284	2825	0.011	0.007
4.75	0.187	−2	2865	6304	0.025	0.017
6.35	0.250	−4	5121	11290	0.045	0.030
7.00	0.276	−6	6223	13720	0.055	0.037
7.92	0.312	−8	7967	17563	0.070	0.045
9.52	0.375	−10	11510	25376	0.101	0.068
10.3	0.404	−12	13396	29532	0.118	0.079
12.7	0.500	−17	20485	45160	0.179	0.120
13.9	0.546	−22	24398	53787	0.213	0.143
15.9	0.625	−30	32028	70608	0.280	0.188
19.1	0.750	−40	46091	101611	0.402	0.270

Ultimate tensile strength: 234 Ksi (1617 MPa)

Density: 0·051 lbs/cu in (1419 Kg/m³)

Modulus of elasticity: 11 Msi (76 GPa)

Turnbuckles for rod rigging

SIZE	⌀ ROD	⌀ PIN	A	⌀ B	⌀ C	⌀ D	E	F	L MIN	L MAX
-2	3.5 4.0	5/16	10	9	15	7.5	167	65	209	278
-4	4.5	3/8	11	10.5	18	9	192	70	241	327
-6	5.0	3/8	11	10.5	18	9	192	70	241	327
-8	5.5 6.0	7/16	13	12.5	20	10.5	215	80	277	375
-10	6.5	1/2	15	14.5	24	12	240	85	315	429
-12	7.0	1/2	15	14.5	24	12	240	85	315	429
-15	7.5	5/8	18	17.5	28	15.5	263	90	350	478
-17	8.5	5/8	18	17.5	28	15.5	263	90	350	478
-22	9.5	3/4	22	19.5	32.5	18.5	291	100	391	536
-30	11.1	7/8	24	23	41	22	337	102	437	618
-40	12.7	1"	26	25.5	41	22	340	107	472	648
-48	14.3	1 1/8	30	28.5	45.5	24	365	112	514	710
-60	16.75	1 1/4	34	34	51	28	420	127	591	817
-66	18.03	1 1/4	34	34	51	28	420	127	591	817
-75	20.6	1 3/8	38	40	62.5	33	475	141	666	919
-90	22.23	1 3/8	38	40	62.5	33	475	141	666	919
-110	25.4	1 1/2	40	45	72	37	535	160	764	1047
-140	28.0	1 3/4	46	52	80	42	550	165	805	1103
-180	30.2	1 7/8	50	58	90	44.5	570	180	880	1140
-220	33.38	2 1/8	56	63	98	48	585	195	915	1168
-260	36.55	2 1/2	64	70	108	54	600	200	950	1200
-300	41.22	2 3/4	70	75	115	60	620	230	985	1230
-400	44.45	2 7/8	74	87	130	64	690	250	1055	1338
-500	50.8	3 1/4	84	100	148	73	765	250	1168	1506

Turnbuckles for half lenticular rod rigging

SIZE	ø ROD	ø PIN	A	ø B	ø C	ø D	E	F	L MIN	L MAX
−2	3.5 4.0	5/16	10	9	15	7.5	132	65	174	208
−4	4.5	3/8	11	10.5	18	9	201	70	200	247
−6	5.0	3/8	11	10.5	18	9	201	70	200	247
−8	5.5 6.0	7/16	13	12.5	20	10.5	175	80	237	295
−10	6.5	1/2	15	14.5	24	12	195	85	270	339
−12	7.0	1/2	15	14.5	24	12	195	85	270	339
−15	7.5	5/8	18	17.5	28	15.5	213	90	290	368
−17	8.5	5/8	18	17.5	28	15.5	213	90	290	368
−22	9.5	3/4	22	19.5	32.5	18.5	241	100	326	421
−30	11.1	7/8	24	23	41	22	267	102	362	473
−40	12.7	1"	26	25.5	41	22	270	107	402	508
−48	14.3	1 1/8	30	28.5	45.5	24	295	112	444	570
−60	16.75	1 1/4	34	34	51	28	330	127	500	637
−66	18.03	1 1/4	34	34	51	28	330	127	500	637
−75	20.6	1 3/8	38	40	62.5	33	365	141	556	700
−90	22.23	1 3/8	38	40	62.5	33	365	141	556	700
−110	25.4	1 1/2	40	45	72	37	405	160	634	787
−140	28.0	1 3/4	46	52	80	42	420	165	675	843
−180	30.2	1 7/8	50	58	90	44.5	470	180	775	935
−220	33.38	2 1/8	56	63	98	48	485	195	810	963
−260	36.55	2 1/2	64	70	108	54	475	200	825	950
−300	41.22	2 3/4	70	75	115	60	500	230	865	990
−400	44.45	2 7/8	74	87	130	64	550	250	915	1058
−500	50.8	3 1/4	84	100	148	73	600	250	1003	1176

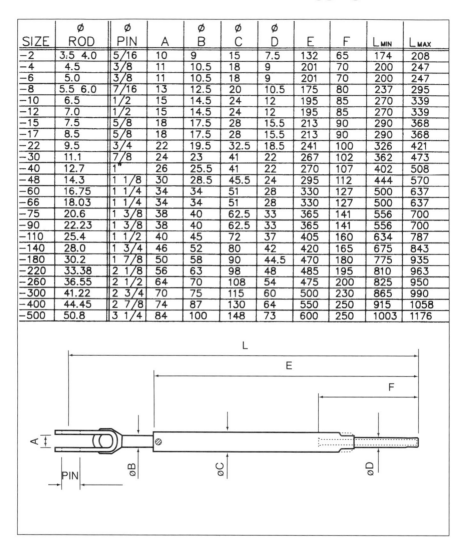

Turnbuckles for wire

Ø WIRE		Ø		Ø	Ø	Ø				
MET	IMP	PIN	A	B	C	D	E	F	L MIN	L MAX
4	5/32	5/16	10	9	15	7.5	207	45	249	318
5	3/16	3/8	11	10.5	18	9.1	241	51	290	376
6	7/32	7/16	13	12.5	20	12.5	279	64	341	439
7	9/32	1/2	15	14.5	24	14.3	315	70	390	504
8	5/16	5/8	18	17.5	28	16.1	355	90	442	570
10	3/8	5/8	18	17.5	28	17.9	385	110	472	600
12	1/2	3/4	22	19.5	32.5	21.4	440	135	540	685
14	9/16	7/8	24	23	41	25.0	515	155	615	796
16	5/8	1"	26	25.5	41	28.1	545	180	677	853
19	3/4	1 1/8	30	28.5	45.5	34.5	600	210	749	945
22	7/8	1 1/4	34	34	51	40.5	700	250	871	1097
26	1"	1 3/8	38	40	62.5	46.0	805	300	996	1249

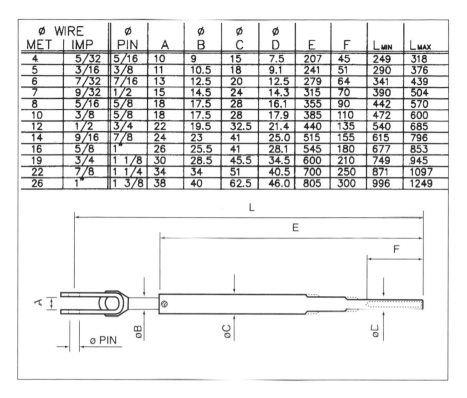

Tip turnbuckles

SIZE	Ø ROD	R	Ø A	Ø B	Ø C	D	E	L MIN	L MAX	TIP CUP EXIT HOLE
-2	3.5 4.0	5.0	9	5.0	12.5	70	10	110	145	6.1
-4	4.5	6.5	12	6.5	15	80	13	135	175	8.0
-6	5.0	6.5	12	6.5	15	80	13	135	175	8.0
-8	5.5 6.0	7.5	13.5	7.5	18	105	15	150	200	9.2
-10	6.5	11	17	9.5	20.5	122	17	165	230	11.6
-12	7.0	11	17	9.5	20.5	122	17	165	230	11.6
-15	7.5	12	20	11.1	23.5	140	20	185	260	15
-17	8.5	12	20	11.1	25	157	22	200	283	15
-22	9.5	13	22.5	12.7	28.5	175	25	225	320	17
-30	11.1	15	25	14.3	32	190	30	240	350	19
-40	12.7	20	34	20.5	36	200	40	230	335	28
-48	14.3	23	38	24	41	210	40	245	350	30
-60	16.75	25	44	27	47	220	45	265	365	34
-66	18.03	25	44	27	47	220	45	265	365	34
-75	20.6	30	46	30	56	260	75	305	420	39
-90	22.23	30	46	30	56	260	75	305	420	39
-110	25.4	38	62	38	65	300	80	350	490	46

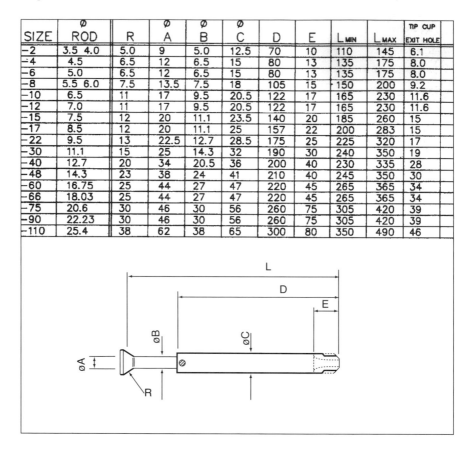

Fork toggles

SIZE	ø ROD	ø PIN	ø A	B	C	D	E	F	G	H
-2	3.5 4.0	5/16	8.5	10	16	30	20	10	20	8.5
-4	4.5	3/8	10	11	17	35	25	15	23	10
-6	5.0	3/8	10	11	17	35	25	15	22	10
-8	5.5 6.0	7/16	11.5	13	21	40	30	17.5	27	11.5
-10	6.5	1/2	13	15	25	50	30	17.5	35	13
-12	7.0	1/2	13	15	25	50	30	17.5	34	13
-15	7.5	5/8	16	18	30	62	40	23	43	16
-17	8.5	5/8	16	18	30	62	40	23	43	16
-22	9.5	3/4	20	22	34	72	50	28	50	18
-30	11.1	7/8	23	24	40	80	50	30	54	22
-40	12.7	1"	26	26	42	90	60	35	62	26
-48	14.3	1 1/8	29	30	54	105	60	35	73	29
-60	16.75	1 1/4	33	34	58	125	70	40	90	33
-66	18.03	1 1/4	33	34	58	125	70	40	90	33
-75	20.6	1 3/8	36	38	68	140	80	45	100	36
-90	22.23	1 3/8	36	38	68	140	80	45	98	36
-110	25.4	1 1/2	39	40	70	160	90	50	113	39
-140	28.0	1 3/4	45	46	86	175	95	60	117	45
-180	30.2	1 7/8	48	50	90	190	110	70	130	48
-220	33.38	2 1/8	54	56	96	205	125	85	140	54
-260	36.55	2 1/2	64	64	114	220	135	90	150	64
-300	41.22	2 3/4	70	70	120	225	155	95	160	70
-400	44.45	2 7/8	74	74	134	250	160	100	165	74
-500	50.8	3 1/4	84	84	144	270	190	115	178	84

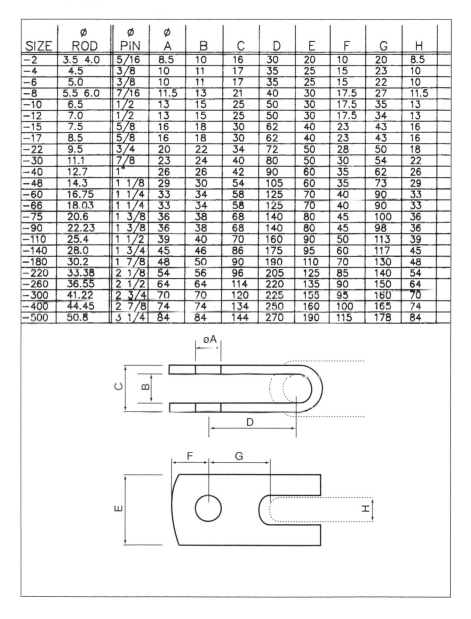

High fatigue jaws

SIZE	ø ROD	ø PIN	ø A	B	C	D	E	F	G	
-2	3.5 4.0	5/16	8.5	10	16	10	20	68	20	
-4	4.5	3/8	10	11	17	15	25	77	23	
-6	5.0	3/8	10	11	17	15	25	81	22	
-8	5.5 6.0	7/16	11.5	13	21	17.5	30	96	27	
-10	6.5	1/2	13	15	25	17.5	30	108	35	
-12	7.0	1/2	13	15	25	17.5	30	113	34	
-15	7.5	5/8	16	18	30	23	40	129	43	
-17	8.5	5/8	16	18	30	23	40	129	43	
-22	9.5	3/4	20	22	34	28	50	148	50	
-30	11.1	7/8	23	24	40	30	50	163	54	
-40	12.7	1"	26	26	42	35	60	185	62	
-48	14.3	1 1/8	29	30	54	35	60	208	73	
-60	16.75	1 1/4	33	34	58	40	70	240	90	
-66	18.03	1 1/4	33	34	58	40	70	243	90	
-75	20.6	1 3/8	36	38	68	45	80	273	100	
-90	22.23	1 3/8	36	38	68	45	80	284	98	
-110	25.4	1 1/2	39	40	70	50	90	309	113	
-140	28.0	1 3/4	45	46	86	60	95	345	117	
-180	30.2	1 7/8	48	50	90	70	110	378	130	
-220	33.38	2 1/8	54	56	96	85	125	420	140	

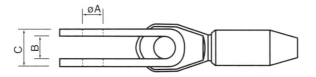

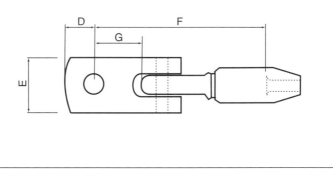

White Kevlar 49 cable

Part No	Strength Tonnes	Diameter mm	Weight K/metre
REG/015T	1.5	6.0	0.027
REG/030T	3.0	7.5	0.045
REG/045T	4.5	9.0	0.065
REG/060T	6.0	10.0	0.079
REG/080T	8.0	11.0	0.098
REG/105T	10.5	12.5	0.119
REG/120T	12.0	13.5	0.145
REG/150T	15.0	15.5	0.189
REG/225T	22.5	18.0	0.259
REG/250T	25.0	19.0	0.289
REG/300T	30.0	20.0	0.321
REG/450T	45.0	25.0	0.522
REG/540T	54.0	27.0	0.574
REG/600T	60.0	29.0	0.626

Kevlar 49 standard lightweight sockets

Part No	Strength Tonnes	Weight Kilos	Thread UNF"
REG/015S	1.5	0.062	$\frac{5}{16}$"
REG/030S	3.0	0.103	$\frac{3}{8}$"
REG/045S	4.5	0.149	$\frac{7}{16}$"
REG/060S	6.0	0.181	$\frac{1}{2}$"
REG/080S	8.0	0.235	$\frac{5}{8}$"
REG/105S	10.5	0.299	$\frac{5}{8}$"
REG/120S	12.0	0.290	$\frac{3}{4}$"
REG/150S	15.0	0.377	$\frac{7}{8}$"
REG/225S	22.5	0.518	1"
REG/250S	25.0	0.578	$1\frac{1}{8}$"
REG/300S	30.0	0.658	$1\frac{1}{4}$"
REG/450S	45.0	1.035	$1\frac{3}{8}$"
REG/540S	54.0	1.148	$1\frac{1}{2}$"
REG/600S	60.0	1.289	$1\frac{3}{4}$"

Kevlar 49 standard lightweight sockets with eyes

Part No	Strength Tonnes	Weight Kilos	Thread UNF"
REG/015E	1.5	0.084	$\frac{5}{16}$"
REG/030E	3.0	0.153	$\frac{3}{8}$"
REG/045E	4.5	0.233	$\frac{7}{16}$"
REG/060E	6.0	0.315	$\frac{1}{2}$"
REG/080E	8.0	0.445	$\frac{5}{8}$"
REG/105E	10.5	0.479	$\frac{5}{8}$"
REG/120E	12.0	0.502	$\frac{3}{4}$"
REG/150E	15.0	0.777	$\frac{7}{8}$"
REG/225E	22.5	1.078	1"
REG/250E	25.0	1.324	$1\frac{1}{8}$"
REG/300E	30.0	1.678	$1\frac{1}{4}$"
REG/450E	45.0	2.801	$1\frac{3}{8}$"
REG/540E	54.0	3.248	$1\frac{1}{2}$"
REG/600E	60.0	4.002	$1\frac{3}{4}$"

Kevlar 49 standard lightweight sockets with bails

Part No	Strength Tonnes	Weight Kilos
REG/015B	1.5	0.062
REG/030B	3.0	0.103
REG/045B	4.5	0.149
REG/060B	6.0	0.181
REG/080B	8.0	0.235
REG/105B	10.5	0.299
REG/120B	12.0	0.290
REG/150B	15.0	0.377

Kevlar 49 standard lightweight sockets with high fatigue jaws

Part No	Strength Tonnes	Weight Kilos	Pin Size"
REG/015J	1.5	0.134	$5/16$"
REG/030J	3.0	0.253	$3/8$"
REG/045J	4.5	0.413	$7/16$"
REG/060J	6.0	0.515	$1/2$"
REG/080J	8.0	0.845	$5/8$"
REG/105J	10.5	0.879	$5/8$"
REG/120J	12.0	1.202	$3/4$"
REG/150J	15.0	1.777	$7/8$"
REG/225J	22.5	2.578	1"
REG/250J	25.0	3.674	$1 1/8$"
REG/300J	30.0	4.428	$1 1/4$"
REG/450J	45.0	6.702	$1 3/8$"
REG/540J	54.0	7.148	$1 1/2$"
REG/600J	60.0	8.222	$1 3/4$"

Kevlar 49 standard lightweight sockets with high fatigue eyes

Part No	Strength Tonnes	Weight Kilos	Thread UNF"
REG/015F	1.5	0.138	5/16"
REG/030F	3.0	0.203	3/8"
REG/045F	4.5	0.333	7/16"
REG/060F	6.0	0.465	1/2"
REG/080F	8.0	0.745	5/8"
REG/105F	10.5	0.779	5/8"
REG/120F	12.0	0.902	3/4"
REG/150F	15.0	1.577	7/8"
REG/225F	22.5	2.328	1"
REG/250F	25.0	2.774	1 1/8"
REG/300F	30.0	3.628	1 1/4"
REG/450F	45.0	5.751	1 3/8"
REG/540F	54.0	6.198	1 1/2"
REG/600F	60.0	7.972	1 3/4"

Kevlar 49 standard lightweight sockets with T terminals

Part No	Strength Tonnes	Weight Kilos	B/plate Size mm
REG/015T	1.5	0.094	4mm
REG/030T	3.0	0.233	5mm
REG/045T	4.5	0.333	6mm
REG/060T	6.0	0.515	7mm
REG/080T	8.0	0.569	10mm

Marine eyes for Kevlar 49

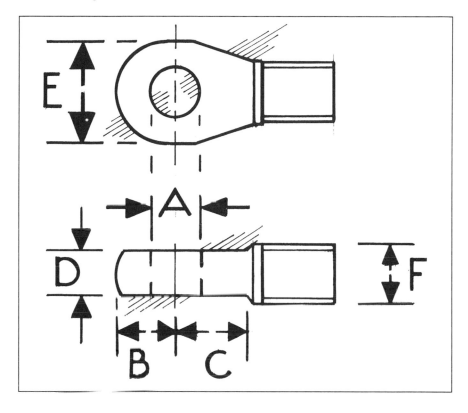

Size Tonnes	A	B	C	D	E	F
1.5	8.5	10.0	12.0	7.0	17.0	⁵⁄₁₆"
3.0	10.0	12.0	13.0	7.0	20.0	³⁄₈"
4.5	11.5	13.0	19.0	10.0	25.0	⁷⁄₁₆"
6.0	13.0	16.0	19.0	11.0	29.0	½"
8.0	16.0	19.0	20.0	14.0	31.0	⁵⁄₈"
10.5	16.0	19.0	20.0	14.0	31.0	⁵⁄₈"
12.0	20.0	22.0	28.0	16.0	37.0	¾"
15.0	23.0	26.0	30.0	20.0	44.0	⅞"
22.5	26.0	28.0	36.0	23.0	47.0	1"
25.0	29.0	32.0	37.0	26.0	54.0	1⅛"
30.0	33.0	33.0	45.0	30.0	62.0	1¼"
45.0	36.0	40.0	50.0	32.0	72.0	1³⁄₈"
54.0	36.0	42.0	50.0	34.0	75.0	1½"
60.0	39.0	46.0	50.0	36.0	83.0	1¾

High fatigue eyes for Kevlar 49

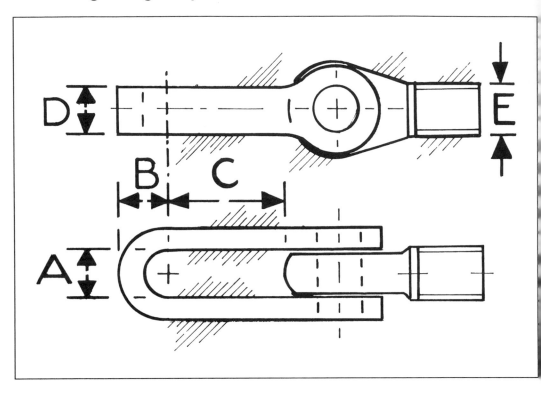

Size Tonnes	A	B	C	D	E
1.5	8.0	8.0	16.0	8.0	⁵⁄₁₆"
3.0	10.0	9.0	21.0	10.0	³⁄₈"
4.5	12.0	10.0	26.0	11.0	⁷⁄₁₆"
6.0	14.0	13.0	29.0	13.0	½"
8.0	17.0	17.0	46.0	16.0	⅝"
10.5	17.0	17.0	46.0	16.0	⅝"
12.0	20.0	18.0	53.0	18.0	¾"
15.0	23.0	22.0	59.0	22.0	⅞"
22.5	26.0	23.0	67.0	25.0	1"
25.0	30.0	27.0	73.0	28.0	1⅛"
30.0	34.0	29.0	92.0	33.0	1¼"
45.0	38.0	35.0	108.0	38.0	1⅜"
54.0	38.0	35.0	108.0	38.0	1½"
60.0	40.0	40.0	114.0	39.0	1¾

High fatigue jaws for Kevlar 49

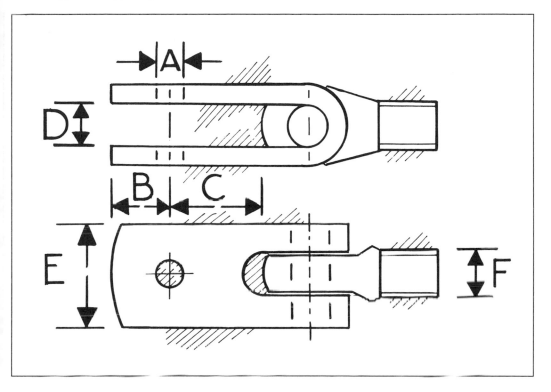

Size Tonnes	A	B	C	D	E	F
1.5	8.5	10.0	20.0	10.0	20.0	$\frac{5}{16}$"
3.0	10.0	15.0	23.0	11.0	25.0	$\frac{3}{8}$"
4.5	11.5	17.5	27.0	13.0	30.0	$\frac{7}{16}$"
6.0	13.0	17.5	35.0	15.0	30.0	$\frac{1}{2}$"
8.0	16.0	25.0	41.0	18.0	40.0	$\frac{5}{8}$"
10.5	16.0	25.0	41.0	18.0	40.0	$\frac{5}{8}$"
12.0	20.0	30.0	48.0	22.0	50.0	$\frac{3}{4}$"
15.0	23.0	30.0	54.0	24.0	50.0	$\frac{7}{8}$"
22.5	26.0	35.0	62.0	26.0	60.0	1"
25.0	29.0	35.0	73.0	30.0	60.0	$1\frac{1}{8}$"
30.0	33.0	40.0	92.0	34.0	70.0	$1\frac{1}{4}$"
45.0	36.0	45.0	100.0	38.0	80.0	$1\frac{3}{8}$"
54.0	36.0	45.0	100.0	38.0	80.0	$1\frac{1}{2}$"
60.0	39.0	50.0	114.0	40.0	90.0	$1\frac{3}{4}$

Shackles – safe working loads

Diameter of pin		Stainless steel						Galvanized tested			
		Normal D shape		Narrow D shape		Harp or bow		D shape		Harp or bow	
mm	ins	kg	lb	kg	lb	kg	lb	kg	lb	kg	lb
3	1/8	140	310			130	290				
4	5/32	320	700								
5	3/16	380	840			190	420				
6	1/4	510	1120			200	450				
8	5/16			790	1700	410	900	200	450	190	420
10	3/8	1400	3080			510	1120	310	670	292	645
11	7/16			1660	3650						
13	1/2	2350	5200			760	1680	410	900	360	780
16	5/8							610	1350	610	1350
19	3/4							1120	2480	1010	2240
22	7/8							1620	3580	1520	3360
25	1							2260	5000	2020	4480
29	1 1/8							3060	6750	2260	5000

Safe working load is approximately a quarter of the distortion load; ie the factor of safety is about four.

Titanium shackles

Typical strength figures though some makes may fall short of these loads.

Diameter of pin		Static load without distortion		Breaking load	
mm	ins	kg	lb	kg	lb
6	1/4	1100	2400	2100	4600
8	5/16	1800	3900	3000	6600
10	3/8	3300	7200	7500	16500
12	1/2	4500	9900	10000	22000
14	9/16	6400	14000	14000	30800
16	5/8	8500	18700	19000	41800
20	3/4	11000	24000	28000	61600
24	1 Nominal	16000	35000	35000	77000

U-bolts – typical dimensions and strengths

Important: Read the notes before using this table.

U-bolts vary according to the makers, so the figures given here are just guide-lines. This is just one reason why big safety factors should be used when specifying or using a U-bolt. It should never be stressed up near its distortion load.

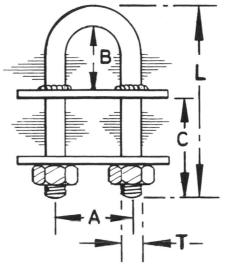

When drilling holes to fit a U-bolt, the washer plate serves as a template or guide. It is important to fit strong backing pads in way of the U-bolt to spread the load over a wide area. Circumstances vary, but as a rough guide, the backing pad typically should be at least four times the T dimensions which is the thickness of the rod forming the U-bolt. Assuming the backing pad is square, then each side should typically be at least of the order of ten times the C dimension.

The U-bolt should be bedded in a water-proof non-hardening compound which should be under the top plate and under the washer plate, also under the doubler pad. This compound must be used so copiously that when the nuts are tightened the compound is seen to squeeze out all round the plates and the backing pad.

T		L		A		B		C		Distortion load		Breaking load	
ins	mm	ins	mm	ins	mm	ins	mm	ins	mm	lb	kg	lb	kg
$5/32$	4	2	50	1	24	$7/8$	21	$1\frac{1}{8}$	27	1300	600	2200	1000
$3/16$	5	$2\frac{3}{8}$	60	$1\frac{1}{8}$	28	1	24	$1\frac{1}{4}$	30	1700	800	4400	2000
$1/4$	6	$2\frac{3}{4}$	70	$1\frac{1}{4}$	32	$1\frac{1}{8}$	27	$1\frac{3}{8}$	35	3500	1600	6300	2900
$1/4$	6	$3\frac{1}{2}$	90	$1\frac{1}{4}$	32	$1\frac{1}{8}$	27	$2\frac{1}{8}$	55	3500	1600	6300	2900
$5/16$	8	$3\frac{1}{8}$	80	$1\frac{3}{8}$	36	$1\frac{1}{4}$	30	$1\frac{5}{8}$	40	6600	3000	10500	4800
$5/16$	8	4	100	$1\frac{3}{8}$	36	$1\frac{1}{4}$	30	$2\frac{3}{8}$	60	6600	3000	10500	4800
$3/8$	10	$3\frac{1}{2}$	90	$1\frac{5}{8}$	40	$1\frac{1}{4}$	32	$1\frac{3}{4}$	45	9900	4500	15400	7000
$3/8$	10	$4\frac{3}{8}$	110	$1\frac{5}{8}$	40	$1\frac{1}{4}$	32	$2\frac{1}{2}$	65	9900	4500	15400	7000
$1/2$	12	$4\frac{3}{8}$	110	$1\frac{3}{4}$	44	$1\frac{3}{8}$	34	2	50	17600	8000	26400	12000
$1/2$	12	$5\frac{1}{8}$	130	$1\frac{3}{4}$	44	$1\frac{3}{8}$	34	$2\frac{3}{4}$	70	17600	8000	26400	12000

Stainless steel flexible wire – breaking load and weight of running rigging

Nominal diameter	Approx diameter	Approx circum	Construction	Nominal breaking load		Approx weight	
mm	ins	ins		kg	lb	kg per 100 m	lb per 100 ft
2	5/64	1/4	6 × 7	270	600	1·5	1·0
2·5	3/32	5/16	7 × 12	410	900	2·4	1·6
3	1/8	3/8	7 × 12	640	1400	3·7	2·5
4	5/32	1/2	7 × 19	950	2100	5·8	3·9
5	3/16	5/8	7 × 19	1500	3300	8·2	5·5
6	1/4	3/4	7 × 19	2100	4800	15·3	10·3
7	9/32	7/8	7 × 19	2900	6500	19·1	12·8
8	5/16	1	7 × 19	3800	8500	23·6	15·9

Stainless steel wire rope – breaking load and weight of standing rigging

| Nominal diameter | Approx diameter | Approx circum | 1 × 19 | | | | 7 × 7 | | | |
| | | | Nominal breaking load | | Weight | | Nominal breaking load | | Weight | |
mm	ins	ins	kg	lb	kg per 100 m	lb per 100 ft	kg	lb	kg per 100 m	lb per 100 ft
2	5/64	1/4	320	700	2·0	1·4	290	650	1·8	1·2
2·5	3/32	5/16	530	1165	3·1	2·1	400	900	2·5	1·7
3	1/8	3/8	760	1680	4·0	2·7	660	1470	3·7	2·5
4	5/32	1/2	1350	3000	7·3	4·9	970	2150	5·7	3·8
5	3/16	5/8	2100	4650	11·3	7·6	1600	3700	8·5	5·7
6	1/4	3/4	3000	6700	16·5	11·1	2300	5200	15·5	10·4
7	9/32	7/8	4150	9150	22·5	15·1				
8	5/16	1	5400	11950	32·7	22·0				
9	3/8	1 1/8	6400	14140	40·9	27·5				
10	13/32	1 1/4	8400	18600	47·5	32·0				
12	15/32	1 1/2	12200	26800	82·0	55·0				
14	9/16	1 3/4	16600	36600	100·1	68·0				
16	5/8	2	21700	47750	132·0	89·0				

Galvanised steel flexible wire – breaking load and weight of running rigging

Nominal diameter	Approx diameter	Approx circum	Construction	Nominal breaking load		Approx weight	
mm	ins	ins		kg	lb	kg per 100 m	lb per 100 ft
2·5	3/32	5/16	7 × 12	340	750	2·3	1·5
3	1/8	3/8	7 × 12	525	1160	3·8	2·5
4	5/32	1/2	7 × 12	880	1940	6·3	4·2
5	3/16	5/8	7 × 12	1130	2510	8·1	5·4
6	1/4	3/4	7 × 19	2180	4890	15·1	10·1
7	9/32	7/8	7 × 19	2820	6280	19·2	12·8
8	5/16	1	7 × 19	3400	7560	23·8	15·9
10	13/32	1 1/4	7 × 19	4930	10900	32·2	21·5

Galvanised steel wire rope – breaking load and weight of standing rigging

Nominal diameter	Approx diameter	Approx circum	1 × 19 Nominal breaking load		Weight		7 × 7 Nominal breaking load		Weight	
mm	ins	ins	kg	lb	kg per 100 m	lb per 100 ft	kg	lb	kg per 100 m	lb per 100 ft
2	5/64	1/4					224	490	1·5	1·0
2·5	3/32	5/16	530	1165	3·1	2·1	322	705	2·3	1·5
3	1/8	3/8	760	1680	4·0	2·7	530	1160	3·8	2·5
4	5/32	1/2	1350	3000	7·3	4·9	1140	2500	5·9	3·9
5	3/16	5/8	2100	4650	11·3	7·6	1810	3950	9·3	6·2
6	1/4	3/4	3000	6700	16·5	11·1	2580	5650	13·4	8·9
7	9/32	7/8	4150	9150	22·5	15·1	3520	7700	18·3	12·2
8	5/16	1	5400	11950	32·7	22·0	4610	10100	23·8	15·9
10	13/32	1 1/4	8400	18600	47·5	32·0	7180	15700	37·2	24·8
12	15/32	1 1/2	12200	26800	82·0	55·0	10300	22600	79·8	53·2

Qualities of man-made fibre ropes

Rope type	Trade names	Uses	Price
Polypropylene	Ulstron Courlene	Dinghy sheets Painters and tow ropes eg for water skiers where rope must float Rescue lines	Low
Polyester	Terylene Dacron	Widely used for all purposes on cruisers	Medium
Nylon	Nylon	Anchor warps Dock lines	Medium
Aramid	Kevlar Twaron Technora		
HMDPE High molecular density polyethylene	Spectra Dyneema	Dinghy ropes Generally, halyards, runners, guys etc on keel boats	High
Vectran	Vectran	Jib and main halyards on yachts over 15m ~ 50 feet	High

Rope damage

A feature of rope with a strong core and an outer protective sheath is that the latter sometimes wears out much sooner than the core. To prevent this the rope should not be secured so that the same length is always subject to chafe. For instance, when leaving the boat after sailing, the halyards should be secured differently each time. As an example, a headsail halyard may have its shackle secured to different positions on the pulpit each week.

When the sheath is stripped off (to save weight and windage), care is needed to ensure the core does not suffer any chafe. For instance a main halyard which has been 'stripped' should have a length of sheathing left where the halyard passes over the sheave both in the 'stowed' position, when on moorings, and in the 'in use' position when the sail is hoisted.

Spinnaker halyards continue to fail, usually at or near the sheave, sometimes after quite a short period of use. When a vessel is involved in a long reach or run which involves having a spinnaker up for days on end, special precautions are needed in the area of the sheave. Sometimes wear occurs on the edges of the sheave cage, sometimes on adjacent fittings. One answer is to use the traditional precaution, namely a short length of chain in the wearing area.

This chain, which must be of the best quality, is heavier than rope, and needs a proper chain-to-rope join, but the added weight is a small penalty to pay for reliability. One accidental spinnaker drop can loose much time, and cause damage to the sail.

Stretch at working load	Resistance to wear	Resistance to ultra-violet light	Notes
A lot	Poor	Poor	Floats Does not absorb water
-%	Good	Good	The most widely available and widely used rope. Hardens with age
A lot	Good	Good	Not widely used because of its high degree of stretch
About 2%	Poor	Poor	No longer widely used due to internal weakening with use causing unexpected failures
.5%	Can be bad	Good	Not ideal for heavily loaded halyards due to 'creep' floats. Does not absorb water
.5%	Excellent	Poor so must have an outer cover	Its high price is widely considered its main disadvantage

Ropes of man-made fibres – diameter, circumference, breaking load, weight

Terylene/Dacron 3-strand
Polyster multifilament.

The recommended working load is ⅓, or for offshore cruising ⅕ of the breaking loads given here.

Diameter		Size Circum	Typical breaking load		Weight	
					kg per	lb per
mm	ins	ins	kg	lb	100 m	100 ft
2	3/32	1/4	140	300	0·37	0·25
4	3/16	1/2	290	650	1·46	0·98
6	1/4	3/4	560	1250	3·0	1·95
8	5/16	1	1020	2240	5·1	3·5
10	3/8	1 1/4	1590	3500	8·1	5·5
12	1/2	1 1/2	2270	5000	11·6	7·8
14	9/16	1 3/4	3180	7000	15·7	10·6
16	5/8	2	4000	9000	20·5	13·8
18	3/4	2 1/4	5000	11200	26·0	17·6
20	13/16	2 1/2	6300	14000	32·0	21·6
22	7/8	2 3/4	7600	17000	38·4	25·9
24	1	3	9000	20000	46·0	31·0
28	1 3/16	3 1/2	12200	27000	63·0	42·3
32	1 3/8	4	15700	35000	82·0	55·0
36	1 1/2	4 1/2	19300	42500	104·0	70·0
40	1 11/16	5	23900	52500	128·0	86·0

Nylon 3-strand (Polyamide multifilament)

The recommended working load is ⅓, or for offshore cruising ⅕ of the breaking loads given here.

Diameter		Size Circum	Breaking load		Weight	
mm	ins	ins	kg	lb	kg per 100 m	lb per 100 ft
4	³/₁₆	¹/₂	320	700	1·1	0·7
6	¹/₄	³/₄	750	1600	2·37	1·67
8	⁵/₁₆	1	1350	2900	4·2	2·85
10	³/₈	1¹/₄	2000	4500	6·5	4·38
12	¹/₂	1¹/₂	3000	6600	9·4	6·4
14	⁹/₁₆	1³/₄	4000	9000	12·8	8·7
16	⁵/₈	2	5300	11600	16·6	11·3
18	³/₄	2¹/₄	6700	14700	21·0	14·2
20	¹³/₁₆	2¹/₂	8300	18000	26·0	17·5
22	⁷/₈	2³/₄	10000	21900	31·5	21·3
24	1	3	12000	26400	37·5	25·3
28	1³/₁₆	3¹/₂	15800	34600	51·0	34·4
32	1³/₈	4	20000	43900	66·5	44·8
36	1¹/₂	4¹/₂	24800	54400	84	56·6
40	1¹¹/₁₆	5	30000	66100	104	70

Ulstron/Courlene 3-strand (Polypropylene multifilament)

The recommended working load is ⅓, or for offshore cruising ⅕ of the breaking loads given here.

Diameter		Size Circum	Breaking load		Weight	
mm	ins	ins	kg	lb	kg per 100 m	lb per 100 ft
4	³/₁₆	¹/₂	250	550	0·93	0·63
6	¹/₄	³/₄	500	1100	1·9	1·3
8	⁵/₁₆	1	900	2000	3·4	2·3
10	³/₈	1¹/₄	1350	3000	5·2	3·5
12	¹/₂	1¹/₂	1900	4200	7·5	5·0
14	⁹/₁₆	1³/₄	2600	5700	10·2	6·9
16	⁵/₈	2	3300	7300	13·2	8·9
18	³/₄	2¹/₄	4300	9500	16·9	11·3
20	¹³/₁₆	2¹/₂	5350	11700	20·6	13·9
22	⁷/₈	2³/₄	6000	13400	25	16·7
24	1	3	7500	16800	30	20·0
28	1³/₁₆	3¹/₂	10000	22400	41	27·3
32	1³/₈	4	12500	28000	53	35·5
36	1¹/₂	4¹/₂	16000	36000	67	45
40	1¹¹/₁₆	5	19200	42500	83	56

Polyester ropes – recommended sizes for running rigging

	up to 5·5 m	5·5–7·3 m	7.3–9 m	9–11 m	11–13·5 m	13·5–16·5 m	16·5–20 m	20–25 m
Length overall	up to 18 ft	18–24 ft	24–30ft	30–36ft	36–44 ft	44–54 ft	54–66 ft	66–80 ft
Thames tonnage	Dinghies and dayboats	2–4 tons	4–8 tons	8–12 tons	12–18 tons	18–30 tons	30–55 tons	55–90 tons
Halyards – Mainsails and masthead jibs	6·5 mm $^1/_4$ in 3 strand	8 mm $^5/_{16}$ in 3 strand	10 mm $^3/_8$ in 3 strand	13 mm $^1/_2$ in 3 strand	13 mm $^1/_2$ in 3 strand	13 mm $^1/_2$ in 3 strand	16 mm $^5/_8$ in 3 strand	21 mm $^{13}/_{16}$ in 3 strand
Halyards – Staysails and mizzen	6·5 mm $^1/_4$ in 3 strand	8 mm $^5/_{16}$ in 3 strand	8 mm $^5/_{16}$ in 3 strand	10 mm $^3/_8$ in 3 strand	13 mm $^1/_2$ in 3 strand	13 mm $^1/_2$ in 3 strand	13 mm $^1/_2$ in 3 strand	16 mm $^5/_8$ in 3 strand
Topping lift – Main boom	5 mm $^3/_{16}$ in plaited	6·5 mm $^1/_4$ in plaited	6·5 mm $^1/_4$ in plaited	10 mm $^3/_8$ in plaited	10 mm $^3/_8$ in plaited	13 mm $^1/_2$ in plaited	13 mm $^1/_2$ in plaited	16 mm $^5/_8$ in plaited
Topping lift – Mizzen	5 mm $^3/_{16}$ in plaited	5 mm $^3/_{16}$ in plaited	6·5 mm $^1/_4$ in plaited	6·5 mm $^1/_4$ in plaited	10 mm $^3/_8$ in plaited	10 mm $^3/_8$ in plaited	10 mm $^1/_2$ in plaited	13 mm $^1/_2$ in plaited
Burgee halyard	2 mm $^1/_{16}$ in plaited	3 mm $^1/_8$ in plaited	3 mm $^1/_8$ in plaited	3 mm $^1/_8$ in plaited	3 mm $^1/_8$ in plaited	5 mm $^3/_{16}$ in plaited	5 mm $^3/_{16}$ in plaited	6·5 mm $^1/_4$ in plaited
Sheets – Mainsail and headsails	11 mm $^7/_{16}$ in plaited	11 mm $^7/_{16}$ in plaited	13 mm $^1/_2$ in plaited	13 mm $^1/_2$ in plaited	16 mm $^5/_8$ in plaited	16 mm $^5/_8$ in plaited	19 mm $^3/_4$ in plaited	22 mm $^7/_8$ in plaited
Sheets – Mizzen and spinnakers	6.5mm $^1/_4$ in plaited	10 mm $^3/_8$ in plaited	11 mm $^7/_{16}$ in plaited	13 mm $^1/_2$ in plaited	13 mm $^1/_2$ in plaited	13 mm $^1/_2$ in plaited	16 mm $^5/_8$ in plaited	19 mm $^3/_4$ in plaited
Spinnaker sheets – Light weather	5 mm $^3/_{16}$ in plaited	6·5 mm $^1/_4$ in plaited	6·5 mm $^1/_4$ in plaited	10 mm $^3/_8$ in plaited	10 mm $^3/_8$ in plaited	10 mm $^3/_8$ in plaited	11 mm $^7/_{16}$ in plaited	11 mm $^1/_2$ in plaited

Note: **All rope sizes are diameters.**
For ocean cruising use one or two sizes larger.

Dinghy running rigging — lengths, diameters, types of rope

Rigging item	Pico	Laser 13	Racing Laser	Standard Laser	Laser Fun	Laser II Regatta	Laser 4000	Laser 5000	Laser 16
Main sheet	12 m 8 mm 8 plait	12 m 9 mm 16 plait	13 m 8 mm Marstron	12·8 m 9 mm 16 plait	9 m† 9 mm 16 plait	9 m† 9 mm 16 plait	6 m† 9 mm 16 plait	9 m† 9 mm 16 plait	12 m† 9 mm 16 plait
Jib sheets		8 m 9 mm 16 plait			7 m† 9 mm 16 plait	7 m† 9 mm 16 plait	10 m 6 mm	11 m 6 mm braid	8 m† 9 mm 16 plait
Spinnaker or jenneker sheet						13·4 m 6 mm braid	12·5 m 8 mm braid	19 m† 8 mm 8 plait	14 m 6 mm braid
Traveller	1·2 m 6 mm 8 plait	1·8 m 5 mm 8 plait	4·25 m 6 mm spectra	3·05 m 7 mm 8 plait	3·3 m 6 mm braid	3·3 m* 6 mm* braid			
Clew outhaul	3·65 m 4 mm 8 plait	3·7 m 6 mm 8 plait	6 m* 5 mm 8 plait	2·3 m 5 mm 8 plait	3·1 m 6 mm 8 plait	3·1 m 6 mm 8 plait			
Clew tie down	0.35 m 4 mm 8 plait	0.7 m 4 mm 8 plait	1 m* 4 mm 8 plait	0.63 m 4 mm 8 plait	0.63 m 4 mm 8 plait	0.63 m 4 mm 8 plait			
Centreboard retaining line			3 m 5 mm shock-cord	2·35 m 5 mm shock-cord	3 m 5 mm shock-cord	3 m 5 mm shock-cord	1.5 m 5 mm shock-cord		
Jenneker bag closure								2·8 m 4 mm 8 plait	
Reef line		3·4 m 5 mm 8 plait			3·7 m 6 mm 8 plait				
Kicking strap	2·7 m 6 mm 8 plait	3·9 m 6 mm 8 plait	5 m 6 mm braid	3·6 m 6 mm 8 plait	3·9 m 6 mm 8 plait		10 m 4 mm 8 plait		5·5 m 6 mm 8 plait
Cunningham line[s]	1·25 m 4 mm 8 plait	2 m 5 mm 8 plait	4·25 m* 5 mm 8 plait	3·7 m 5 mm 8 plait	2·3 m 5 mm 8 plait		10 m†† 4 mm 8 plait		
Spinnaker pole up-haul and downhaul									7 m 5 mm 3 m 5 mm
Cunninghams 1 and 2							1·25 m 4·5 mm 1·2 m 4 mm	5·6 m 4 mm 2·2 m 4 mm	2 m 5 mm 0·75 m 5 mm

*Pre stretched   †Matt   ‡Second one 1·6 m 6 mm   ††Control line

Running rigging – typical lengths for small craft

Class	Sheets					Halyards			
	Mainsails			Foresails		Mainsails		Foresails	
	Metres	Ft	No of Sheaves	Metres	Ft	Metres	Ft	Metres	Ft
Albacore	7·35	24	4	9·15	30	13·40	44	9·15	30
Bobcat	14·65	48	4	9·15	30	20·15	66	18·30	60
Cadet	6·40	21	2	6·10	20	10·35	34	8·25	27
Enterprise	7·95	26	2	7·35	24	12·80	42	9·45	31
Finn	8·25	27	3			14·65	48		
Fireball	7·65	25	3	7·65	25	14·65	48	10·70	35
Firefly	6·70	22	2	6·75	22	13·70	45	10·05	33
505	10·70	35	4	9·15	30	14·05	46	10·40	34
Fleetwind	6·40	21	2	5·50	18	12·20	40	7·65	25
Flying Dutchman	9·15	30	4	14·02	46	14·65	48	11·00	36
Flying 15	7·35	24	5	7·35	24				
470	9·75	32	4	8·85	29	14·05	46	10·40	34
GP14	7·95	26	2	7·35	24	13·75	45	10·10	33
Graduate	7·35	24	2	7·35	24	11·00	36	7·95	26
Heron	7·35	24	2	6·10	20	7·95	26	7·95	26
Hornet	9·75	32	4	7·05	23	13·75	45	8·85	29
Jollyboat	11·00	36	5	8·26	27	9·75	32	13·75	45
Merlin Rocket	7·95	26	4	6·75	22	14·65	48	10·70	35
National 12	7·65	25	2	6·75	22	13·75	45	11·00	36
OK	8·55	28	2			11·00	36		
Shearwater	9·15	30	4	9·15	30	14·65	48	7·95	26
Signet	7·35	24	2	5·50	18	11·00	36	8·55	28
Silhouette	12·20	40	3	7·95	26	12·20	40	13·45	44
Snipe	7·95	26	3	8·55	28	11·90	39		
Solo	11·00	36	3			11·90	39		
Tempest	10·05	33	5	12·20	40	16·30	55	14·65	48
Topper	7·00	23				10·67	35		
Vagabond	7·35	24	2	6·1	20	7·95	26	7·95	26
Wayfarer	12·80	42	3	9·75	32	14·05	46	10·70	35
Zenith	10·05	33	3	8·23	27	15·25	50	11·60	38

Sheave sizes – for rope cordage

Rope diameter size		Recommended sheave diameter		Minimum sheave diameter	
mm	ins	mm	ins	mm	ins
2 & 3	1/16 & 1/8	25	1	16	5/8
5	3/16	38	1 1/2	25	1
6.5	1/4	45	1 3/4	25	1
8	5/16	50	2	29	1 1/8
10	3/8	57	2 1/4	32	1 1/4
11	7/16	64	2 1/2	45	1 3/4
13	1/2	70	2 3/4	57	2 1/4
14	9/16	83	3 1/4	67	2 5/8
16	5/8	90	3 1/2	73	2 7/8

Note: **Rope sizes are diameters**

117

5 ENGINES AND POWERING

Fuel tank design

For small craft all fuel tanks should be made in accordance with the principles shown here. Though this sketch is based on British official recommendations, similar rules apply in other countries.

Key: 1 The deck filler must be fully watertight and sealed all round so that:
a) There is no chance of rain or spray getting into the fuel and,
b) There is no chance that spillage will get below decks.
2 Stainless steel hose clips.
3 Short length of oil resistant hose.
4 Electric conductor between the engine and tank.

Note: The fuel feed pipe is normally made the same size as the connection on the engine.

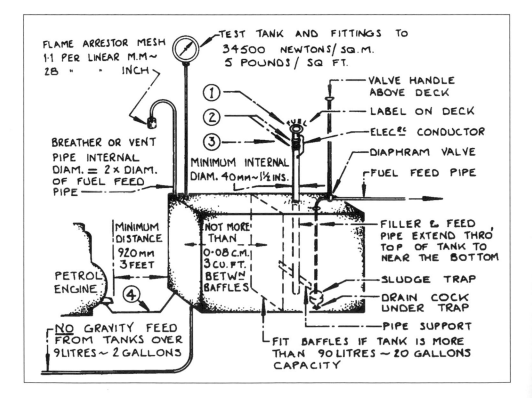

Engine room exhaust system

A particularly attractive way of sucking hot foul air from an engine room is to use the power of the engine exhaust. The ejector type of combined exhaust and ventilator must be carefully proportioned if it is to work well. Two alternative layouts are shown here based on recommendations by Caterpillar Diesels Limited.

Key: 1 The exhaust pipe with a gently sweeping elbow.

2 The ejector mixing section.

3 The ejector entrance.

4 The funnel or exhaust stack, with hot air from the engine room rising up outside the engine exhaust pipe. The cross-sectional area of the funnel should exceed $(4D)^2$.

5 Exhaust pipe extension. Minimum length = D.

6 Partial bell-mouth formed by the end piece cut at 45° and added to lower end of ejector mixing section.

7 Water drains formed by transverse slots cut in the under side of the pipe. Edges of slot bent as shown. Transverse length of slot = D/2.

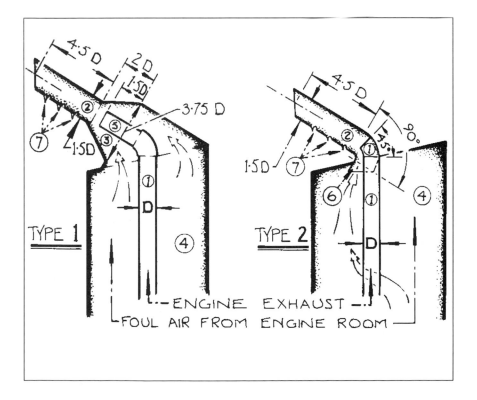

Fuel – consumption, weight, tankage

Consumption	Litres	Pints
	BHP × Hours	BHP × Hours
High speed diesel engines	0·23	0·4
Low speed diesel engines	0·21	0·37
Petrol engines	0·34	0·6
TVO (kerosene or paraffin)	0·40	0·7

Weight	One litre weighs	One gallon weighs
Diesel	0·84 kilograms	8·5 pounds
Petrol	0·73 kilograms	7·4 pounds
TVO (kerosene or paraffin)	0·81 kilograms	8·2 pounds

Tankage	1 tonne is approx	1 ton is approx
Diesel	1180 litres	1200 litres
		264 galls
Petrol	1340 litres	1360 litres
		300 galls
TVO (kerosene or paraffin)	1250 litres	1270 litres
		280 galls

Fuel and gas piping

Fuel and bottled gas pipes should have the minimum number of joins. If possible pipes should be run in one unbroken length from the tank to the units served. Junctions, taps etc should be accessible. Seamless annealed copper piping should always be used, except where flexible piping is essential. Flexible piping should be as short as possible and protected from sharp edges and from rubbing with the craft's movement. Bottled gas flexible piping should be to BSS 3212: 1960 or the equivalent.

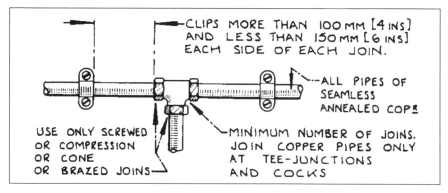

CLIPS MORE THAN 100 MM [4 INS] AND LESS THAN 150 MM [6 INS] EACH SIDE OF EACH JOIN.

ALL PIPES OF SEAMLESS ANNEALED COPE

USE ONLY SCREWED OR COMPRESSION OR CONE OR BRAZED JOINS

MINIMUM NUMBER OF JOINS. JOIN COPPER PIPES ONLY AT TEE-JUNCTIONS AND COCKS

Electric cables – current capacity

Wire specifications for rubber insulated twin and single core cables.

Current rating in amps	Cable
5	1/·044 or 3/·029
10	1/·064 or 3/·036
15	7/·029
24	7/·036
31	7/·044
37	7/·052
46	7/·064
53	19/·044
64	19/·052
83	19/·064
118	19/·083

Fuse wire – current capacity

Diameter		SWG	Current capacity in amps
mm	ins		
0·213	0·0084	35	5
0·345	0·0136	29	10
0·510	0·020	25	15
0·610	0·024	23	20
0·815	0·033	21	30
1·02	0·040	19	38
1·43	0·056	17	65
1·83	0·072	15	77
2·03	0·080	14	100

Power/ speed ratios

The nomograph opposite, based on work by Borner & Witte, gives a rough but useful preliminary guide to the power needed for a given speed, over a range of craft from 4·5 to 40m (15 to 130 ft).

The start is from line 1, which is the load-waterline, and for an example, 18 m (60 ft) has been selected. A line is drawn through the displacement scale (2), where the example displaces 10 tons, and extended to the baseline on the right (3). A new line runs leftwards from the right-hand baseline and through the estimated horsepower (4), at 200 hp, to the left-hand baseline (5). From this point a new straight line is drawn to the appropriate hull form graph (6) where the example is a round bilge hull form with a beam/draft ratio of 4. The speed is read off on the scale (7) and in the example is 13·5 knots. If this speed is inadequate, then the line from the right-hand baseline (3) to the left-hand one (5) is slid up through a higher horsepower.

Experienced designers always treat this sort of exercise with caution as they know that the engine(s) may not deliver their predicted power, or the propellers may be slightly imperfect, or the hull built overweight due to inattention to detail, and so on. If in doubt, it is best to assume the finished craft will be, say, 5% overweight, and the engines give perhaps 8% less than their stated power. Also, of course, wise naval architects always aim for a slightly higher speed than the owner requires.

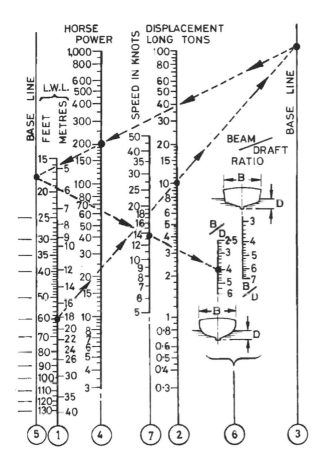

This nomograph assumes that the propeller efficiency will be about 65%. It tends to be less accurate at the higher lengths, ie near the bottom of scale (1), especially when associated with the upper end of the displacement scale (2). It is important to remember that no craft will achieve its expected speed if trials are carried out in shallow water or in bad weather.

Speed – Power – Weight graphs

The approximate graphs below are used when a design is being prepared and the horsepower for a given speed is needed. A full powering calculation cannot always be done during the early stages of a design, and these curves are valuable then. They should not be relied upon, especially as rough seas, a badly aligned shaft, a fouled hull, or one floating below her designed waterline are just some of the things which will reduce a vessel's speed.

An example of how the graphs are used is shown by looking at a boat 21·3 m (70 ft) long. This length is shown bottom left, at point A. The vertical line from there is followed up to the required speed, which in this case is 12 knots, seen at point B. The horizontal dotted line is followed to the right till it crosses the correct displacement curve, which in the example is 60 tons, at point C. From there a vertical line downwards is drawn to give the required horsepower at D. This is 325 hp when the block coefficient is 0·36 and 350 hp when the block coefficient is 0·4. If the block coefficient is 0·44 then 370 hp is required. Because these graphs are approximate, a safety factor must always be added.

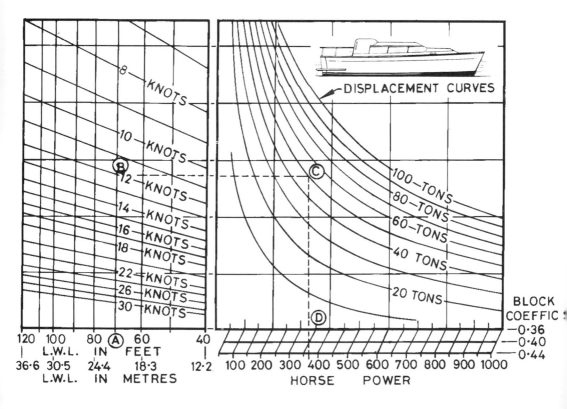

Speed/horsepower – launches and workboats (1)

These speeds are reduced, often considerably, by head winds, rough seas, damaged propeller blades, a weed-covered under-body and so on.

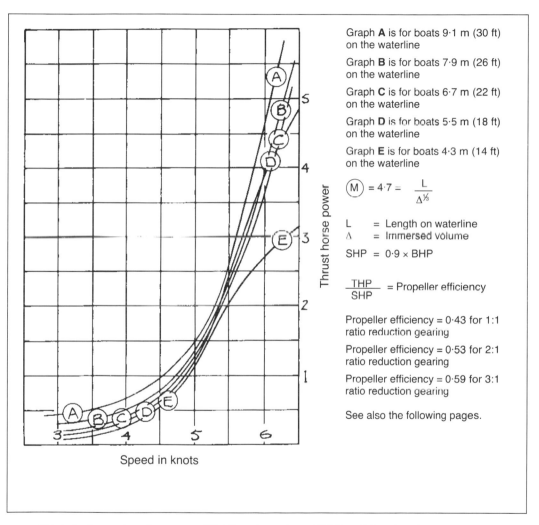

Speed in knots

Graph **A** is for boats 9·1 m (30 ft) on the waterline

Graph **B** is for boats 7·9 m (26 ft) on the waterline

Graph **C** is for boats 6·7 m (22 ft) on the waterline

Graph **D** is for boats 5·5 m (18 ft) on the waterline

Graph **E** is for boats 4·3 m (14 ft) on the waterline

$$\text{\textcircled{M}} = 4\cdot7 = \frac{L}{\Delta^{\frac{1}{3}}}$$

L = Length on waterline
Λ = Immersed volume

$$\text{SHP} = 0\cdot9 \times \text{BHP}$$

$$\frac{\text{THP}}{\text{SHP}} = \text{Propeller efficiency}$$

Propeller efficiency = 0·43 for 1:1 ratio reduction gearing

Propeller efficiency = 0·53 for 2:1 ratio reduction gearing

Propeller efficiency = 0·59 for 3:1 ratio reduction gearing

See also the following pages.

This and subsequent graphs on pages 126–133 are by courtesy of R A Lister & Co Ltd.

Speed/horsepower – launches and workboats (2)

These speeds are reduced, often considerably, by head winds, rough seas, damaged propeller blades, a weed-covered under-body and so on.

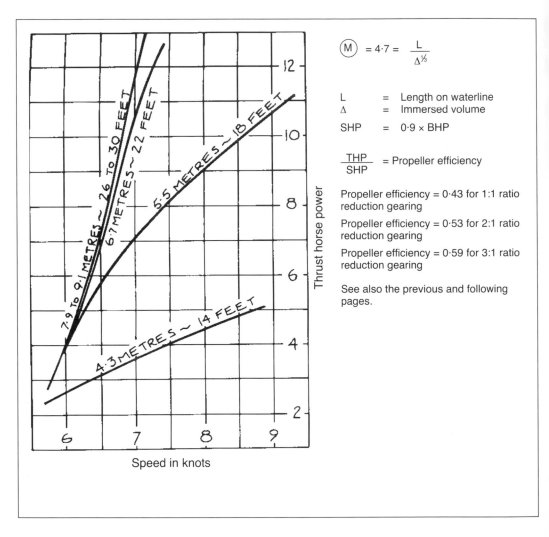

$$\textcircled{M} = 4{\cdot}7 = \frac{L}{\Delta^{1/3}}$$

L	=	Length on waterline
Δ	=	Immersed volume
SHP	=	$0{\cdot}9 \times$ BHP

$\dfrac{THP}{SHP}$ = Propeller efficiency

Propeller efficiency = $0{\cdot}43$ for 1:1 ratio reduction gearing

Propeller efficiency = $0{\cdot}53$ for 2:1 ratio reduction gearing

Propeller efficiency = $0{\cdot}59$ for 3:1 ratio reduction gearing

See also the previous and following pages.

Thrust horse power

Speed in knots

Speed/horsepower – launches and workboats (3)

These speeds are reduced, often considerably, by head winds, rough seas, damaged propeller blades, a weed-covered under-body and so on.

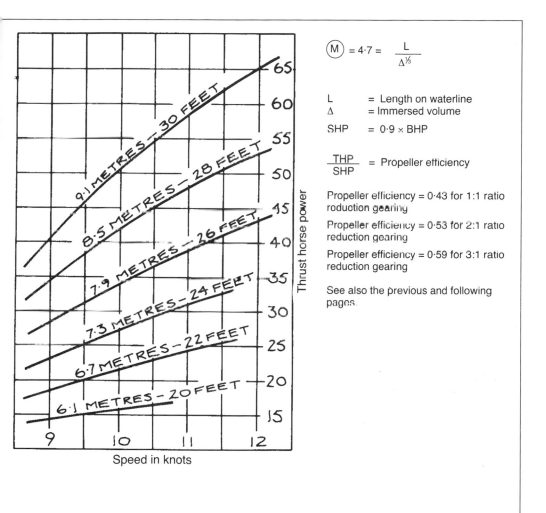

$$\text{\textcircled{M}} = 4\cdot7 = \frac{L}{\Delta^{1/3}}$$

L = Length on waterline
Δ = Immersed volume
SHP = 0·9 × BHP

$\dfrac{\text{THP}}{\text{SHP}}$ = Propeller efficiency

Propeller efficiency = 0·43 for 1:1 ratio reduction gearing

Propeller efficiency = 0·53 for 2:1 ratio reduction gearing

Propeller efficiency = 0·59 for 3:1 ratio reduction gearing

See also the previous and following pages.

Speed in knots

Speed/horsepower – auxiliary yachts (1)

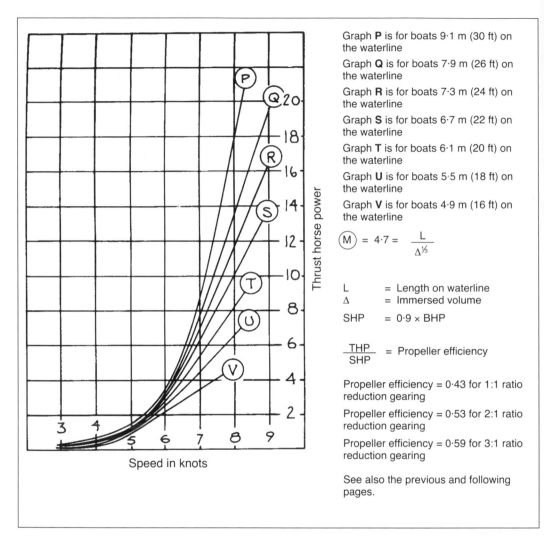

Speed in knots

Thrust horse power

Graph **P** is for boats 9·1 m (30 ft) on the waterline

Graph **Q** is for boats 7·9 m (26 ft) on the waterline

Graph **R** is for boats 7·3 m (24 ft) on the waterline

Graph **S** is for boats 6·7 m (22 ft) on the waterline

Graph **T** is for boats 6·1 m (20 ft) on the waterline

Graph **U** is for boats 5·5 m (18 ft) on the waterline

Graph **V** is for boats 4·9 m (16 ft) on the waterline

$$\text{M} = 4\cdot7 = \frac{L}{\Delta^{1/3}}$$

L   = Length on waterline
Δ   = Immersed volume
SHP   = 0·9 × BHP

$$\frac{\text{THP}}{\text{SHP}} = \text{Propeller efficiency}$$

Propeller efficiency = 0·43 for 1:1 ratio reduction gearing

Propeller efficiency = 0·53 for 2:1 ratio reduction gearing

Propeller efficiency = 0·59 for 3:1 ratio reduction gearing

See also the previous and following pages.

Speed/horsepower – auxiliary yachts (2)

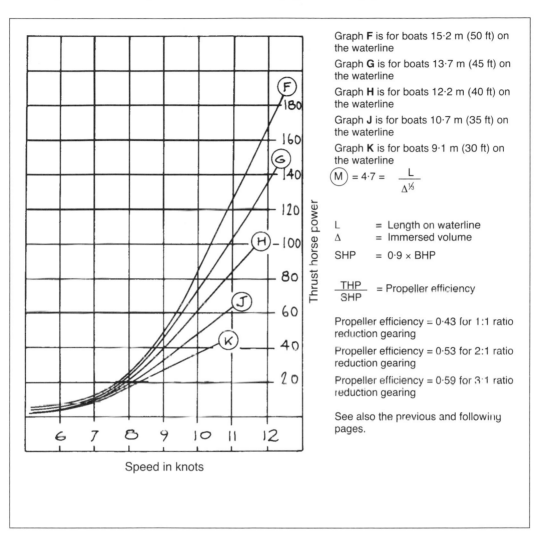

Graph **F** is for boats 15·2 m (50 ft) on the waterline

Graph **G** is for boats 13·7 m (45 ft) on the waterline

Graph **H** is for boats 12·2 m (40 ft) on the waterline

Graph **J** is for boats 10·7 m (35 ft) on the waterline

Graph **K** is for boats 9·1 m (30 ft) on the waterline

$$\text{M} = 4·7 = \frac{L}{\Delta^{\frac{1}{3}}}$$

L   = Length on waterline
Δ   = Immersed volume
SHP = 0·9 × BHP

$$\frac{THP}{SHP} = \text{Propeller efficiency}$$

Propeller efficiency = 0·43 for 1:1 ratio reduction gearing

Propeller efficiency = 0·53 for 2:1 ratio reduction gearing

Propeller efficiency = 0·59 for 3·1 ratio reduction gearing

See also the previous and following pages.

129

Outboard engines (1) – for small power craft

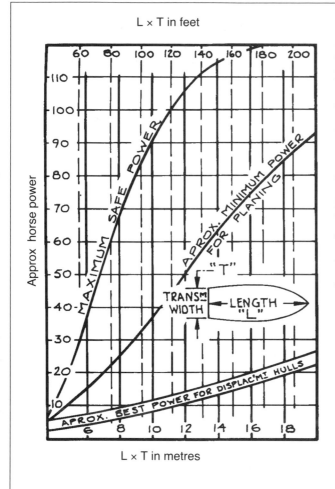

L × T in feet

L × T in metres

Approx horse power

Maximum Safe Power.
Before using this type of power make sure that the transom is strong enough. Weak points are usually along the top edge and at the junction with the topsides.

Power of this order will be expensive on fuel and more than is needed for general cruising or water skiing.

Minimum Planing Power.
Should be exceeded for planing types of craft, especially for water skiing. For rough water use, too, some extra power is needed to overcome the additional resistance.

On the graph the upper scale and the dotted vertical lines represent *Length* in feet (L) × *Transom width* in feet (T).

The bottom scale and the solid vertical lines represent *Length* in metres (L) × *Transom width* in metres (T).

Outboard engines (2) – for inflatable boats

The speed to be expected from an inflatable boat depends on the horse power of the engine, the number of people and the amount of luggage to be carried, and the weather conditions etc. This graph shows typical speeds against loading for inflatable craft between 2·7 metres (9 ft) and 5 metres (16 ft 6 in).

To get the best speed the inflatable must be pumped up hard and the outboard engine has to be in first class condition, using the correct fuel and the right propeller.

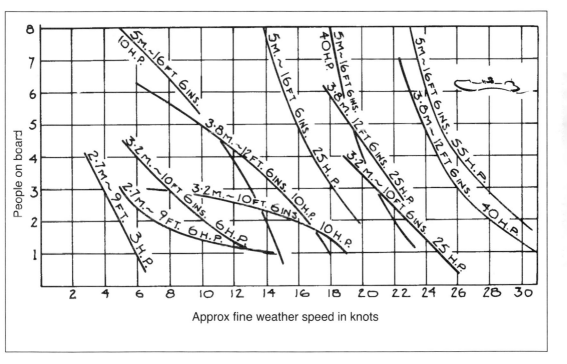

Approx fine weather speed in knots

Outboard engines (3) – for 10 kph (6mph)

This graph is for small sailing boats, day boats and centreboard dinghies.

The following conditions apply:

1 The waterline length is the basis.
2 A 50% overload has been allowed for.
3 With headwinds or steep seas the speed will drop. In very severe conditions double the horse power shown may be scarcely adequate to maintain way.
4 This graph is a guide only. Easily driven hulls and those lightly laden may need less power. Heavy boats with deeply immersed transoms and a lot of windage are likely to need more power.

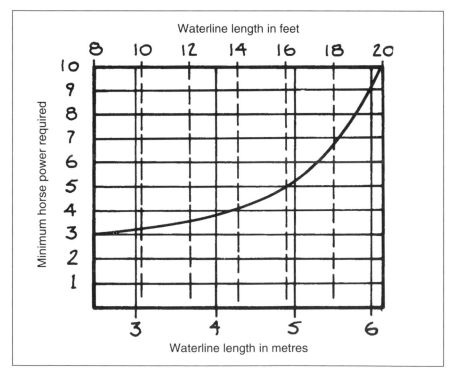

The graph is based on the Manual of the BIA, Chicago, to whom acknowledgement is made.

Outboard engines (4) – speed-v-weight in runabouts

The speed of an outboard runabout very largely depends on the weight of the craft when under way and the horse power of the engine. With the accompanying graph a probable speed for a typical boat of about 4 m (13 ft) can be predicted.

Alternatively a boat with a known weight and engine which does not achieve something like the indicated speed is likely to be suffering from a defect such as a poor bottom shape, or marine growth fouling, or the engine may not be putting out its advertised horse power.

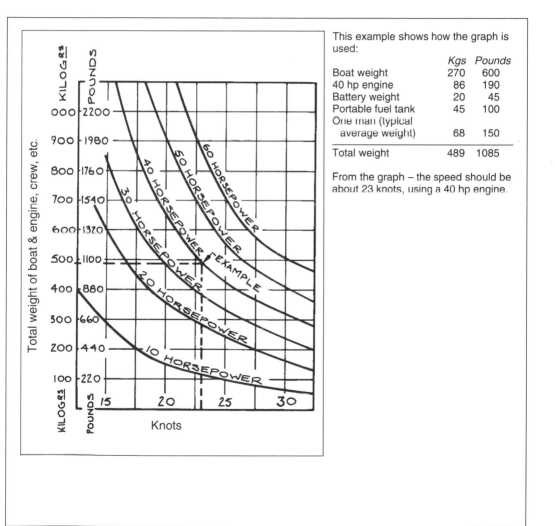

This example shows how the graph is used:

	Kgs	Pounds
Boat weight	270	600
40 hp engine	86	190
Battery weight	20	45
Portable fuel tank	45	100
One man (typical average weight)	68	150
Total weight	489	1085

From the graph – the speed should be about 23 knots, using a 40 hp engine.

Outboard engine weights

Typical weights of engines and equipment

Engine horse power			Engine and controls		Battery		Portable fuel tank	
			kg	lb	kg	lb	kg	lb
up to	–	3½	16	35				
4	–	5	25	55			11	25
5½	–	10	32	70	9	20	23	50
10½	–	30	48	105	20	45	23	50
30½	–	50	86	190	20	45	45	100
50½	–	75	110	240	20	45	45	100
75½	–	140	140	300	20	45	45	100

Lead/acid batteries

Battery condition

	Temperature						
	43°C	38°C	32°C	27°C	21°C	16°C	10°C
	110°F	100°F	90°F	80°F	70°F	60°F	50°F
Charge condition	Reading on hydrometer						
Fully discharged	1·094	1·098	1·102	1·106	1·110	1·114	1·118
Half discharged	1·184	1·188	1·192	1·196	1·200	1·204	1·208
Charged fully	1·264	1·268	1·272	1·276	1·280	1·284	1·288

Propeller graphs – medium and slow speed craft

The graphs (shown on pages 138–147), which can be used in a number of ways, are first approximation guides for propellers on small craft. They should not be taken as precise, but then the selection of propellers for boats only approaches an exact science on racing and other very high-speed power boats. To find the right propeller for a given boat:

Decide on the wake factor:

1 This will be between 30% and zero. This depends mainly on the location of the propeller relative to the hull. A sailing cruiser with a propeller well sheltered behind a wide stern-post, or a heavy displacement hull-form with full aft sections, will have wake factors equal to about 30% of the vessel's speed. A power boat with a propeller well exposed below the whole hull should have a very small wake factor.

2 Subtract from the boat's speed the wake factor.

   For example if the craft is designed for 10 knots and the wake factor is 20%:

   20% of 10 knots   = 2 knots.

   10 minus 2 = 8 knots.

   Select the graph for 8 knots 'water-past-propeller' speed.

3 Determine the propeller rpm at the vessel's full speed. If the engine achieves a peak of 2 800 rpm and there is a 2:1 reduction gear the propeller rpm is

   $$\frac{2\,800}{2} = 1\,400 \text{ rpm}$$

4 Select the *diameter* curve relating to *shaft* horse power (see note in later section) and work along it until it crosses the correct rpm axis. Read across to get the correct diameter (left side in mm, right side in inches).

5 Then select the *pitch* curve relating to the *shaft* horse power and work along it until it crosses the correct rpm axis. Read across for the correct pitch (left side for mm, right side for inches).

6 The resulting figures will be a first approximation. The diameter figure should suffice for determining such matters as propeller aperture size allowing for tip clearance. This latter should be 15% of the diameter, and never less than 8%. The diameter figure should also be adequate for making a propeller cost estimate.

The graphs can also be used to discover if a fitted propeller is correct. For instance, knowing the propeller on the boat, if the speed seems inadequate it is easy to discover if the fault is due to the wrong pitch or diameter. To do this:

1 Determine the actual diameter and pitch of the propeller. As the figures stamped on the boss are not always correct the propeller should be measured.

2 Determine the true boat speed by running accurately over a measured mile. Correct this for the 'speed-past-propeller' by subtracting the wake factor.

3 Select the graphs corresponding to the calculated speed of water past the propeller. (One graph for *diameter,* one for *pitch.)*

4 On the graphs select the horse power curve relating to the shaft horse power of the engine (see note re shaft horse power).

5 On the vertical ordinate of the propeller rpm (not the same as the engine rpm if a reduction gear is fitted) read off the recommended propeller diameter, or pitch on the respective graph.

6 Compare the recommended diameter and pitch with the actual measurements of the propeller. Any serious difference suggests that the wrong propeller is fitted.

If the true propeller size agrees with the charts then the indications are that there is some reason not connected with the propeller which is causing the loss of speed.

In practice a loss of speed is often caused by more than one factor. The propeller may be partly to blame, but the hull may also be covered with marine growth, extra weights may have been added since the boat was built, there may be shaft wear, poor trim, and so on, which can all contribute.

Above all it must be appreciated that these graphs are preliminary guides and not final selection recommendations.

Note: Shaft horse power.

The published output of an engine will normally be the horse power of the engine with its auxiliaries, such as water-pump and alternator, coupled up. But as some manufacturers still publish the output without the load from these essential components, the horse power figures should be checked with the maker. The shaft horse power is the actual horse power delivered to the propeller. It will be less than the published figure since there are losses at the stern gland, stern bearing in the gear-box due to vibration, at plummer blocks and so on. The losses are greater if the engine is not properly aligned. It is usual for the shaft horse power in small craft to be between 90% and 70% of the published horse power. A bad installation or an abused engine may result in greater losses. Naturally the assumption must be that the engine is in reasonable and fairly new condition.

Propeller weights

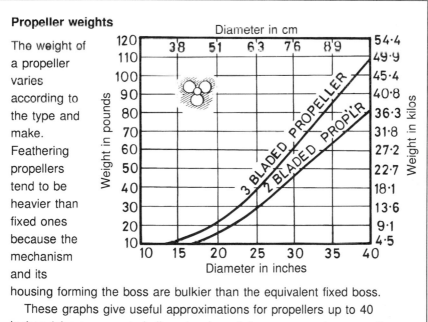

The weight of a propeller varies according to the type and make.

Feathering propellers tend to be heavier than fixed ones because the mechanism and its housing forming the boss are bulkier than the equivalent fixed boss.

These graphs give useful approximations for propellers up to 40 inches (about one metre) diameter. Imperial measurements are on the left and along the bottom, metric up the right side and across the top.

If precise figures are required, the makers should be consulted, and the propeller weights reconfirmed when they are delivered.

Propeller graphs – for 6 knots water velocity past propeller

PROPELLER DIAMETER

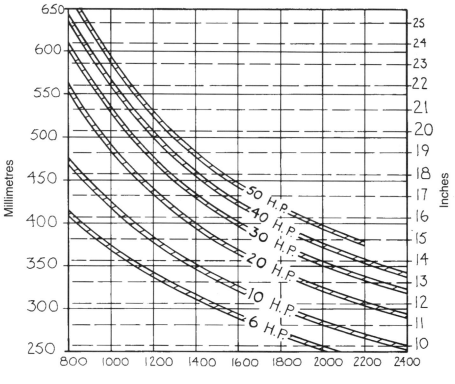

Propeller RPM

PROPELLER PITCH

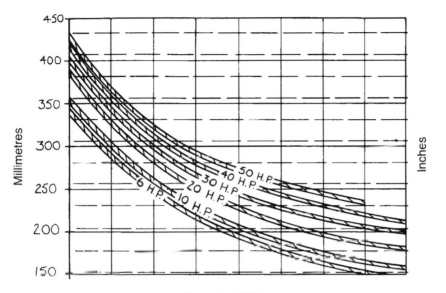

Propeller graphs – for 8 knots water velocity past propeller

PROPELLER DIAMETER

Propeller RPM

PROPELLER PITCH

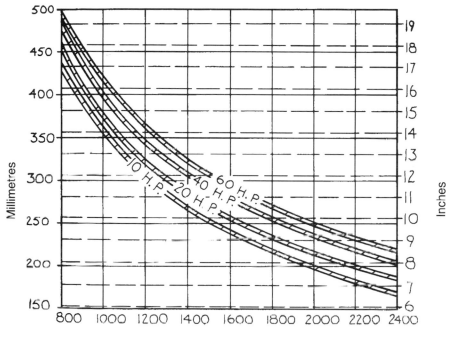

Propeller RPM

Propeller graphs – for 10 knots water velocity past propeller

PROPELLER DIAMETER

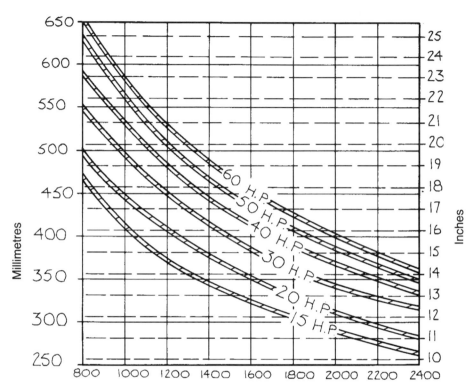

Propeller RPM

PROPELLER PITCH

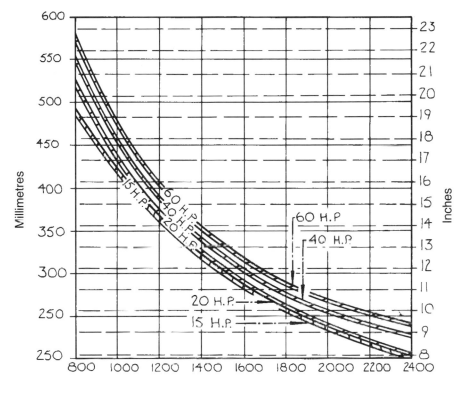

Propeller RPM

Propeller graphs – for 12 knots water velocity past propeller

PROPELLER DIAMETER

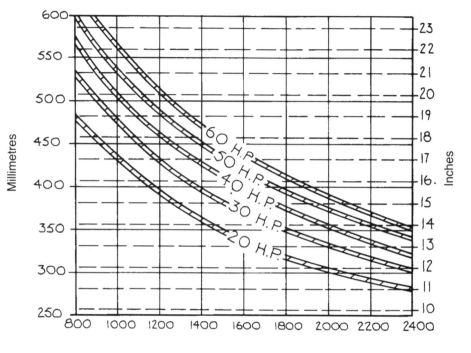

Propeller RPM

PROPELLER PITCH

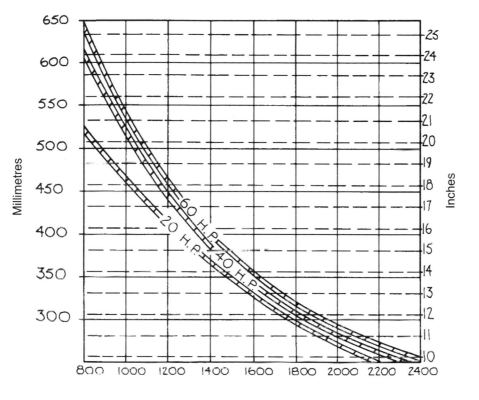

Propeller RPM

Propeller graphs – for 14 knots water velocity past propeller

PROPELLER DIAMETER

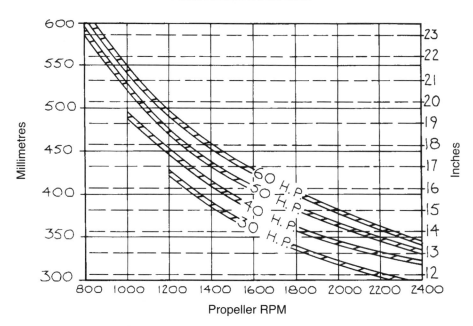

Propeller RPM

PROPELLER PITCH

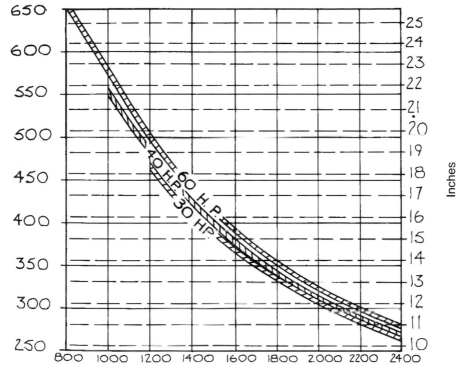

Propeller RPM

Stern gear – propeller shafts, glands, stern tubes etc

The proportions and sizes of flanges etc vary according to the manufacturer. When designing, planning, ordering and fitting it is often desirable, and sometimes essential, to know how much space to allow.

The table gives a guidance to typical manufacturing sizes and proportions and is based on common small craft usage but is not suitable for racing power craft.

Information supplied by courtesy of J M Macdonald and Co, Byron Street, Glasgow.

Shaft diameter		A		B		C	
mm	ins	mm	ins	mm	ins	mm	ins
15·9	5/8	95·3	3³/4	79·4	3¹/8	50·8	2
19·1	3/4	95·3	3³/4	79·4	3¹/8	50·8	2
25·4	1	108	4¹/4	101·6	4	55·6	2³/16
28·6	1¹/8	108	4¹/4	101·6	4	55·6	2³/16
31·8	1¹/4	101·6	4	88·9	3¹/2	diameter	
34·9	1³/8	114·3	4¹/2	114·3	4¹/2	diameter	
38·1	1¹/2	114·3	4¹/2	114·3	4¹/2	diameter	
41·3	1⁵/8	109·5	4⁵/16	114·3	4¹/2	88·9	3¹/2
44·5	1³/4	109·5	4⁵/16	114·3	4¹/2	88·9	3¹/2
50·8	2	139·7	5¹/2	139·7	5¹/2	101·6	4
57·2	2¹/4	177·8	7	165·1	6¹/2	diameter	
63·5	2¹/2	177·8	7	165·1	6¹/2	diameter	

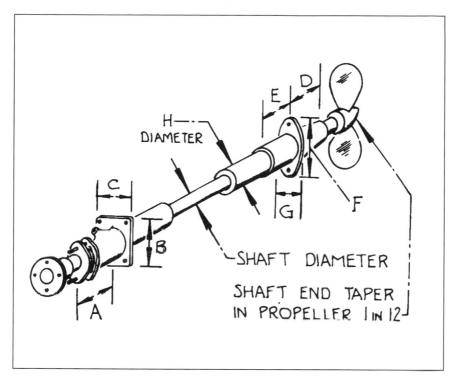

D		E		F		G		H	
mm	ins	mm	ins	mm	ins	mm	ins	mm	ins
69·9	2³/₄			79·4	3¹/₈	69·9	2³/₄	28·6	1¹/₈
69·9	2³/₄			79·4	3¹/₈	69·9	2³/₄	28·6	1¹/₈
108	4¹/₄			101·6	4	82·6	3¹/₄	38·1	1¹/₂
108	4¹/₄			101·6	4	82·6	3¹/₄	38·1	1¹/₂
95·3	3³/₄	63·5	2¹/₂	114·3	4¹/₂	69·9	2³/₄	44·5	1³/₄
114·3	4¹/₂	76·2	3	139·7	5¹/₂	82·6	3¹/₄	50·8	2
114·3	4¹/₂	76·2	3	139·7	5¹/₂	82·6	3¹/₄	50·8	2
152·4	6	76·2	3	165·1	6¹/₂	101·6	4	63·5	2¹/₂
152·4	6	76·2	3	165·1	6¹/₂	101·6	4	63·5	2¹/₂
152·4	6	114·3	4¹/₂	177·8	7	120·7	4³/₄	76·2	3
190·5	7¹/₂	120·7	4³/₄	203·2	8	133·4	5¹/₄	88·9	3¹/₂
190·5	7¹/₂	120·7	4³/₄	203·2	8	133·4	5¹/₄	88·9	3¹/₂

Propeller shaft – sizes-v-bhp and rpm

	RPM				
BHP	3000	2000	1500	1000	500
3	12	14	15·5	17·5	22
6	15·5	17·5	19·5	22	28
10	18	21	23	26·5	33
20	23	26·5	29	33	42
30	26·5	30	33	38	48
40	29	33	36·5	42	53
50	31	35·5	39·5	45	56·5
75	35·5	41	45	51·5	65
100	39·5	45	49·5	56·5	71·5
125	42·5	48·5	53	61	77
150	45	51·5	56·5	65	82
200	49·5	56·5	62·5	71·5	90
250	53	61	67	77	97
300	56·5	65	71·5	82	103
350	59·5	68·5	75	86	108
400	62·5	71·5	78·5	90	113
500	67·5	77	85	97	122

Shaft diameter in mm

	RPM				
BHP	3000	2000	1500	1000	500
3	1/2	9/16	5/8	11/16	7/8
6	5/8	11/16	3/4	7/8	1 1/8
10	11/16	13/16	7/8	1 1/16	1 5/16
20	7/8	1 1/16	1 1/8	1 5/16	1 5/8
30	1 1/16	1 3/16	1 5/16	1 1/2	1 7/8
40	1 1/8	1 5/16	1 7/16	1 5/8	2 1/16
50	1 1/4	1 3/8	1 9/16	1 3/4	2 1/4
75	1 3/8	1 5/8	1 3/4	2	2 9/16
100	1 9/16	1 3/4	1 15/16	2 1/4	2 13/16
125	1 11/16	1 15/16	2 1/16	2 3/8	3
150	1 ¾	2	2 1/4	2 9/16	3 1/4
200	1 15/16	2 1/4	2 7/16	2 13/16	3 9/16
250	2 1/16	2 3/8	2 5/8	3	3 13/16
300	2 1/4	2 9/16	2 13/16	3 1/4	4 1/16
350	2 5/16	2 11/16	2 15/16	3 3/8	4 1/4
400	2 7/16	2 13/16	3 1/16	3 9/16	4 7/16
500	2 11/16	3	3 5/16	3 13/16	4 13/16

Shaft diameter in inches

Rubber shaft bearings

Water lubricated. Recommended especially for use in shallow and gritty waters.

Shaft diameter		Outside diameter		Length	
mm	*ins*	*mm*	*ins*	*mm*	*ins*
19·1	3/4	31·8	1 1/4	76·2	3
22·2	7/8	34·9	1 3/8	88·9	3 1/2
25·4	1	38·1	1 1/2	101·6	4
28·6	1 1/8	41·3	1 5/8	114·3	4 1/2
31·8	1 1/4	44·5	1 3/4	127	5
34·9	1 3/8	47·6	1 7/8	139·7	5 1/2
38·1	1 1/2	50·8	2	152·4	6
41·3	1 5/8	54	2 1/8	165·1	6 1/2
44·5	1 3/4	60·3	2 3/8	177·8	7
47·6	1 7/8	66·7	2 5/8	190·5	7 1/2
50·8	2	66·7	2 5/8	203·2	8
57·2	2 1/4	76·2	3	228·6	9
60·3	2 3/8	79·4	3 1/8	241·3	9 1/2
63·5	2 1/2	82·6	3 1/4	254	10
63·5	2 1/2	85·7	3 3/8	254	10
66·7	2 5/8	88·9	3 1/2	266·7	10 1/2
69·9	2 3/4	88·9	3 1/2	279·4	11
69·9	2 3/4	95·3	3 3/4	279·4	11
76·2	3	95·3	3 3/4	304·8	12
76·2	3	101·6	4	304·8	12

Propeller shaft bearings – spacing

To find the spacing of propeller shaft bearings:

1 Rule a line from the shaft size on scale 2 to modulus on scale 4.
2 Rule a line from point of intersection on scale 3 to connect with propeller Revs per Minute on scale 1.
3 Extend this last line to scale 5 and read off the answer.

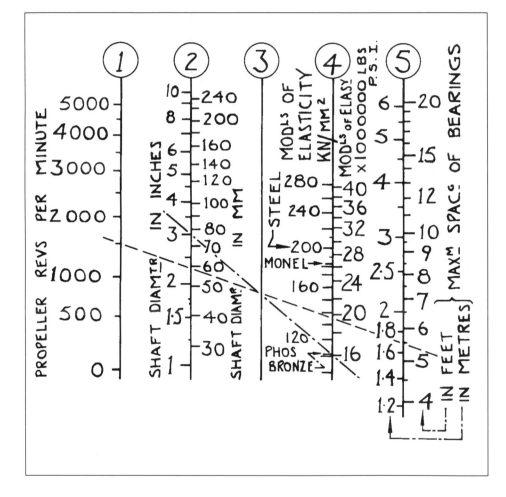

6 DESIGN

British Standard Specifications (BS numbers)

This section includes a wide range of British Standard Specifications which relate to small craft etc. However there are so many Specifications (some of which are out-of-date, some nearly so), so it has therefore not been possible to include every one which has a bearing on the building and maintenance of small craft.

BS MA 16:1971	Specification for inflatable boats
ISBN 0 580 06677 0	(Manual or motor propelled.)
BS MA 28:1973 (1980)	Specification for dimensions of tracks for mast and deck fittings.
ISBN 0 580 07576 − 1	Tracks for internal fittings in 16 mm to 25 mm widths and for external fittings in 25 mm, 32 mm and 50 mm widths.
BS MA 29:1982	Specification for steel wire rope and strand for yachts.
ISBN 0 580 12858X	Zinc coated and stainless steel.
BS 370 316 S16	Stainless steel. Mirror polished.
BS 729	Hot dip galvanising. (Recommended for long term resistance to
ISO 1459-61	rust.)
BS 903 A2	Fender test method.
BS 1470–1475 1 to 30	Wrought aluminium alloy.
BS 1490 LM1 to 30	Aluminium casting alloy.
BS 1088 & 4079 1966 (AMD 3)	WBP marine grade plywood.
BS 1400 LG2	Gunmetal castings.
BS 1400 HTB1	High tensile brass castings.
BS 1400 AB2c	Nickel aluminium bronze castings
BS 1475	Aluminium sprayed on steel.
BS 1615 AA 25	Anodising for masts etc. Heavy specification.
BS 1706	Electroplating (zinc and cadmium). Must be Class A.
ISO 2081-2	
BS 2569	Sprayed aluminium and zinc. Class I is the one to select for marine use.
BS 3014	Grades 3, 4 or 5. Stainless steel pipes and tubes.
BS 3382	Zinc plated nuts and bolts.
BS 3396	Fibreglass woven roving.
BS 3436	Zinc sprayed on steel.
BS 3496	Fibreglass chopped strand mat.
BS 3532	Polyester resins.
BS 3534	Epoxide resins.
BS 3643	Fastening threads.
BS 4224 1982	Specification for yachtsman's safety harnesses and safety lines.
ISBN 0 580 13035 5	
BS 4232	Blast cleaning of steel. Equivalent to Swedish SA 2½.
BS 4360	Grade A mild steel for shipbuilding.
BS 4474:1979	Specification for safety harnesses and safety lines for use by
ISBN 0 580 10719 1	children in yachts.
BS 4921	Sheradising.
ISO 2063	
BS 5083	Marine Grade aluminium (NS 8).
BS 5315	Stainless steel hose clamps.
BS 5482:Part 3 1979	Domestic butane and propane-gas-burning installations in boats
ISBN 0 580 10491 5 AMD 4067	and other vessels.
Sept. 1982. AMD 5026 June 1986. AMD 6316 June 1991.	
BS 7162	Waste water fittings on yachts. Waste water pump-out fittings.
ISBN 0 580 18718	
BS 7163 1990	Specification for wire rope and pulley steering systems on small craft. Construction, operation and installation.
BS 7814	Bolts and screws incorporating either underhead locking or anti-rotating features.
BS 7828	Small craft: seacocks and through hull fittings.
ISO 9093 1 1994 PART 1 1995	Metallic fittings.
BS 7842 1996	Bolts, screws, studs, thread-setting feature.

Beam-v-waterline length

The graph opposite has Imperial measurements, that is feet, on the left and at the bottom, shown with continuous lines. On the right and across the top are metric scales in metres, shown by dotted lines.

The graph is an indication of typical beam/length ratios, based on the overall maximum beam without rub rails, and the designed waterline length. It is handy for many people; for instance a buyer can see if a yacht is wider or narrower than average. A designer wanting a quick reference to contemporary proportions can read off these figures to save doing a lot of research.

Like so many diagrams of this type it needs using with care, as it is based on a large number of craft, but does not cover racing machines or shallow draft extra-wide boats. Nor does it cover specialist craft such as those which have extra-wide beam associated with water-ballast tanks, and craft built to a rating rule which strongly encourages a wide beam.

The hatched area covers a large number of yachts, but by no means the whole range of craft currently in production. Where a designer needs a lot of internal space he will be attracted to the top of the hatched area. Generally speaking, for good performance to windward, the bottom of the hatched area is favoured, other things being equal.

The curve, labelled TRADITIONAL, is a mean line through points plotted taking the dimensions from boats built between 1920 and 1940. Currently the tendency is towards a wider beam, often associated with a ballast ratio of the order of 30% to 35%.

This graph can be a help in assessing whether a yacht has a beam/length ratio which is, for whatever reason, outside normal current practice. By itself this graph cannot show whether a boat has ample or inadequate stability.

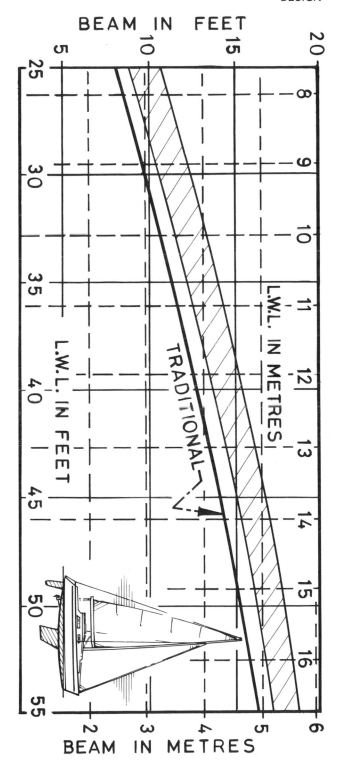

Draft-v-waterline length

The graph opposite has Imperial measurements, that is feet, on the left and at the bottom, shown with continuous lines. On the right and across the top are metric scales in metres, shown by dotted lines.

The graph is an indication of typical draft/length ratios, based on the maximum draft, and the designed waterline length. It is handy for a boat-buyer, who can see if a yacht is shallower than average. Such boats tend to perform less well to windward, other things being equal. However, they put less strain on their hull structures. Also they are easier to handle, as well as safer in shallow waters. If they run aground they tend to do themselves less damage, other things (as always) being equal.

A designer or builder wanting a quick reference to contemporary proportions can read off these figures to save doing a lot of research. The top of the shaded area indicates that the vessel's performance to windward should be above average, and her cost may be likewise. Also she will not be able to get into small creeks and may be too deep to be hauled up in some boatyards or marinas. Or it may be that she can only be taken out of the water on a high tide.

Like so many diagrams of this type, it needs using with care, as is based on a large number of craft, but does not cover racing machines (which tend to be extra deep drafted) or unusually shallow draft boats. Nor does it cover specialist craft such as pure centre-boarders with no substantial protruding keel.

The hatched area covers a large number of yachts, but by no means the whole range of craft currently in production.

The curve, labelled TRADITIONAL, is a mean line through points plotted taking the dimensions from boats built between 1920 and 1940. In those days there were plenty of small shipyards where deep yachts could be slipped. Since the closure of many of these yards, big yachts have not had the same choice of facilities. Also the introduction of 'winged' and other specialist keels has resulted in a tendency to build large sailing yachts with more limited draft.

This graph can be a help in assessing whether a yacht has a draft/length ratio which is, for whatever reason, outside of, or on the edge of normal current practice. By itself this graph cannot show whether a boat has a good or average windward ability. However if the rig is not high and efficient, the vessel's windward performance may be disappointing if her dimensions put her near the bottom of the shaded area.

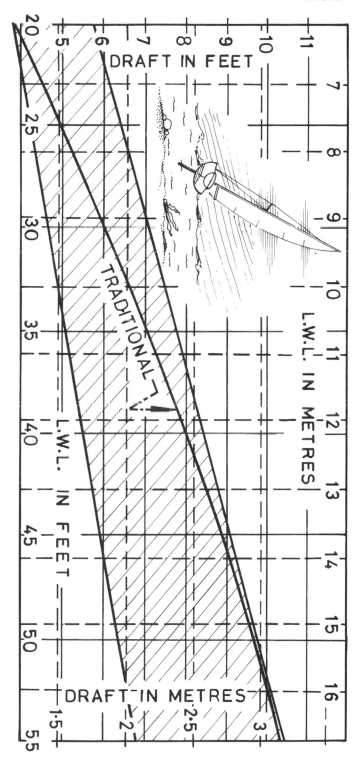

DRAFT IN FEET

DRAFT IN METRES

L.W.L. IN METRES

L.W.L. IN FEET

TRADITIONAL

Displacement-v-waterline length

The left side of the graph opposite is the scale in long tons, of 2240 lb. This is close to metric tons of 1000 kilogrammes. For many purposes the difference between the Imperial and metric tons can be ignored. The small difference between the two figures can often be accepted when assessing yachts with a view to buying, or when doing preliminary design work. One Imperial ton equals 1·12 US (short) tons.

The bottom scale is the water-line length in feet and this, like the displacement, is shown by the continuous lines. The top scale is the waterline length in metres and is shown by dotted vertical lines.

As with all graphs of this nature, it is important to realise its limitations. Broadly speaking if a yacht lies on or near the top of the shaded area she is probably heavily built with big tanks for fuel and water, lots of spares and emergency equipment, plenty of winches and ground tackle, a substantial, reliable engine and so on. However she *may* be crudely built, with material used indiscriminately.

A boat with a displacement on or near the bottom of the hatched area tends to be lightly built for racing, with a small engine, minimum accommodation, minimum tankage, light-weight spars and so on. But caution is needed, since she *may* be under-built and lacking in adequate strength.

Materials and techniques used in construction affect the final displacement a lot. Steel is heavy, but a cleverly-built steel yacht need not be right at the top end of the displacement curve. Aluminium construction is normally light, but if the vessel has to carry a lot of equipment for long range cruising the final displacement will be well up.

Heavily ballasted yachts, designed to have a good performance going to windward in moderate and strong breezes, often come high on the scale. In contrast, the current trend in production cruisers is to cut the displacement to save money since the sail plan and engine (with all its related gear) can be small and therefore cheap.

Some yachts will fall outside the limits of the hatched area, including ultra-light racing boats, boats with no accommodation and no engine, experimental boats, massive motor-sailers, craft-built by some old-fashioned methods, and so on.

As always it is essential to use this graph with caution, bearing in mind relevant factors like fabrication and end use.

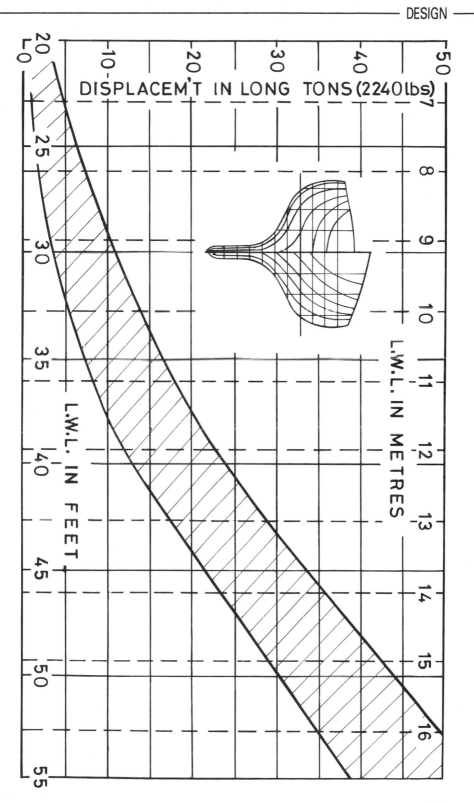

DISPLACEM'T IN LONG TONS (2240 lbs)

L.W.L. IN METRES

L.W.L. IN FEET

Ballast-v-waterline length

The bottom of the graph opposite is in Imperial measurements, namely feet, shown by continuous lines. The top is in metric measurements of metres, shown with dotted lines.

The right hand scale is in long tons of 2240 lb. This is, for many practical purposes, the same as metric tons of 1000 kilogrammes. For instance when assessing two comparable yachts with a view to purchase, differences of less than 2% in the ballast are unlikely to have practical consequences. And during preliminary design studies, small differences in the ballast seldom affect the broad issues. One Imperial ton of 2240 lb is the same as 1·12 US (Short) tons.

Very broadly speaking, Line A is an average of heavy yachts with high ballast ratios. Line B indicates typical heavy yachts with low ballast ratios, and motor-sailers tend to be in this area, especially if they have heavy hulls, big tanks, and lots of equipment.

Line C is a mean of light yachts with a high ballast ratio, and Line D the same general type of yacht with a low ballast ratio. Many modern production yachts built of fibreglass come between lines C and D, but some are above line C and some below line D.

These curves are drawn for a selection of typical yachts, but very light, unusually heavy and exceptional yachts often fall well clear of these curves.

Racing yachts tend to have a lot of ballast, especially if there is little or no accommodation or furniture or cruising gear in and on the hull. The more staid the yacht, the less ballast she is likely to have, though here, as in many situations where these curves are being used, there are a substantial number of factors which affect the issue.

It is always essential to use this type of graph with considerable caution, bearing in mind relevant factors like the sophistication of the vessel, the standard of construction, her purpose, cost, operating area and so on. However in this instance extra care is needed, because there are so many factors which affect the ballasting of yachts. For example, the type and weight of the rig, the 'form' stability (or lack of it), the depth of the ballast, the type, location and weight of the engine(s), the number, size and type of tanks, and so on. In addition, water ballast can make a substantial difference to the ballasting. Water ballast is not taken into account here.

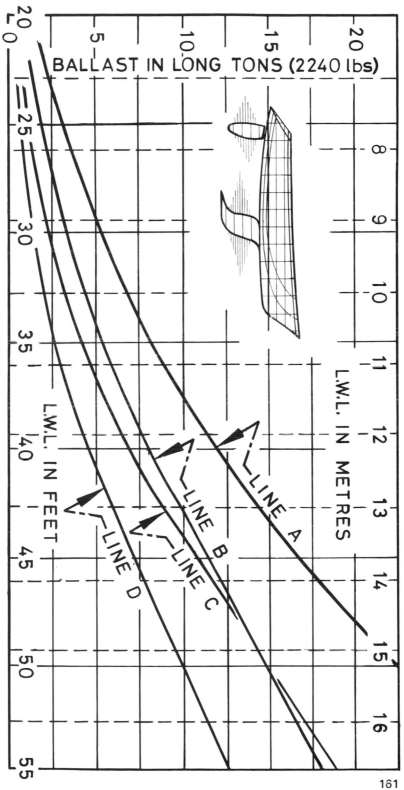

BALLAST IN LONG TONS (2240 lbs)

L.W.L. IN METRES

L.W.L. IN FEET

LINE A

LINE B

LINE C

LINE D

Engine power-v-waterline length

The left side and bottom of the graph opposite are in Imperial measurements of horsepower and feet, shown by continuous lines. The top and right side are in metric measurements of metres and kilowatts, shown with dotted lines. Where two engines are fitted, the horsepower/kilowatt figures are for the total output of both.

The middle curve, labelled BROAD AVERAGE, is the mean of a large number of yachts, with plenty coming above and below this line. A vessel with an engine which comes on this line should have enough power to make progress to windward in rough but perhaps not very severe conditions.

This middle line assumes that the hull form is fair and gives a good flow of water to a well-immersed propeller of average size and good design. It is based on craft with a clean bottom, average windage, and no serious adverse factors such as poor engine line-up.

This BROAD AVERAGE line takes into account the rise in engine power which has occurred year by year. However the engine power put in small craft of all types continues to increase.

The upper curve, marked CRITERION 1 shows the engine size found in powerful motor-sailers and yachts intended for cruising with no thought to racing. Such craft often have more than one alternator on the engine, hydraulic and water pump power-take-offs, and so on. The main engine is expected to deal with large electrical loads, such as those imposed by radar, freezers and winches.

A yacht with an engine on the upper curve should be able to make adequate progress to windward in severe conditions offshore, provided the hull and other components are reliable. She should be able to turn into winds of force 9 (and perhaps more), provided the stern gear and other features are satisfactory, including adequate stability to give the engine a chance to work properly.

A yacht with an engine of the power shown by the upper line will need big fuel tanks, and to work adequately offshore in all conditions may need a feathering propeller. She will certainly need a large propeller, and if this cannot be folded or feathered she will not sail well in all conditions due to propeller drag.

The bottom curve, labelled CRITERION 2 shows the size of engine sometimes fitted on racing craft, and on sailing yachts with good light weather performance. It should give power to charge the batteries and get the yacht home in windless conditions. It is economical but may not be powerful enough to deal with adverse tides. In quite small waves, progress may be halted.

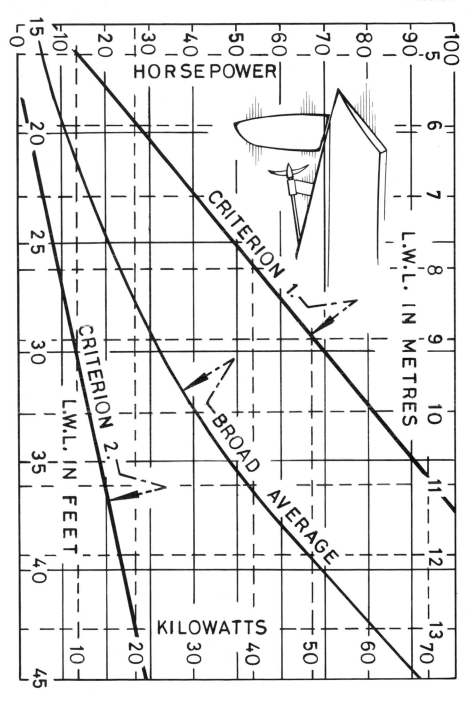

As always it is essential to use this graph with caution, bearing in mind relevant factors like the sophistication of the vessel and sea conditions. For instance a poorly made propeller near the surface coupled to a badly installed engine may reduce the effective horse-power to less than half the stated figure.

Sail area-v-waterline length

The left side and bottom of the graph opposite are in Imperial measurements of square feet and feet, shown by continuous lines. The top and right side are in metric measurements of metres and square metres, shown with dotted lines.

The sail area is taken as the whole of the mainsail plus 100% of the foretriangle. This foretriangle is defined as the height of the top of the outer forestay up the mast from deck level, and the distance from the fore side of the mast to the bottom of the outer forestay. Sometimes spinnakers are set above the top of the outer forestay, but this graph ignores these.

As with all graphs of this nature, it is important to realise its limitations. Broadly speaking if a yacht lies on or near the top of the shaded area she is probably intended for racing. If she is towards the bottom of the hatched area she may be designed for safe family use, or she may be a motor-sailer; or she may be very light and only require a small sail plan to give her a reasonable performance. However, she may then be hampered in light airs unless she has large light sails which extend outside the foretriangle.

Craft which are outside the limits of these double curves include racing machines, some heavy vessels which need a lot of sail area to move them, some traditional vessels, motor-sailers with the emphasis on the engine, and so on.

As the sail plan is the motive power of a sailing boat, then other things being equal (as always when using graphs of this general type) the bigger the sail plan, the higher the expected average speed. When designing for high performance there is seldom any substitute for sheer area.

As always it is essential to use this graph with caution, bearing in mind relevant factors like the sophistication level and end use of the craft.

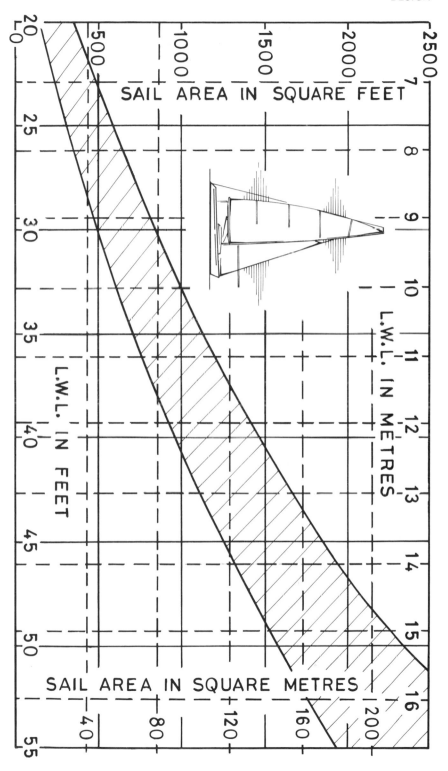

SAIL AREA IN SQUARE FEET

L.W.L. IN METRES

L.W.L. IN FEET

SAIL AREA IN SQUARE METRES

Camber and sheer – how to calculate

Camber

To work out the camber curve. The half beam is taken as 'B'. The maximum camber of a deckhead, 'C', is a height chosen by the designer depending on such factors as headroom, appearance, strength, the need to shed water quickly in rough conditions, the advantage of levelling up the weather side deck when the vessel is heeled if she is a sailing yacht, etc.

The camber 'a' at a distance 'd' off the centreline is:

$$a = C \times \frac{d^2}{B^2}$$

NB 'a' is the *downward* measurement from the level of maximum camber, as shown in the top sketch.

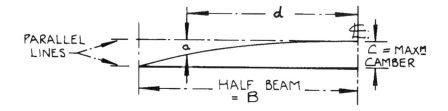

EXAMPLE: To find the drop in the camber curve at quarter beam width (1·1 m off centreline) when the maximum camber height is 0·15 metres and the half beam is 2·2 metres:

$$a = 0{\cdot}15 \times \frac{1{\cdot}1^2}{2{\cdot}2^2} \quad \text{metres}$$

$$= 0{\cdot}0375 \text{ metres, measured downwards.}$$

Camber normally extends evenly from the centreline to the sheer though occasionally there is a flat horizontal section either side of the centreline. In such a case the half-beam (B) in the formula will extend from the side of the flat centre section to the deck edge.

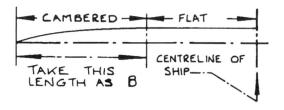

Sheer

The same formula is used for measuring sheer, but the measurement is upwards from a horizontal line through the lowest point of the sheer. This point may be at 3/4 of the length from the bow on a typical yacht and amidship on a traditional merchant vessel

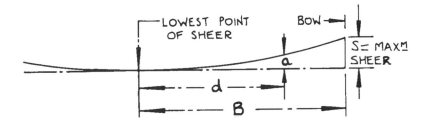

If 'S' is the maximum height of the sheer above the lowest point ('S' will naturally be at the bow) and 'B' is the distance from the lowest point to the highest point measured horizontally, then to find the height of the sheer ('a') at a distance 'd' from the lowest point:

$$a = S \times \frac{d^2}{B^2}$$

The formula can be used for the curve aft of the lowest point.

Diagrammatic method

1. Draw out the full maximum beam AC.
2. Erect the maximum camber height on the centreline BD.
3. Erect a perpendicular from A.
4. Draw a straight line from C to D and continue it to meet the perpendicular from A at X.
5. Divide AB into a number of equal parts.
6. Divide AX into the same number of equal parts.
7. Erect perpendiculars dividing the parts along AB, that is at p, q, r and s.
8. Join C to the dividing points on AX, that is at k, l, m and n.
9. The intersections of the perpendiculars from p, q, r and s with the respective diagonals from C give the points on the camber curve.

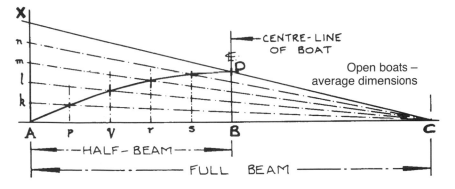

Dinghy sizes, weights and sail areas

Imperial dimensions – in feet, square feet and pounds

Dinghy class	Overall length	Beam	Hull weight	Sail area ex spinnaker	Spinnaker area
Topper	11·15 ft	3·94 ft	95 lb	56 sq ft	
Pico	11·48 ft	4·69 ft		63 sq ft	
Byte	11·98 ft	4·27 ft	99 lb	60 sq ft	
Laser 13	13·29 ft	5·64 ft		102 sq ft	113 sq ft
Blaze	13·78 ft	4·92–6·56 ft	143 lb	97 sq ft	
Buzz	13·78 ft	6·30 ft	198 lb	138 sq ft	187 sq ft
Laser Radial	13·88 ft	4·49 ft		62 sq ft	
Laser	13·88 ft	4·49 ft		76 sq ft	
Cruz	14·27 ft	5·91 ft	265 lb	111 sq ft	
Classic	14·27 ft	5·91 ft	265 lb	118 sq ft	156 sq ft
Laser Fun	14·40 ft	4·66 ft		124 sq ft	133 sq ft
Laser Regatta	14·40 ft	4·66 ft		124 sq ft	110 sq ft
Sport 14	14·60 ft	5·91 ft	265 lb	138 sq ft	187 sq ft
Laser 4000	15·22 ft	4·92–7·55 ft		158 sq ft	184 sq ft
ISO	15·55 ft	5·74–7·38 ft	220 lb	154 sq ft	202 sq ft
Boss	16·08 ft	5·58–6·56–7·78 ft	187 lb	192 sq ft	355 sq ft
Laser 5000	16·41 ft	6·23–10 ft		227 sq ft	323 sq ft
Laser 16	17·03 ft	6·76 ft		151 sq ft††	124 sq ft
Breeze 6	19·69 ft	6·56–9·02 ft	353 lb*	258 sq ft	355 sq ft

*838 lb incl keel.   †'Unifurl' version: 136 sq ft and no spinnaker.

Metric dimensions – in metres, square metres and kilograms

Dinghy class	Overall length	Beam	Hull weight	Sail area ex spinnaker	Spinnaker area
Topper	3·4 m	1·2 m	43 kg	5·20 sq m	
Pico	3·5 m	1·43 m		5·90 sq m	
Byte	3·65 m	1·3 m	45 kg	5·60 sq m	
Laser 13	4·05 m	1·72 m		9·50 sq m	10·50 sq m
Blaze	4·2 m	1·5–2·0 m	65 kg	9·00 sq m	
Buzz	4·2 m	1·92 m	90 kg	12·85 sq m	17·40 sq m
Laser Radial	4·23 m	1·37 m		5·76 sq m	
Laser	4·23 m	1·37 m		7·06 sq m	
Cruz	4·35 m	1·8 m	120 kg	10·30 sq m	
Classic	4·35 m	1·8 m	120 kg	11·00 sq m	14·50 sq m
Laser Fun	4·39 m	1·42 m		11·52 sq m	12·40 sq m
Laser Regatta	4·39 m	1·42 m		11·52 sq m	10·20 sq m
Sport 14	4·45 m	1·8 m	120 kg	12·85 sq m	17·40 sq m
Laser 4000	4·64 m	1·5–2·3 m		14·70 sq m	17·10 sq m
ISO	4·74 m	1·75–2·25 m	100 kg	14·30 sq m	18·80 sq m
Boss	4·9 m	1·70–2·0–2·37 m	85 kg	17·85 sq m	33·00 sq m
Laser 5000	5·0 m	1·9–3·05 m		21·10 sq m	30·00 sq m
Laser 16	5·19 m	2·06 m		14·02 sq m†	11·54 sq m
Breeze 6	6·0 m	2·0–2·75 m	160 kg*	24·00 sq m	33·00 sq m

*380 kg incl keel.   †'Unifurl' version: 12·62 sq m and no spinnaker.

Sports boat sizes, weights and sail areas

Imperial dimensions – in feet, pounds and square feet

Class name	Overall length	Beam	Weight	Mainsail area	Headsail area	Spinnaker area	Notes
AV Breeze	19·69 ft	6·23–9·84 ft	840 lb	167 sq ft	91 sq ft	323 sq ft asymmetric	Crew 2–3, 463 lb maximum
AV Bull	24·6 ft	8·04 ft	2200 lb	226 sq ft	118 sq ft	591 sq ft asymmetric	Crew 4
Beneteau First Class 8	27·89 ft	8·17 ft	3090 lb	218 sq ft	199 sq ft	527 sq ft non-asymmetric	Crew 4–5
H22	22 ft	8·2 ft	1630 lb	210 sq ft	99 sq ft	247 sq ft asymmetric	Boat supplied in kits, crew 2–6
Hunter 707	23·2 ft	8·17 ft	2340 lb	220 sq ft	100 sq ft	550 sq ft asymmetric	Crew 3 or 4, 728 lb maximum
International 11 metre OD	33·79 ft	8·2 ft	1600 lb	282 sq ft	139 sq ft	817 sq ft	Crew 4–5, 754 lb maximum
J24	24 ft	8·21 ft	2800 lb	137 sq ft	198 sq ft	231 sq ft non-asymmetric	Crew 4 or 5
J80	26·25 ft	8·2 ft	3150 lb	226 sq ft	215 sq ft	559 sq ft asymmetric	Crew 4
Magic 25	24·48 ft	7·55 ft	1870 lb	278 sq ft	137 sq ft	521 sq ft asymmetric	Crew 4, 3 on trapeze
Melges 24	24 ft	8·2 ft	1750 lb	254 sq ft	126 sq ft	Asymmetric	Crew maximum 762 lb
Melges 30	31·99 ft	9·84 ft	3300 lb	353 sq ft	302 sq ft	1290 sq ft asymmetric	Crew 7
Mount Gay (Rogers) 30	31·63 ft	10·99 ft	5070 lb	710 sq ft	1462 sq ft	Masthead asymmetric	Crew 4 with water ballast. 8 crew without
Mumm 30	30·94 ft	10·15 ft	4500 lb	398 sq ft	215 sq ft	Asymmetric and non-asymmetric	Crew maximum 1158 lb
Projection 762	25 ft	8·53 ft	2870 lb	215 sq ft	194 sq ft	591 sq ft	Crew 4–5
Reflex 21	21 ft	7 ft deck 12 ft racks	990 lb	248 sq ft	96 sq ft	548 sq ft asymmetric	Crew 4
Reflex 28	27·72 ft	8·65 ft	2870 lb	246 sq ft	224 sq ft	688 sq ft asymmetric and non-asymmetric	Crew 6
Sigma 8m OD	26·25 ft	8·17 ft	2540 lb	271 sq ft	153 sq ft	818 sq ft non-asymmetric	Crew 5, 937 lb
Tripp 26	26·67 ft	8·67 ft	2760 lb	(combined main and headsail 410 sq ft)			Crew 4–5
1720	26·25 ft	8·2 ft	3010 lb	295 sq ft	172 sq ft	742 sq ft asymmetric	Crew 4–5
7·5m One Design	24·16 ft	6·56 ft	1760 lb	161 sq ft	86 sq ft	430 sq ft non-asymmetric	Crew 3, 496 lb

Metric dimensions – in metres, kilograms and square metres

Class name	Overall length	Beam	Weight	Mainsail area	Headsail area	Spinnaker area	Notes
AV Breeze	6 m	1·9–3 m	380 kg	15·5 sq m	8·5 sq m	30 sq m asymmetric	Crew 2–3, 210kg maximum
AV Bull	7·5 m	2·45 m	1000 kg	21 sq m	11 sq m	55 sq m asymmetric	Crew 4
Beneteau First Class 8	8·5 m	2·49 m	1400 kg	20·3 sq m	18·5 sq m	49 sq m non-asymmetric	Crew 4–5
H22	6·7 m	2·5 m	740 kg	19·53 sq m	9·18 sq m	23 sq m asymmetric	Boat supplied in kits, crew 2–6
Hunter 707	7·07 m	2·49 m	1060 kg	19·8 sq m	9 sq m	49·5 sq m asymmetric	Crew 3–4, 330 kg maximum
International 11 metre OD	10·03 m	2·5 m	725 kg	26·2 sq m	12·9 sq m	Open	Crew 4–5, 342 kg maximum
J24	7·32 m	2·5 m	1207 kg	12·7 sq m	18·4 sq m	21·5 sq m non-asymmetric	Crew 4 or 5
J80	8 m	2·5 m	1430 kg	21 sq m	20 sq m	52 sq m asymmetric	Crew 4
Magic 25	7·46 m	2·3 m	850 kg	25 sq m	12·33 sq m	46·9 sq m asymmetric	Crew 4, 3 on trapeze
Melges 24	7·32 m	2·5 m	794 kg	22·9 sq m	11·34 sq m	59·4 sq m asymmetric	No crew limit except maximum weight 345·5 kg
Melges 30	9·75 m	3 m	1500 kg	32·8 sq m	28·1 sq m	120 sq m asymmetric	Crew 7
Mount Gay (Rogers) 30	9·64 m	3·35 m	2300 kg	66 sq m	36 sq m	Masthead asymmetric	Crew 4 with water ballast. 8 without
Mumm 30	9·43 m	3·08 m	2040 kg	37 sq m	20 sq m	Asymmetric and non-asymmetric	Crew maximum weight 525 kg
Projection 762	7·62 m	2·6 m	1300 kg	20 sq m	18 sq m	55 sq m	Crew 4–5
Reflex 21	6·4 m	2·14 m deck 3·66 racks	450 kg	22·32 sq m	8·64 sq m	49·3 sq m asymmetric	Crew 4
Reflex 28	8·45 m	2·65 m	1300 kg	22·9 sq m	20·8 sq m	64 sq m asymmetric and non-asymmetric	Crew 6
Sigma 8m OD	8 m	2·49 m	1150 kg	25·2 sq m	14·23 sq m	76·07 sq m non-asymmetric	Crew 5, 937 lb
Tripp 26	8·1 m	2·64 m	1250 kg	(Main and headsail together 36·9 sq m)			Crew 4–5
1720	8 m	2·5 m	1365 kg	27·44 sq m	15·96 sq m	69 sq m asymmetric	Crew 4–5
7·5m One Design	7·5 m	2 m	800 kg	15 sq m	8 sq m	40 sq m non-asymmetric	Crew 3, 225 kg

Open boats – average dimensions

Boats intended for rowing, for small outboards or for sailing should not be too extreme if they are to be safe. The graph opposite shows typical dimensions based on the load waterline. The bottom and left hand side of the graph are calibrated in metres while the top and right hand side are in feet. These dimensions are shown in the plan and elevation below, and for each dimension there is a graph.

In general the freeboard at the bow should be at least 115% of the freeboard at half LWL. The freeboard at the stern should be at least 85% of the freeboard at half LWL.

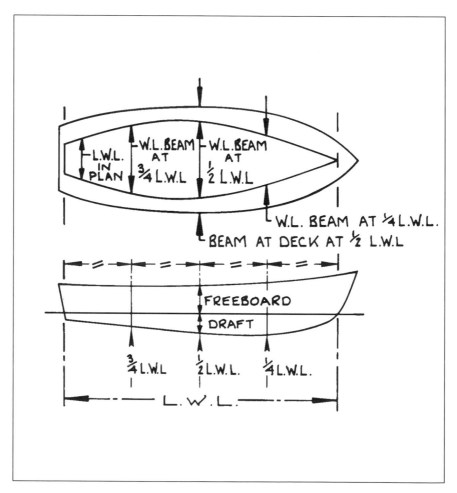

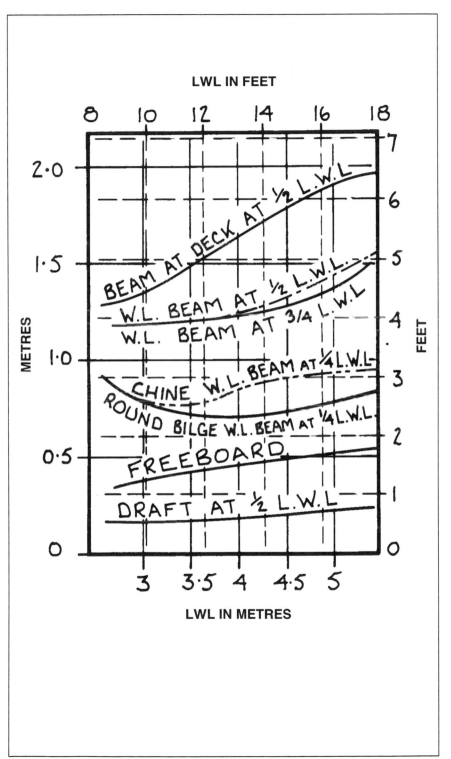

LWL IN FEET

LWL IN METRES

Open boats – typical sail areas

The graph below shows safe sail areas for general use on boats
between 3 and 5·5 metres and is calibrated in metres at the bottom
and on the left hand side, in feet at the top and right hand side.
Beginners may require less sail area than those shown but racing
boats are likely to have somewhat greater sail areas. Sails should
have reefs.

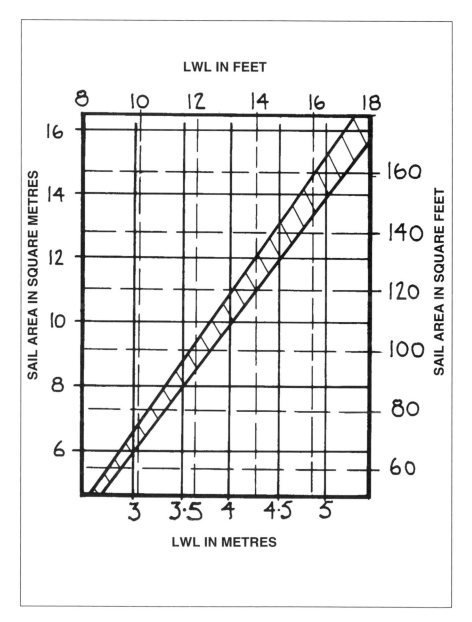

Strip plank wood construction

A combined graph of strip dimensions-v-boat length and plank nail spacing-v-boat length is given below. Owing to shortage of space, this graph is entirely in metric measurements. Down the left is the overall length of the vessel in metres.

The top is in millimetres and is used for the four dimensions of the strip planks, namely the thickness 't', the plank breadth 'b', the convex radius, 'Q', and the concave radius, 'R' (see the inset sketch).

The bottom of the graph is in millimetres and gives the maximum and minimum nail centres. For a light racing yacht the number of nails may be kept to a minimum by using the maximum spacing, to save weight.

Some boatbuilders use a modern technique which involves tongued and grooved strip planks, and these normally have no nails. However this type of planking is not always available. Also at awkward turns it may be advisable to add nails.

Whatever technique is used, the strips of planking should be strongly glued together using a gap-filling glue to exclude water.

Further information about strip plank boatbuilding is published in *Cold Moulded and Strip Plank Wood Boatbuilding* by Ian Nicolson.

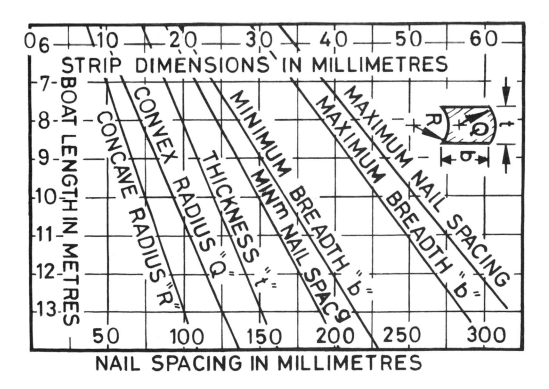

Common welding symbols

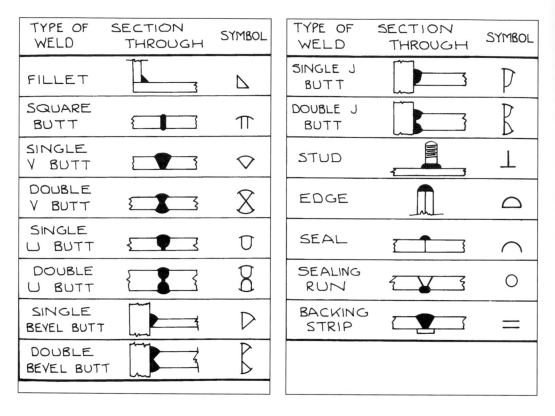

TYPE OF WELD	SECTION THROUGH	SYMBOL
FILLET		△
SQUARE BUTT		Π
SINGLE V BUTT		▽
DOUBLE V BUTT		✕
SINGLE U BUTT		∪
DOUBLE U BUTT		૪
SINGLE BEVEL BUTT		▷
DOUBLE BEVEL BUTT		ᐳᐸ

TYPE OF WELD	SECTION THROUGH	SYMBOL
SINGLE J BUTT		▷
DOUBLE J BUTT		૪
STUD		⊥
EDGE		◠
SEAL		⌒
SEALING RUN		○
BACKING STRIP		=

The human figure – space required

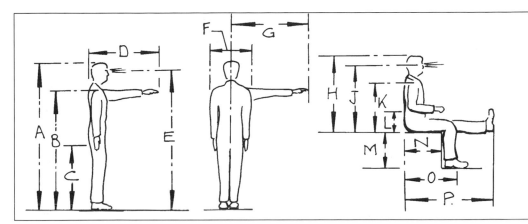

Key dimensions and typical use	Tall man		Average man		Small woman	
	mm	ft & in	mm	ft & in	mm	ft & in
A Headroom*	1880	6 – 2	1740	5 – 8½	1455	4 – 9¼
B Shoulder height – for restricted or shaped doorways	1435	4 – 8½	1400	4 – 7	1200	3 – 11¼
C Hand height – for tiller when standing	840	2 – 9	740	2 – 5	655	2 – 1¾
D Reach forward – engine controls from helmsman's seat†	925	3 – 0½	845	2 – 9¼	600	1 – 11½
E Eye height standing – window level	1745	5 – 8¾	1630	5 – 4¼	1310	4 – 1¾
F Shoulder width – narrow or shaped doorways	505	1 – 7¾	465	1 – 6¼	375	1 – 2¾
G Side reach – instrument controls beside chart table†	925	3 – 0½	885	2 – 11	765	2 – 6
H Headroom above seat – settees under side deck*	960	3 – 1¾	900	2 – 11½	740	2 – 5¼
J Eye height above seat – deckhouse saloon windows	845	2 – 9¼	730	2 – 4¾	620	2 – 0½
K Shoulder above seat – back rests behind seats	640	2 – 1¼	580	1 – 10¾	480	1 – 7
L Elbow above seat – arm rest above seat	270	10¾	220	8¾	145	5¾
M Seat above sole level – seat heights	470	1 – 6½	420	1 – 4½	365	1 – 2¼
N Thigh length—seat width	520	1 – 8½	480	1 – 7	420	1 – 4½
O Back to knee – helmsman's seat space above toe space	660	2 – 0½	590	1 – 11¼	520	1 – 8½
P Back to outstretched foot – cockpit well width	1185	3 – 10¾	1060	3 – 5¾	890	2 – 11

* Allow 100mm (4 in) for hats etc   † Reduce by about 150 mm (6 in) for full grasp

Clothing and boots – space required

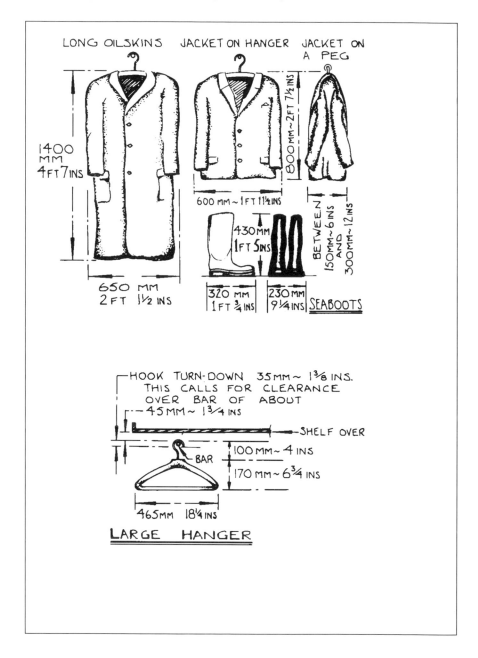

Bunk sizes

Minimum comfortable seagoing berth to fit a large (but not exceptional) man

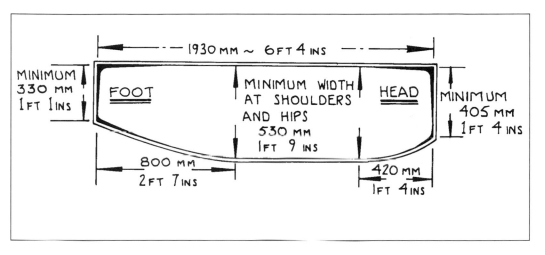

Note: One berth in four could be made 1855 mm (6 ft 1 in) in length in a typical small craft since it is very exceptional to find more than three out of any four men over this size. For comfort there should be at least 25 mm (1 in) beyond the head and feet of the sleeper.

All the dimensions given in the plan are to the *inside* of the berth. Where the ship's side slopes out the width dimensions can be reduced a little.

Chart table, chair – recommended sizes

Especially in boats under about 10 metres (32 ft) it is often hard to fit in a proper chart table and seat. The dimensions here are the minimum practicable. If the seat has to be lowered it will probably be best to lower the chart table almost the same amount, and extra foot-room should be worked in.

Chart table
Big charts may be 1300 mm (4 ft 3 in) when opened out, so the table top should be at least this size where possible.

Chart drawer
Folded charts require a drawer in excess of 712 mm (28 in) by 535 mm (21 in). The depth and number of drawers depends on how many charts are to be carried. 25 folded charts make a pile 12 mm (¹/₂ in) thick.

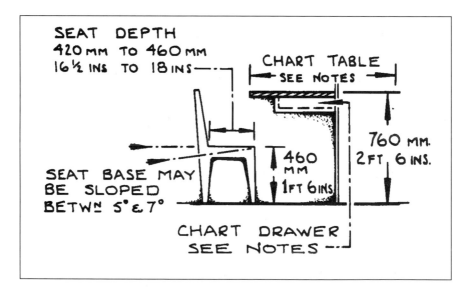

Desk, dressing table, stool – sizes

Desk or dressing table
The height of a desk or dressing table should not be varied just because there is less headroom over it, or because the cabin space round it is limited. There have been fashions for lower levels for

these working surfaces but they tend to conflict with convenience and comfort.

If necessary desks can be much smaller than the one shown in the plan view. In large yachts' engine rooms, for example, an under-size desk is better than none. However the dimensions given here should not be under-cut without good reason.

Likewise the seat size of 250 mm (10 in) wide by 150 mm (6 in) deep at the top can be reduced, especially if there is good padding. But small seats become uncomfortable sooner than large ones.

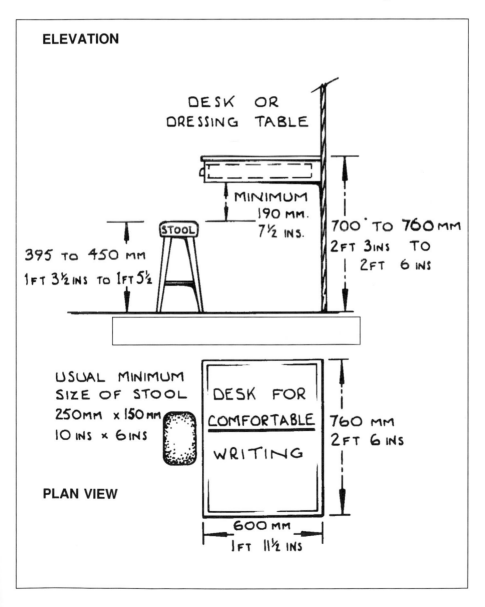

ELEVATION

DESK OR
DRESSING TABLE

MINIMUM
190 MM.
7½ INS.

700 TO 760 MM
2FT 3INS TO
2FT 6 INS

STOOL

395 TO 450 MM
1FT 3½ INS TO 1FT 5½

USUAL MINIMUM
SIZE OF STOOL
250MM x 150MM
10 INS x 6INS

DESK FOR
COMFORTABLE

WRITING

760 MM
2FT 6 INS

PLAN VIEW

600 MM
1FT 11½ INS

Upholstery and bookcase – sizes

Upholstery thicknesses – plastic and rubber materials

Thickness	As mattress or cushion	As backrest
25 mm/1 in	For use on cot or root berths and other berths where there is a canvas or cloth base	Scarcely comfortable. May be used where weight saving is important
50 mm/2 in	For use on dished, radiussed or scooped out bases	Used to save space, weight and cost. Fairly common in very small craft
75 mm/3 in	In general use on very small craft. and inexpensive boats. Adequately comfortable	Widespread. Fully comfortable
100 mm/4 in	Much preferred to 75 mm. General in quality craft	Widespread. Very comfortable
150 mm/6 in	Sumptuous but may be too deep for hot climates. Note that full headroom is still needed over the top surface	May be inconveniently thick and may look wrong on craft under 12 m (40ft)

Book case and book rack (design notes)

For an average book allow 38 mm (1½ in) width
For a paper-back book allow 16 mm (⅝ in) width
For large books and magazines allow 300 mm (11¾ in) height, H_1
For paper-back books allow 185 mm (7¼ in) height, H_2
For large books and magazines allow 215 mm (8½ in) depth, D_1
For paper-back books allow 115 mm (4½ in) depth, D_2

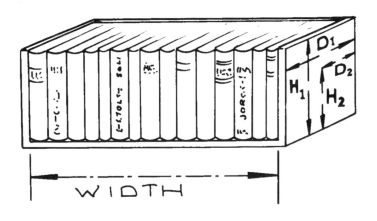

Tables and seats – minimum area

Tables and seats

Table size for four places

This should be considered the minimum to allow adequate comfort and space for crockery etc, at least in harbour.

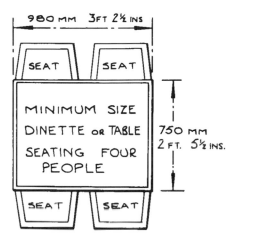

Table size for five or more places

For comfortable meals in harbour, or in a large boat at sea, the dimensions shown are a minimum.

The size of table needed for seven, nine, eleven etc can be worked out from the drawing.

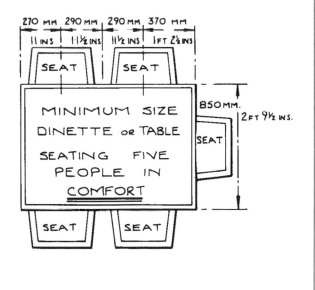

Galley – recommended dimensions

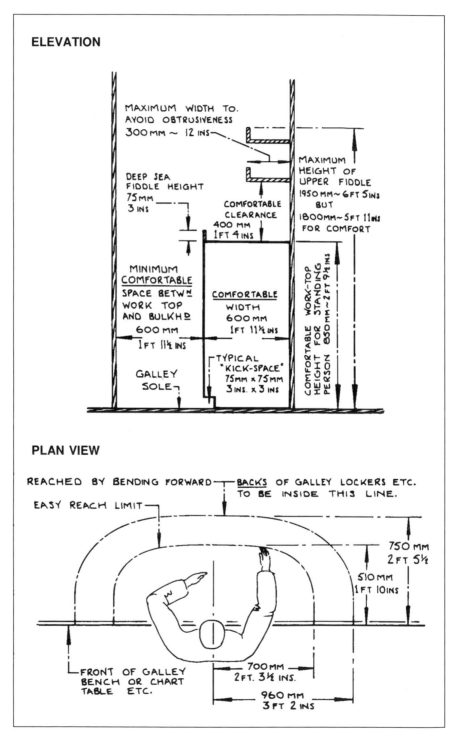

ELEVATION

MAXIMUM WIDTH TO.
AVOID OBTRUSIVENESS
300 mm ~ 12 INS

MAXIMUM
HEIGHT OF
UPPER FIDDLE
1950 mm ~ 6 FT 5 INS
BUT
1800 mm ~ 5 FT 11 INS
FOR COMFORT

DEEP SEA
FIDDLE HEIGHT
75 mm
3 INS

COMFORTABLE
CLEARANCE
400 mm
1 FT 4 INS

MINIMUM
COMFORTABLE
SPACE BETW^N
WORK TOP
AND BULKH^D
600 mm
1 FT 11½ INS

COMFORTABLE
WIDTH
600 mm
1 FT 11½ INS

COMFORTABLE WORK-TOP
HEIGHT FOR STANDING
PERSON 850 mm ~ 2 FT 9¼ INS

GALLEY
SOLE

TYPICAL
"KICK-SPACE"
75 mm x 75 mm
3 INS. x 3 INS

PLAN VIEW

REACHED BY BENDING FORWARD

BACKS OF GALLEY LOCKERS ETC.
TO BE INSIDE THIS LINE.

EASY REACH LIMIT

750 mm
2 FT 5½

510 mm
1 FT 10 INS

FRONT OF GALLEY
BENCH OR CHART
TABLE ETC.

700 mm
2 FT. 3½ INS.

960 mm
3 FT 2 INS

Toilet dimensions

Toilet type	SL400 Minimum size Low price		SL401 Small compact Low price		SL396 Standard Good quality Pricey		SL391 Kentigern Top quality Expensive		Typical chemical toilet with no sea connections Cheap	
Dimensions	in	mm	in	mm	in	mm	in	mm	in	mm
A Overall height	10	255	16¹/₂	420	23⁵/₈	600	38¹/₄	970	16¹/₈	410
B Base to cover top	10	255	13³/₄	350	14	356	16	390	16¹/₈	410
C Overall width	16¹/₂	420	17¹/₂	445	18¹/₈	460	22⁷/₈	580	13³/₄	350
D Front to back	19¹/₂	495	20¹/₂	520	17³/₈	440	18¹/₂	460	17¹/₈	435

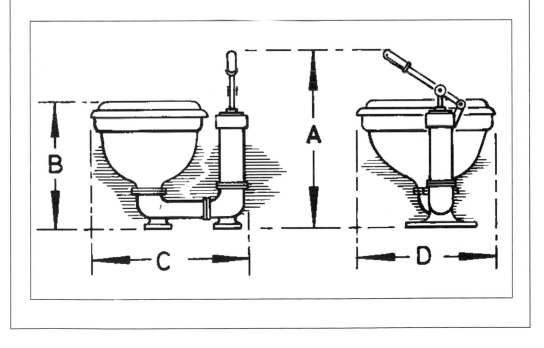

Note: These are overall dimensions. However space must be allowed all round for installation, access to piping, cleaning etc. SL in the table refers to Simpson Lawrence.

Gas cylinders – size and weight

Calor gas

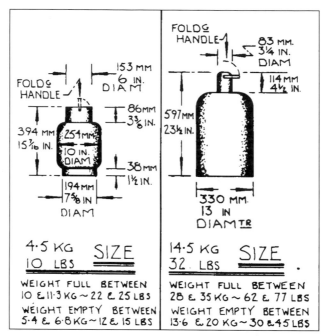

WEIGHT FULL BETWEEN
10 & 11·3 KG ~ 22 & 25 LBS
WEIGHT EMPTY BETWEEN
5·4 & 6·8 KG ~ 12 & 15 LBS

WEIGHT FULL BETWEEN
28 & 35 KG ~ 62 & 77 LBS
WEIGHT EMPTY BETWEEN
13·6 & 20 KG ~ 30 & 45 LBS

Camping gaz

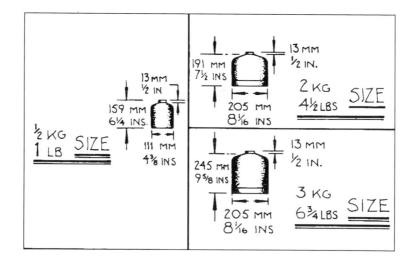

Crockery, glassware, bottles – standard dimensions

The dimensions given here are the maximum sizes for normal crockery. Lockers and shelves built to these sizes will take any normal set of crockery and glassware. (See also drawings on page 186).

Note Dimension A is the height of one plate. B is the increment for further stacking plates.

Handle thicknesses are given because cups and mugs may be stowed in special racks or lockers with slots to take the handles. These slots should be extended well down as some handles protrude from near the bottom of the cup and mug body.

Traditionally the crockery was bought before the galley was made so that the galley racks could be designed round the crockery. Nowadays it is advisable to check that the crockery intended for a particular boat will fit the galley, which is likely to be a mass-produced compartment with standard fittings.

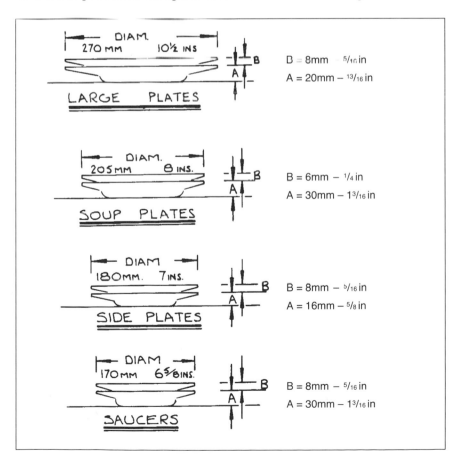

DIAM.
270 mm   10½ INS

LARGE   PLATES

B = 8mm   5/16 in
A = 20mm – 13/16 in

DIAM.
205mm   8 INS.

SOUP   PLATES

B = 6mm – 1/4 in
A = 30mm – 13/16 in

DIAM
180mm.   7INS.

SIDE   PLATES

B = 8mm – 5/16 in
A = 16mm – 5/8 in

DIAM
170mm   6⅝INS.

SAUCERS

B = 8mm – 5/16 in
A = 30mm – 13/16 in

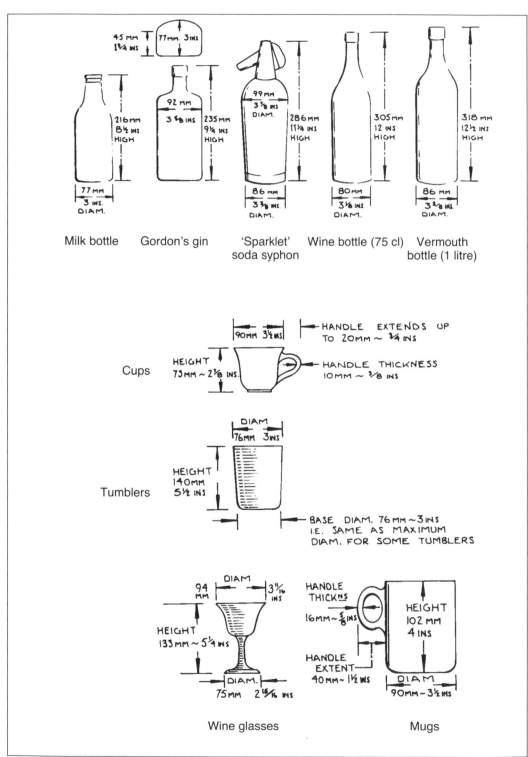

45 mm 1¾ ins · 77 mm. 3 ins

216 mm 8½ ins HIGH

77 mm 3 ins. DIAM.

Milk bottle

92 mm 3⅝ ins · 235 mm 9¼ ins HIGH

Gordon's gin

99 mm 3⅞ ins DIAM. · 286 mm 11¼ ins HIGH

86 mm 3⅜ ins. DIAM.

'Sparklet' soda syphon

305 mm 12 ins HIGH

80 mm 3⅛ ins DIAM.

Wine bottle (75 cl)

318 mm 12½ ins HIGH

86 mm 3⅜ ins. DIAM.

Vermouth bottle (1 litre)

Cups

90 mm 3½ ins

HANDLE EXTENDS UP TO 20mm ~ ¾ ins

HEIGHT 73 mm ~ 2⅞ ins.

HANDLE THICKNESS 10 mm ~ ⅜ ins

Tumblers

DIAM 76 mm 3 ins

HEIGHT 140 mm 5½ ins

BASE DIAM. 76 mm ~ 3 ins I.E. SAME AS MAXIMUM DIAM. FOR SOME TUMBLERS

DIAM 94 mm 3¹¹⁄₁₆ ins

HEIGHT 133 mm ~ 5¼ ins

DIAM. 75 mm 2¹⁵⁄₁₆ ins

Wine glasses

HANDLE THICKNSS 16 mm ~ ⅝ ins

HANDLE EXTENT 40 mm ~ 1½ ins

HEIGHT 102 mm 4 ins

DIAM 90 mm ~ 3½ ins

Mugs

Liferaft container sizes

Different makers of liferafts produce a variety of shapes and sizes of container. The dimensions shown here are typical, but when planning space for a liferaft, it is best to allow a little extra all round, to be safe. Also some containers have protuberances such as handles which extend beyond the sides or ends.

A raft in a deep locker must not be a tight fit. Room is needed to get hands down the sides to grip the container when it has to be pulled out. Even where there appears to be ample space for getting the raft out the job can be so difficult that it is best to have straps (with loops at each end) led under the raft.

Size	SOFT VALISE		FIBREGLASS CONTAINER	
	L × B × D	weight	L × B × D	weight
4 Person	$31^1/_2$ × $13^1/_2$ × $11^3/_4$ ins 80 × 34 × 30 cms	53lbs 24 kilos	$26^1/_2$ × $18^1/_2$ × $8^1/_4$ ins 67 × 47 × 21 cms	66lbs 30 kilos
6 Person	33 × 14 × $12^1/_2$ ins 84 × 36 × 32 cms	$68^1/_2$lbs 31 kilos	$29^1/_2$ × $20^1/_2$ × $8^1/_4$ ins 75 × 52 × 21 × cms	$81^1/_2$ lbs 37 kilos
8 Person	$33^1/_2$ × 15 × $13^1/_2$ ins 85 × 38 × 34 cms	$79^1/_2$ lbs 36 kilos	$29^1/_2$ × $20^1/_2$ × $9^1/_2$ ins 75 × 52 × 24 cms	93lbs 42 kilos

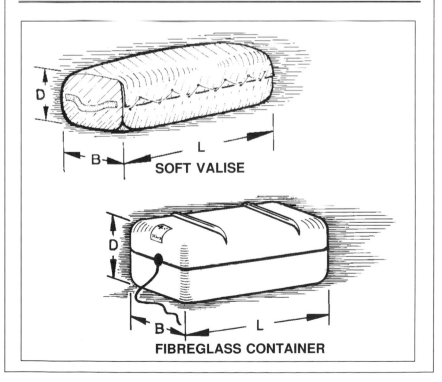

SOFT VALISE

FIBREGLASS CONTAINER

Small power boat seats

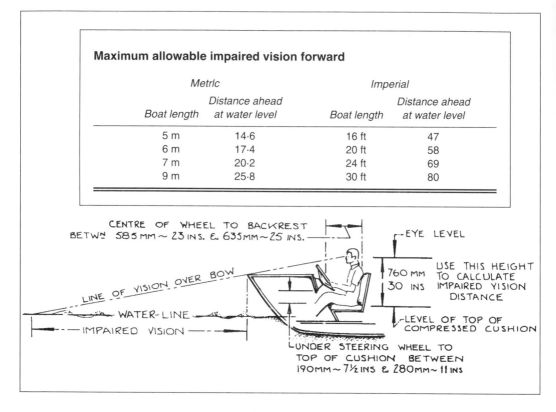

Maximum allowable impaired vision forward

	Metric		Imperial	
	Distance ahead			Distance ahead
Boat length	at water level		Boat length	at water level
5 m	14·6		16 ft	47
6 m	17·4		20 ft	58
7 m	20·2		24 ft	69
9 m	25·8		30 ft	80

The wheel rim, windshield framing or other structure should not obstruct forward vision.

Hatch size, cockpit locker lid size and sail locker bin size

The graph opposite is used for selecting the minimum size of hatch through which a yacht's sails can be passed. Normally the fore hatch is the one used, though it can be useful (and in severe weather possibly essential) to be able to get all the sails through the main hatch as well. The graph is based on the probable size of the largest sail on board, normally the No 1 genoa. This size depends on the 'I' and 'J' measurements, namely the height and base length of the fore triangle as shown in the sketch, top left.

This graph is drawn for imperial and metric measurements. The bottom and left vertical sides are in feet with solid lines across and up the graph. The top and right vertical sides are in metres with

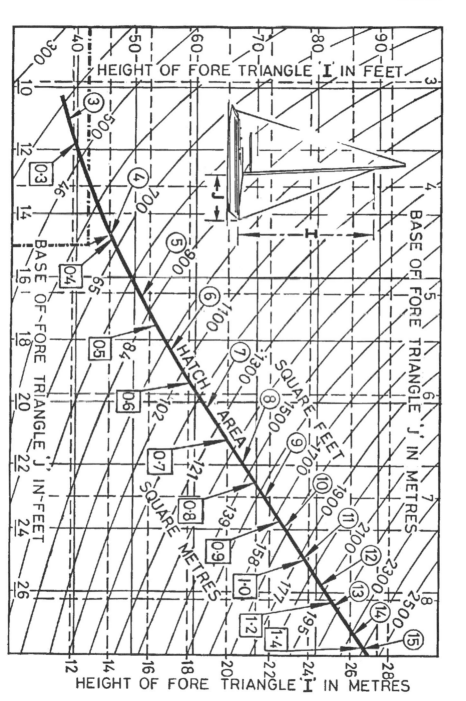

(This graph is based on original work by Roger Marshall, to whom credit is given.)

dotted lines drawn across and down the graph. The hatch area (or cockpit locker lid area, or sail bin top size) is the heavy line running bottom left to top right. It has the sizes in square feet circled above the line, and in square metres in square boxes below the line.

An example is shown in chain dotted lines, bottom left. The height of the fore triangle in this example is 42 ft, and the base 15 ft. Drawing horizontal and vertical lines at these figures gives an area of 630 sq ft. The curved diagonal lines going from bottom right to top left are the fore triangle area lines, but only alternate lines are marked with the area dimension. Above the 'hatch area' line is the area in square feet; below it, the area in square metres. From the intersection in the example the hatch area is read off. It is always best to increase the hatch size at least a little, and in this case a hatch 2 x 2 ft (4 sq ft) is selected.

This graph assumes the sail will be properly flaked down in a 'sausage' sail bag. A sail loosely bundled into an old-fashioned tub shaped bag will need a much bigger hatch.

Also in practice:

- It is rare to fit a hatch less than about 2 x 2 ft (60 x 60) cm) in size, partly because this is about the smallest hatch which a person clad in bulky oilskins can get through without too much of a struggle. As a result the 2 x 2 ft hatch is the popular standard size.
- Hatches are often found to be too small when it comes to getting sails through, and it is best to work on the basis that this graph gives minimum sizes.
- This graph is also useful for determining the size of cockpit locker lids when sails are stowed in these lockers.

The graph can also be used to give an idea of the size of sail bin tops, for instance in a foc's'le. However here again the sizes given should be taken as minimal. Where sails are just stuffed haphazardly into tub shaped traditional bags the top of the bin, or the size of the hatch must be substantially larger.

Sail covers – measurement plan

It is possible to make a sail cover without a drawing but in practice the best approach is to make a sail cover drawing and this means putting the sail on its boom. It should be stowed in the normal way, with the battens in and the slides on the mast track if this is the owner's practice.

Coloured chalk is used to mark off the locations of the girths (distances round the sail-and-boom or, in the case of GE, GF and GH, distance round sail-and-mast).

All dimensions prefixed G on the diagram below are girths. Their locations are based on ordinates (distances off) from the fore side of the mast, in line with the under side of the boom.

Halyard winches are located by height and if they are not exactly on the fore side, or exactly athwartships, this must be shown. The diameter (shown as X) and the distance off the mast (shown as Z) must be detailed.

Other obstructions like spinnaker boom cups must be marked in, with their size and exact location.

A sail cover needs to be cut full, in fact slightly baggy, so that water on a wet sail will drain away and the bottom should be sufficiently open to allow a circulation of air to dry up surface moisture. But the cover must not be cut so full that it flaps in the breeze and destroys itself in a season.

A cover should extend along the boom at least 75 mm (3 in) beyond the extreme aft end of the sail. If the boom diameter is more than 125 mm (5 in), the cover should extend the boom's diameter beyond the sail.

At the top the cover must extend up the mast beyond the sail for enough to allow the lashing to be secured tightly round the mast. This will normally be of the order of 50 mm (2 in) but the dimension depends partly on the lashing method used.

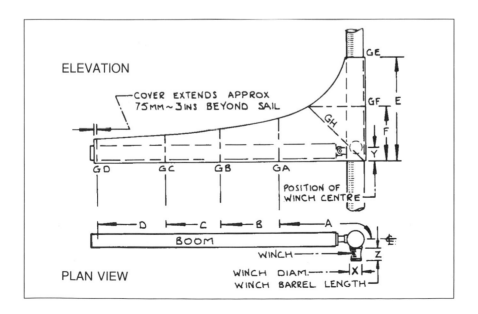

Unshaped mainsail cover

This is a simple modern type of cover, used on racing craft and on sails which come off the mast when the sail is lowered. The advantages of this type of sail cover are:

- Simple shape, and hence low cost.
- Sometimes there is not even a taper towards the end, so the cover is made from a rectangular piece of cloth.
- It fits the type of mainsail which comes off the mast when lowered, that is, a sail with a luff-rope in a mast groove.
- It is quickly and easily fitted over a furled sail.

Measuring

Taking the measurements for this type of sail cover is quick and easy. The length of the sail foot from the back of the mast to the aft end of the clew is taken. To this must be added the aft end overlap. This should be of the order of 3 in (75 mm) per 20 ft (6 metres) of boat length. Alternatively it can be three-quarters of the distance from the aft end of the sail to the haul-out point. The aim is to have plenty of overlap so that sunlight cannot get at the clew of the sail.

   The sail may be flaked down as shown in the sketch, or it may

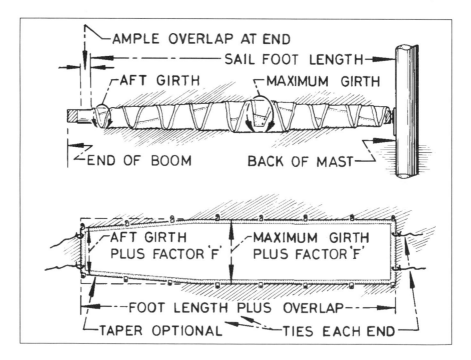

be flaked with the battens in, in which case it tends to bunch aft, as the leech is kept 'on top of itself' all the way up, and the battens lie snugly parallel with the boom. If the sail is rolled up, the same applies. When the battens are left in, the bulk of the sail is aft because the leech is rolled up 'on itself' and the luff gradually works aft away from the mast.

The girth measurement is the maximum one, whichever way the sail is stowed. This girth forms the width of the cover, but a factor 'F' is added to ensure the cover can be fitted even when the sail is slightly rumpled as the result of a bad stow, perhaps due to windy conditions. The factor 'F' is typically 2 in (50 mm) per 20 ft (6 metres) of yacht length. Some sailmakers have no taper aft, but do have one forward. This will take into account the smaller girth forward when the sail is rolled or flaked with the leech kept tight together, as described above.

Seacock sizes

Seacocks are measured by the bore of the pipe to which they are attached. At present the sizes are not standardized therefore it is sensible to buy the cock and the fittings at the same time from the same maker. Approximate guide:

Toilets
Small craft Discharge: 38 mm (1½ in); Inlet: 20 mm (¾ in).
Over 15 m/50 ft Discharge: 50 mm (2 in); Inlet: 25 mm (1 in).

Basins and sinks
Small size wastes: 20 mm (¾ in).
Average size wastes: 32–38 mm (1¼–1½ in).
Special care should be taken to avoid small waste pipe sizes for sinks because they block so easily. Even 20 mm (¾ in) is often considered too small.

Steering – rudder, wheel etc

Rudder
Rudder stops should normally be fitted at 33° each side, since beyond this angle the steering effect is lessened. Sometimes however, rudder stops are fitted beyond this angle to allow the rudder to swing to say 60° and act as a partial brake. If so the

rudder, its stock and controls have to be made extra strong to withstand the pressure on the rudder when going astern.

Normally rudder stall will occur at about 17° if the rudder is put over violently. Therefore where the helm is very light, eg where there is a tiller on a small craft, consideration should be given to introducing a light resisting pressure, or marking helm positions at 17°.

A balanced rudder normally has about ¹/₆ of the area ahead of the centreline of the stock. More than ¹/₆ can be dangerous.

Wheel

A steering wheel should be as large as possible. About 75 mm (3 in) is needed outside a rim or spoke for knuckle clearance. The minimum practical diameter for continuous use is about 350 mm (14 in) and the larger the better. It is generally better to have a large diameter ungeared wheel than a small one with gearing.

Anchor cable and stowage space

Points to note: Ample reserve space should always be allowed. The compartment for chain cable should taper towards the bottom. No overhang or other structure should protrude into the space. The clench plate for securing the end of the cable should always be above the stowed chain. Approximate stowage space for 20 metres (66 ft or 11 fathoms):

Cable diameter		Approx stowage space	
mm	ins	cubic m	cubic ft
5	3/16	0·005	0·16
6·5	1/4	0·008	0·27
8	5/16	0·010	0·35
10	3/8	0·015	0·56
11	7/16	0·021	0·76
13	1/2	0·030	1·0
14	9/16	0·037	1·3
16	5/8	0·048	1·7
19	3/4	0·070	2·5

Formulae for anchor chains

Breaking strain in tons $= (\text{Diameter in ins})^2 \times 27$

Proof strain in tons $= (\text{Diameter in ins})^2 \times 18$

Weight of chain in pounds per fathom $= (\text{Diameter in ins})^2 \times 54$

'Standard' bollards/fairleads
(See design on page 197)

It can be difficult and sometimes impossible to buy reliable bollards and fairleads from chandlers. Even when they are available, they may only be offered in small sizes. The diagram on page 197 shows an easily made 'standard' bollard which also serves as a fairlead, because a rope can be passed under the top bar and between the two uprights. This type of fairlead is called an 'enclosed' type and it has the advantage that a rope cannot accidentally lift out of it.

The recommended sizes fit yachts used for coastal cruising (see following pages). Light-weight craft, may use one size smaller. For heavy duty use, one or even two sizes larger are recommended.

An owner, builder or designer can save time when a new set of bollards/fairleads are needed by simply photocopying these pages from *Boat Data Book*, marking what bollard size is required and giving them to the boatbuilder. This saves a lot of time and trouble, because this sketch and notes form a complete specification.

Quite another use of this diagram and table of dimensions is for checking the standard of deck fittings on a vessel. Many craft are built with the cheapest fittings and as a result bollards are sometimes inadequate even for limited cruising. Using the data here, it is easy to see if the bollards on a boat are correct for her size.

Design notes
1 For craft subject to heavy duty use such as fishing boats and ocean cruisers the bollard should be increased by one or two sizes.
2 The material used will normally be marine quality stainless steel, but it can be mild steel, in which case the fitting should be galvanised on completion and after the holes have been drilled.
3 Dimension 'A' is the tube diameter. It applies to the top bar, the two upright support tubes and the half tube on the base-plate, between the two uprights.
4 Dimension 'A' can be the inside or outside diameter of the tube.
5 Oval tubing may be used, but it is normally more expensive and it is often hard to obtain.
6 The ends of the top tube must be blanked off. If this is not done the tube may 'whistle' in the wind; in fog this can sound like the fog-horn of an approaching craft.
7 All welds are full, continuous and 'round the ends'.
8 The vertical tubes may be tilted 20 degrees as shown by the dotted lines. This triangulates the whole fitting and slightly lengthens the tube end welds.

'Standard' bollards/fairleads

For vessels up to: (See note 1)	Bollard-fairlead size	Dimensions in inches						
		A Tube diameter	B Length	C Base-plate width	D Height	E Base-plate thickness	F Fairlead width	G Holding-down bolt diameter
34 feet	1	1	9	2⅞	3	³⁄₁₆	2½	⁵⁄₁₆
43 feet	2	1½	12	4	4	¼	3⅜	⅜
52 feet	3	2	15	5⅛	5	¼	4⅜	½
61 feet	4	2½	19	6¼	6	⁵⁄₁₆	5¼	⅝
70 feet	5	3	24	7½	7½	⅜	6⅝	¾

For vessels up to: (See note 1)	Bollard-fairlead size	Dimensions in millimetres						
		A Tube diameter	B Length	C Base-plate width	D Height	E Base-plate thickness	F Fairlead width	G Holding-down bolt diameter
10·4 metres	1	25	225	70	75	5	65	8
13 metres	2	40	300	100	100	6	85	10
16 metres	3	50	375	130	125	6	110	12
18·6 metres	4	60	475	160	150	8	135	16
21·3 metres	5	80	600	190	190	10	170	18

9 Six holding-down bolts are fitted. They should be round-head ones to reduce the chance of chaffing warps. Alternatively they may be counter-sunk, but this will call for the next thickness up in base-plate size, or the holes will need washers welded round them on top of the base-plate, prior to drilling the counter-sinking.

10 The base-plate may have to be widened to ensure that the bolts can be easily fitted and clear the top bar as they go in. For instance if oval tubes are used the top one may overhang the bolt holes, in which case a wider base-plate and wider spaced bolt holes will be needed.

11 The length of half-tubing between the vertical tubes is to prevent warps chaffing when the fitting is being used as a fairlead. It also strengthens the whole fitting.

12 All edges and corners must be well rounded.

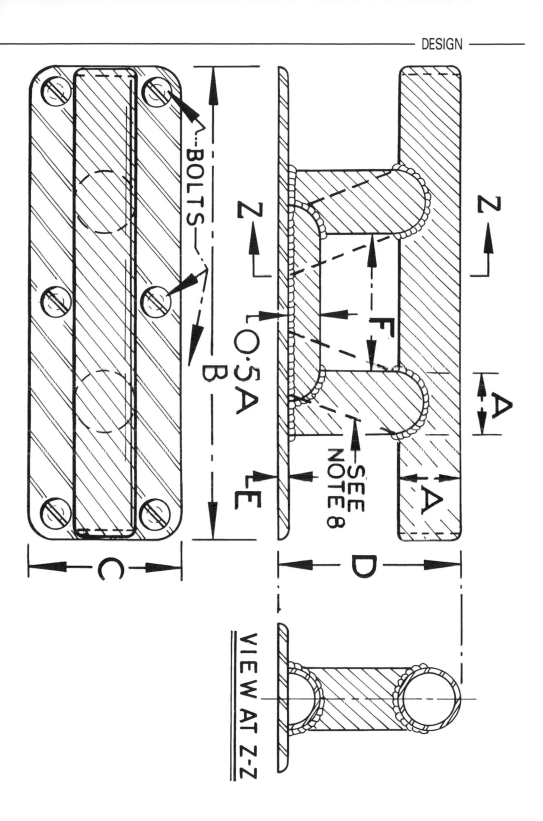

BOLTS

Z

0.5A

B

Z

C

SEE NOTE 8

E

D

Z

A

A

F

VIEW AT Z-Z

Davit strengths and sizes

The graphs on page 199 can be used to calculate the size of dinghy or anchor davits. It can be used to check if davits are strong enough, and it is handy for checking the strength of the structure which supports davits.

The strength of a davit depends on its outside diameter and whether it is made of solid bar, standard pipe or a stronger grade of tubing. The point which is most highly stressed is at the upper bearing, so if a davit is too weak an outside tube welded to it at this point will increase the strength.

The basis of davit strength calculations are the two figures which must be known, namely W and L. W is the weight being lifted, and here it is important to take a pessimistic view. For instance it should always be assumed that a dinghy will have a lot of water in it and that this water will run to one end so that most of the load will be lifted by one davit. An anchor davit not only lifts the anchor but also a length of chain attached to the anchor, and maybe some mud or kelp on the anchor too.

L is the outreach length. It is best to assume the vessel heels 30° so that the outreach is not just the length of the bent top of the davit. L is the length of the line from the top davit bearing, at right angles to the rope extending down from the end of the davit to the load, as shown in the sketch.

This set of curves is in imperial and metric dimensions. The left hand vertical side gives the outside diameter of the davit in inches, with solid horizontal lines. The right hand vertical side gives the diameter in millimetres, with dotted horizontal lines. The bottom line gives M, which is W × L, in pounds and inches. At 10 000, and 20 000 and so on, there are vertical solid lines. One quarter of the way up from the bottom are M values in kilogrammes (for W) and centimetres (for L). Vertical dotted lines are shown at 10 000, 20 000 and so on.

EXAMPLE: A davit made of solid steel 50 mm in diameter has an M value of 10 000. It will therefore just be able to lift a load of 100 kilos at an arm's length of 1 metre. This assumes a standard safety factor.

EXAMPLE: A dinghy which, with rain water or spray over the floorboards, may weigh as much as 800 lbs. This boat has a half-beam of 50 inches, so the davit must have an outreach of that plus a margin. A simple preliminary sketch of the davit viewed from forward or aft shows that when the vessel heels 30°, the outreach will be about 60 inches. M = 800 × 60 = 48 000. This is divided between two davits, so each should be able to carry 24000 lbs/inches. To be safe assume much of the bilge-water slops to one end, and take M as 35000. A double extra strong pipe 3·5 inches diameter should be safe, or a solid bar davit, 3·25 inches diameter will cope.

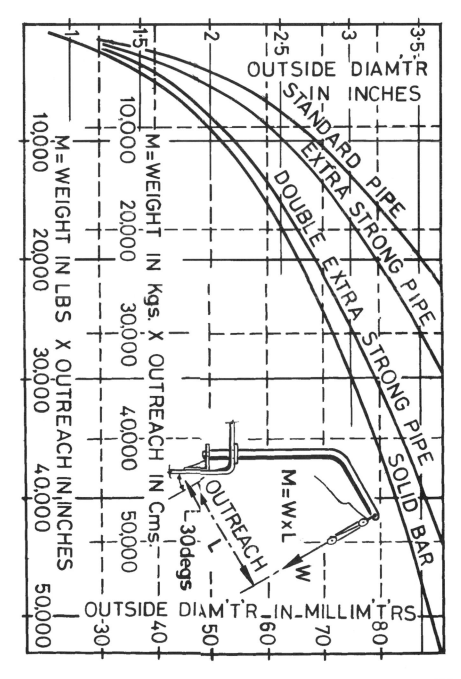

Ventilation

Ventilator diameter	Cross sectional area		Notes
50mm (2 in)	1900 mm²	3in²	Too small. Promotes little ventilation especially in calm weather
75 mm (3 in)	4400 mm²	7 in²	Suitable for craft below about 9 m (29 ft) overall
100 mm (4 in)*	7800 mm²	12·5 in²	Smallest reliable size for all round effectiveness*
150 mm (6 in)	17700 mm²	28 in²	Recommended for craft over about 13 m (43 ft) overall

*This is the 'Standard vent' size included in the table below

As a guide, each person needs 0·4 cubic metres of air per minute (14 cu ft).

An engine requires about 0·07 cubic metres per horse power per minute for combustion (2·5 cu ft).

In temperate climates air intake should approximately equal exhaust but if the trunking is long or tortuous extra should be allowed for. Inflowing air will not travel as fast as exhaust gases and so extra area must be allowed for also.

Engine room ventilation is needed for the crew and the engine plus additional area of 650 sq mm (1 sq in) per horse power if the inlet is of the low speed type without fan assistance.

For personnel an air speed of about 900 mm/sec (3 ft/sec) is comfortable.

For hot weather an air speed of 1500 mm/sec (5 ft/sec) is pleasant.

Changes per hour and suggested ventilation

Compartment	Temperate climate	Hot climate	Very hot climate	Notes
Saloon cabins, etc	8 ch/hr 1 'Standard vent' per 2 people	16 ch/hr 2 'Standard vents' per 2 people	24 ch/hr 3 'Standard vents' per 2 people	In hot climates vents will need wind scoops plus hatches and bigger than standard vents
Toilets of size 2 m x 2 m x 2 m (6·5 ft cube)	15 ch/hr	25 ch/hr	30 ch/hr	Extractor fan recommended when the compartment is occupied. Flow required 4·5 m/sec (15 ft/sec) with 'Standard vent'
Galley	30 ch/hr	36 ch/hr	40 ch/hr	Extractor fan required over cooker to draw off steam and smells and to ensure the required number of changes
Engine room	Depends on horse power and crew (see above). Inlet area should be 1·5 times exhaust plus 950 sq mm (1·4 sq in) per horse power of all engines			Minimum two cowls. One to be trunked to the bilge. Ventilation is often found to be inadequate in engine spaces

Colour coding of pipes, cables, conduits, notices etc

Colour coding may be applied using paint or coloured tape. There are basic identification colours (eg green for water) with a safety or reference colour (eg a short mid-length blue strip to show it is drinking water) as an addition.

On small craft it is usual to use a simple system involving only single colours, as shown in the list at the bottom of the page. It is seldom considered necessary to paint the full length of a pipe with the colour code. Colour coding paints or tapes are normally just applied near junctions, valves, bulkheads, by access hatches and so on. Typically the basic colour will extend along the pipe for 150 mm (6 in) and there will be a band of the safety or reference colour 100 mm (4 in) long, followed by another length of the basic identification colour.

Water pipes			
Pipe contents	Basic colour	Colour code indication	Basic colour
	Approx 150 mm (6 in)	Approx 100 mm (4 in)	Approx 150 mm (6 in)
Drinking water	Green	Blue	Green
Cooling water	Green	White	Green
Boiler feed	Green	Crimson / white / crimson	Green
Condensate	Green	Crimson / green / crimson	Green
Hot water	Green	White / crimson / white	Green
Hydraulic power	Green	Salmon pink	Green
Sea-water (untreated)	Green	Green	Green
Fire extinguishing	Green	Red	Green

Oil pipes			
Diesel fuel	Brown	White	Brown
Furnace fuel	Brown	Brown	Brown
Lubricating oil	Brown	Emerald Green	Brown
Hydraulic power	Brown	Salmon pink	Brown

Other piping			
Compressed air	Light blue	Light blue	Light blue
Vacuum	Light blue	White	Light blue
Steam	Silver grey	Silver grey	Silver grey
Drainage	Black	Black	Black
Electrical conduits & vent ducts	Orange	Orange	Orange
Acids and alkalis	Violet	Violet	Violet

Based on BS 1710 and BS 4800, to which acknowledgement is made

Simple colour coding			
Fresh water	Light green	Bilge suctions	Dark grey
Salt water	Dark green	Diesel fuel	Light brown
Fire extinguishing water	Medium red	Lubricating oil	Dark brown
Fire CO_2	Dark red	Hydraulic pipelines	Fawn
Soil drainage or 'grey' water	Light grey	Steering hydraulic lines	Salmon pink
WC drainage	Black	Air and venting	Pale blue
		AC electrics	Bright blue

Notices, tally plates etc	
Fire systems	Bright red
Rescue and life-saving items	Yellow
Pumping and flooding	Dark blue
AC electrics	Bright blue
General	Black or white

New colour coding for fire extinguishers

The whole of the exterior of the extinguisher has to be red, apart from up to 5 per cent of the area which may be used to identify the extinguishing compound or agent in the container. The following colours show the contents and their uses:

Blue	Indicates dry powder. Suitable for flammable liquids. Safe up to 1000 volts.
Cream	Indicates foam. Suitable for flammable liquids. Unsafe at all voltages.
Black	Indicates CO_2 (carbon dioxide). Suitable for flammable liquids. Safe for high voltages.
Green	Vapourising liquids. Suitable for flammable liquids. Safe for high voltages.
White	Water CO_2 (soda acid). Suitable for wood, paper, textiles, etc. Unsafe for all voltages.

Old types of fire extinguisher — use and colour coding

Type	Colour code	Type of fire	Precautions
Water	Red	Wood, paper, fabrics etc	Dangerous on electrical and flammable liquid fires
Foam	Yellow	Flammable liquids, oils, fats, spirits etc	Dangerous on electrical fires
AFFF	Grey	Wood, paper, fabrics, flammable liquids, vehicle protection and mixed 'office' areas etc	
Powder	Blue	All risks. Flammable liquids and gaseous fires, if no risk of explosion	
CO_2	Black	Electrical and flammable liquids	
BCF halon	Green	Electrical and flammable liquids	Compartment must be evacuated before using this type of extinguisher, and not re-entered until it is fully ventilated

7 TABLES AND FORMULAE

Conversion factors

The reciprocal is used to convert the quantity in the second column into that in the first:

$$\text{eg Inches} \times 25\cdot4 = \text{millimetres}$$
$$\text{Millimetres} \times 0\cdot0394 = \text{inches}$$

To convert inches	into millimetres	Multiplier 25·4	Reciprocal 0·0394
Length			
⅛ ths of inches	Millimetres	3·175	0·315
¹⁄₁₆ ths of inches	Millimetres	1·587	0·630
Inches	Metres	0·025	39·37
Feet	Metres	0·305	3·281
Yards	Metres	0·914	1·094
Miles	Kilometres	1·609	0·621
Sea miles	Metres	1853·1	0·000539
Miles	Metres	1609·3	0·000621
Area			
Square inches	Square centimetres	6·4516	0·155
Square feet	Square metres	0·0929	10·764
Volume			
Cubic inches	Cubic centimetres	16·387	0·061
Cubic inches	Litres	0·016	62·5
Cubic feet	Cubic metres	0·028	35·315
Cubic yards	Cubic metres	0·765	1·308
Imperial gallons	Litres	4·546	0·220
USA gallons	Litres	3·785	0·264
Imperial gallons	USA gallons	1·205	0·830

To convert	into	Multiplier	Reciprocal
Weight			
Grammes	Ounces	0·035	28·35
Pounds (lbs)	Kilogrammes	0·454	2·205
Hundredweights (cwt)	Kilogrammes	50·802	0·020
Tons	French tonnes	1·016	0·984
Density			
Pounds per cubic foot	Kilograms per cubic metre	16·019	0·0624
Speed			
Kilometres per hour	Metres per second	0·278	3·6
Metres per second	Knots	1·943	
Feet per second	Metres per second	0·305	3·281
Feet per second	Miles per hour	0·682	1·467
Feet per minute	Kilometres per hour	0·018	54·68
Miles per hour	Metres per second	0·447	2·237
Miles per hour	Kilometres per hour	1·609	0·621
Knots	Miles per hour	1·151	
Stress, Work, Energy			
Kilograms per sq metre	Pounds per sq foot	0·205	4·88
Kilogram-metres	Foot-pounds	7·23	0·138
Horsepower (metric)	Horsepower (British)	0·986	1·014
Kilowatts (kW)	Horsepower British	1·340	0·746
Watts	B Th U per second	0·00095	1055·36

Thames tonnage

$$\text{Thames tonnage} = \frac{[L - B] \times B \times 0 \cdot 5B}{94}$$

Where L is the Thames tonnage length from fore side of stem to aft side of stern-port (or fore side of rudder post), and B is the beam to the outside of the planking or plating. All dimensions are in feet.

Temperatures – Fahrenheit/Centigrade

0 to 100						0 to 1000						1000 to 2000					
C.		F.	C.		F.	C.		F.	C.		F.	C.		F.	C.		F.
-17.8	0	32	10.0	50	122.0	-17.8	0	32	260	500	932	538	1000	1832	816	1500	2732
-17.2	1	33.8	10.6	51	123.8	-12.2	10	50.0	266	510	950	543	1010	1850	821	1510	2750
-16.7	2	35.6	11.1	52	125.6	-6.67	20	68.0	271	520	968	549	1020	1868	827	1520	2768
-16.1	3	37.4	11.7	53	127.4	-1.11	30	86.0	277	530	986	554	1030	1886	832	1530	2786
-15.6	4	39.2	12.2	54	129.2	4.44	40	104.0	282	540	1004	560	1040	1904	838	1540	2804
-15.0	5	41.0	12.8	55	131.0	10.0	50	122.0	288	550	1022	566	1050	1922	843	1550	2822
-14.4	6	42.8	13.3	56	132.8	15.6	60	140.0	293	560	1040	571	1060	1940	849	1560	2840
-13.9	7	44.6	13.9	57	134.6	21.1	70	158.0	299	570	1058	577	1070	1958	854	1570	2858
-13.3	8	46.4	14.4	58	136.4	26.7	80	176.0	304	580	1076	582	1080	1976	860	1580	2876
-12.8	9	48.2	15.0	59	138.2	32.2	90	194.0	310	590	1094	588	1090	1994	866	1590	2894
-12.2	10	50.0	15.6	60	140.0	38	100	212	316	600	1112	593	1100	2012	871	1600	2912
-11.7	11	51.8	16.1	61	141.8	43	110	230	321	610	1130	599	1110	2030	877	1610	2930
-11.1	12	53.6	16.7	62	143.6	49	120	248	327	620	1148	604	1120	2048	882	1620	2948
-10.6	13	55.4	17.2	63	145.4	54	130	266	332	630	1166	610	1130	2066	888	1630	2966
-10.0	14	57.2	17.8	64	147.2	60	140	284	338	640	1184	616	1140	2084	893	1640	2984
-9.44	15	59.0	18.3	65	149.0	66	150	302	343	650	1202	621	1150	2102	899	1650	3002
-8.89	16	60.8	18.9	66	150.8	71	160	320	349	660	1220	627	1160	2120	904	1660	3020
-8.33	17	62.6	19.4	67	152.6	77	170	338	354	670	1238	632	1170	2138	910	1670	3038
-7.78	18	64.4	20.0	68	154.4	82	180	356	360	680	1256	638	1180	2156	916	1680	3056
-7.22	19	66.2	20.6	69	156.2	88	190	374	366	690	1274	643	1190	2174	921	1690	3074
-6.67	20	68.0	21.1	70	158.0	93	200	392	371	700	1292	649	1200	2192	927	1700	3092
-6.11	21	69.8	21.7	71	159.8	99	210	410	377	710	1310	654	1210	2210	932	1710	3110
-5.56	22	71.6	22.2	72	161.6	104	220	428	382	720	1328	660	1220	2228	938	1720	3128
-5.00	23	73.4	22.8	73	163.4	110	230	446	388	730	1346	666	1230	2246	943	1730	3146
-4.44	24	75.2	23.3	74	165.2	116	240	464	393	740	1364	671	1240	2264	949	1740	3164
-3.89	25	77.0	23.9	75	167.0	121	250	482	399	750	1382	677	1250	2282	954	1750	3182
-3.33	26	78.8	24.4	76	168.8	127	260	500	404	760	1400	682	1260	2300	960	1760	3200
-2.78	27	80.6	25.0	77	170.6	132	270	518	410	770	1418	688	1270	2318	966	1770	3218
-2.22	28	82.4	25.6	78	172.4	138	280	536	416	780	1436	693	1280	2336	971	1780	3236
-1.67	29	84.2	26.1	79	174.2	143	290	554	421	790	1454	699	1290	2354	977	1790	3254
-1.11	30	86.0	26.7	80	176.0	149	300	572	427	800	1472	704	1300	2372	982	1800	3272
-0.56	31	87.8	27.2	81	177.8	154	310	590	432	810	1490	710	1310	2390	988	1810	3290
0	32	89.6	27.8	82	179.6	160	320	608	438	820	1508	716	1320	2408	993	1820	3308
0.56	33	91.4	28.3	83	181.4	166	330	626	443	830	1526	721	1330	2426	999	1830	3326
1.11	34	93.2	28.9	84	183.2	171	340	644	449	840	1544	727	1340	2444	1004	1840	3344
1.67	35	95.0	29.4	85	185.0	177	350	662	454	850	1562	732	1350	2462	1010	1850	3362
2.22	36	96.8	30.0	86	186.8	182	360	680	460	860	1580	738	1360	2480	1016	1860	3380
2.78	37	98.6	30.6	87	188.6	188	370	698	466	870	1598	743	1370	2498	1021	1870	3398
3.33	38	100.4	31.1	88	190.4	193	380	716	471	880	1616	749	1380	2516	1027	1880	3416
3.89	39	102.2	31.7	89	192.2	199	390	734	477	890	1634	754	1390	2534	1032	1890	3434
4.44	40	104.0	32.2	90	194.0	204	400	752	482	900	1652	760	1400	2552	1038	1900	3452
5.00	41	105.8	32.8	91	195.8	210	410	770	488	910	1670	766	1410	2570	1043	1910	3470
5.56	42	107.6	33.3	92	197.6	216	420	788	493	920	1688	771	1420	2588	1049	1920	3488
6.11	43	109.4	33.9	93	199.4	221	430	806	499	930	1706	777	1430	2606	1054	1930	3506
6.67	44	111.2	34.4	94	201.2	227	440	824	504	940	1724	782	1440	2624	1060	1940	3524
7.22	45	113.0	35.0	95	203.0	232	450	842	510	950	1742	788	1450	2642	1066	1950	3542
7.78	46	114.8	35.6	96	204.8	238	460	860	516	960	1760	793	1460	2660	1071	1960	3560
8.33	47	116.6	36.1	97	206.6	243	470	878	521	970	1778	799	1470	2678	1077	1970	3578
8.89	48	118.4	36.7	98	208.4	249	480	896	527	980	1796	804	1480	2696	1082	1980	3596
9.44	49	120.2	37.2	99	210.2	254	490	914	532	990	1814	810	1490	2714	1088	1990	3614
10.0	50	122.0	37.8	100	212.0	260	500	932	538	1000	1832	816	1500	2732	1093	2000	3632

Read known temperature in bold typeface. Corresponding temperature in degrees Fahrenheit will be found in column to the right. Corresponding temperature in degrees Centigrade will be found in column to the left.

For intermediate values add the following

C		F	C		F
0·56	1	1·8	3·33	6	10·8
1·11	2	3·6	3·89	7	12·6
1·67	3	5·4	4·44	8	14·4
2·22	4	7·2	5·00	9	16·2
2·78	5	9·0	5·56	10	18·0

Temperature conversion formulae : $°C = °F − 32 × \frac{5}{9}$
$°F = °C × \frac{9}{5} − 32$

Standard wire gauge – metric and Imperial equivalents

MM.	IMPERIAL STANDARD W.G.	DECIMAL EQUIVALENTS INCHES	FRACTIONS INCHES	MM.	IMPERIAL STANDARD W.G.	DECIMAL EQUIVALENTS INCHES	FRACTIONS INCHES
0·314	30	·0124		3·17		·125	$\frac{1}{8}$
0·345	29	·0136		3·251	10	·128	
0·375	28	·0148		3·571		·1406	$\frac{9}{64}$
0·396		·0156	$\frac{1}{64}$	3·657	9	·144	
0·416	27	·0164		3·97		·1562	$\frac{5}{32}$
0·457	26	·018		4		·1575	
0·508	25	·020		4·064	8	·160	
0·558	24	·022		4·365		·1718	$\frac{11}{64}$
0·609	23	·024		4·470	7	·176	
0·711	22	·028		4·76		·1875	$\frac{3}{16}$
0·790		·0312	$\frac{1}{32}$	4·876	6	·192	
0·812	21	·032		5		·1968	
0·914	20	·036		5·159		·2031	$\frac{13}{64}$
1		·039		5·384	5	·212	
1·016	19	·040		5·56		·2187	$\frac{7}{32}$
1·190		·0469	$\frac{3}{64}$	5·892	4	·232	
1·219	18	·048		5·952		·2343	$\frac{15}{64}$
1·422	17	·056		6		·2362	
1·59		·0625	$\frac{1}{16}$	6·35		·250	$\frac{1}{4}$
1·625	16	·064		6·400	3	·252	
1·828	15	·072		7		·2756	
2		·0781	$\frac{5}{64}$	7·010	2	·276	
2·032	14	·080		7·14		·2812	$\frac{9}{32}$
2·336	13	·092		7·620	1	·300	
2·38		·0937	$\frac{3}{32}$	7·94		·3125	$\frac{5}{16}$
2·640	12	·104		8		·3150	
2·778		·1093	$\frac{7}{64}$	8·229	0	·324	
2·946	11	·116		8·73		·3437	$\frac{11}{32}$
3		·118		8·839	2/0	·348	

MM.	IMPERIAL STANDARD W.G.	DECIMAL EQUIVALENTS INCHES	FRACTIONS INCHES
9		·3543	
9·448	3/0	·372	
9·52		·375	$\frac{3}{8}$
10		·3937	
10·16	4/0	·400	
10·32		·4062	$\frac{13}{32}$
10·97	5/0	·432	
11		·4331	
11·11		·4375	$\frac{7}{16}$
11·8	6/0	·464	
11·91		·468	$\frac{15}{32}$
12		·472	
12·70	7/0	·500	$\frac{1}{2}$
13		·5118	
14		·5512	
14·29		·5625	$\frac{9}{16}$
15		·5905	
15·87		·625	$\frac{5}{8}$
16		·6299	
17		·6693	
17·46		·6875	$\frac{11}{16}$
18		·7087	
19		·7480	
19·05		·750	$\frac{3}{4}$
20		·7874	
20·64		·8125	$\frac{13}{16}$
22·22		·875	$\frac{7}{8}$
23·81		·9375	$\frac{15}{16}$
25·40		1·000	1

Metal gauges – metric and Imperial equivalents

Gauge No	Thickness		Gauge No	Thickness	
	mm	*inches*		*mm*	*inches*
1	7·61	0·300	16	1·62	0·064
2	7·00	0·276	17	1·42	0·056
3	6·39	0·252	18	1·22	0·048
4	5·88	0·232	19	1·01	0·040
5	5·38	0·212	20	0·91	0·036
6	4·87	0·192	21	0·81	0·032
7	4·46	0·176	22	0·71	0·028
8	4·06	0·160	23	0·61	0·024
9	3·66	0·144	24	0·56	0·022
10	3·25	0·128	25	0·51	0·020
11	2·94	0·116	26	0·46	0·018
12	2·64	0·104	27	0·41	0·016
13	2·34	0·092	28	0·36	0·014
14	2·00	0·080	29	0·33	0·013
15	1·83	0·072	30	0·30	0·012

Millimetres in decimals of an inch

MM.	INCHES	MM.	INCHES	MM.	INCHES	MM.	INCHES	MM.	INCHES
·01	·00039	·21	·00827	·41	·01614	·61	·02402	·81	·03189
·02	·00079	·22	·00866	·42	·01654	·62	·02441	·82	·03228
·03	·00118	·23	·00906	·43	·01693	·63	·02480	·83	·03268
·04	·00157	·24	·00945	·44	·01732	·64	·02520	·84	·03307
·05	·00197	·25	·00984	·45	·01772	·65	·02559	·85	·03346
·06	·00236	·26	·01024	·46	·01811	·66	·02598	·86	·03386
·07	·00276	·27	·01063	·47	·01850	·67	·02638	·87	·03425
·08	·00315	·28	·01102	·48	·01890	·68	·02677	·88	·03465
·09	·00354	·29	·01142	·49	·01929	·69	·02717	·89	·03504
·10	·00394	·30	·01181	·50	·01969	·70	·02756	·90	·03543
·11	·00433	·31	·01220	·51	·02008	·71	·02795	·91	·03583
·12	·00472	·32	·01260	·52	·02047	·72	·02835	·92	·03622
·13	·00512	·33	·01299	·53	·02087	·73	·02874	·93	·03661
·14	·00551	·34	·01339	·54	·02126	·74	·02913	·94	·03701
·15	·00591	·35	·01378	·55	·02165	·75	·02953	·95	·03740
·16	·00630	·36	·01417	·56	·02205	·76	·02992	·96	·03780
·17	·00669	·37	·01457	·57	·02244	·77	·03032	·97	·03819
·18	·00709	·38	·01496	·58	·02283	·78	·03071	·98	·03858
·19	·00748	·39	·01535	·59	·02323	·79	·03110	·99	·03898
·20	·00787	·40	·01575	·60	·02362	·80	·03150	1	·0394

Inches to decimal parts of a foot

Inches	Feet	Inches	Feet
1/8	0·01	1	0·083
1/4	0·021	2	0·167
3/8	0·031	3	0·250
1/2	0·042	4	0·333
5/8	0·052	5	0·417
3/4	0·062	6	0·500
7/8	0·073	7	0·583
		8	0·667
		9	0·750
		10	0·833
		11	0·017

MM.	INCHES	MM.	INCHES	MM.	INCHES	MM.	INCHES	MM.	INCHES
2	·0787	22	·8661	42	1·6535	62	2·4409	82	3·2283
3	·1181	23	·9055	43	1·6929	63	2·4803	83	3.2677
4	·1575	24	·9449	44	1·7323	64	2·5197	84	3·3071
5	·1968	25	·9842	45	1·7716	65	2·5590	85	3·3464
6	·2362	26	1·0236	46	1·8110	66	2·5984	86	3·3858
7	·2756	27	1·0630	47	1·8504	67	2·6378	87	3·4252
8	·3150	28	1·1024	48	1·8898	68	2·6772	88	3·4646
9	·3543	29	1·1417	49	1·9291	69	2·7165	89	3·5039
10	·3937	30	1·1811	50	1·9685	70	2·7559	90	3·5433
11	·4331	31	1·2205	51	2·0079	71	2·7953	91	3·5827
12	·4724	32	1·2598	52	2·0472	72	2·8346	92	3·6220
13	·5118	33	1·2992	53	2·0866	73	2·8740	93	3·6614
14	·5512	34	1·3386	54	2·1260	74	2·9134	94	3·7008
15	·5905	35	1·3779	55	2·1653	75	2·9527	95	3·7401
16	·6299	36	1·4173	56	2·2047	76	2·9921	96	3·7795
17	·6693	37	1·4567	57	2·2441	77	3·0315	97	3·8189
18	·7087	38	1·4961	58	2·2835	78	3·0709	98	3·8583
19	·7480	39	1·5354	59	2·3228	79	3·1102	99	3·8976
20	·7874	40	1·5748	60	2·3622	80	3·1496	100	3·9370
21	·8268	41	1·6142	61	2·4016	81	3·1890		

Millimetres to inches and inches to millimetres

Millimetres versus inches   1 millimetre = 0·039370 inches

Millimetres	0 mm	1 mm	2 mm	3 mm	4 mm
0	0	0·039370	0·078740	0·118110	0·157481
10	0·393701	0·433072	0·472442	0·511812	0·551182
20	0·787403	0·826773	0·866143	0·905513	0·944884
30	1·18110	1·22047	1·25984	1·29291	1·33858
40	1·57481	1·61418	1·65355	1·69292	1·73229
50	1·96851	2·00788	2·04725	2·08662	2·12599
60	2·36221	2·40158	2·44095	2·48032	2·51969
70	2·75591	2·79528	2·83465	2·87402	2·91339
80	3·14961	3·18898	3·22835	3·26772	3·30709
90	3·54331	3·58268	3·62205	3·66142	3·70079
100	3·93701	3·97638	4·01575	4·05513	4·09450

Inches versus millimetres   1 inch = 25·4mm

Inches	0 in	1 in	2 in	3 in	4 in
0	0	25·4	50·8	76·2	101·6
10	254·0	279·4	304·8	330·2	355·6
20	508·0	533·4	558·8	584·2	609·6
30	762·0	787·4	812·8	838·2	863·6
40	1016·0	1041·4	1066·8	1092·2	1117·6
50	1270·0	1295·4	1320·8	1346·2	1371·6
60	1524·0	1549·4	1574·8	1600·2	1625·6
70	1778·0	1803·4	1828·8	1854·2	1879·6
80	2032·0	2057·4	2082·8	2108·2	2133·6
90	2286·0	2311·4	2336·8	2362·2	2387·6
100	2540·0	2565·4	2590·8	2616·2	2641·6

5 mm	6 mm	7mm	8mm	9mm
0·196851	0·236221	0·275591	0·314961	0·354331
0·590552	0·629922	0·669292	0·708663	0·748033
0·984254	1·02362	1·06299	1·10236	1·14173
1·37796	1·41733	1·45670	1·49607	1·53544
1·77166	1·81103	1·85040	1·88977	1·92914
2·16536	2·20473	2·24410	2·28347	2·32284
2·55906	2·59843	2·63780	2·67717	2·71654
2·95276	2·99213	3·03150	3·07087	3·11024
3·34646	2·38583	3·42520	3·46457	3·50394
3·74016	3·77953	3·81890	3·85827	3·89764
4·13387	4·17324	4·21261	4·25198	4·29135

5 in	6 in	7 in	8 in	9 in
127·0	152·4	177·8	203·2	228·6
381·0	406·4	431·8	457·2	482·6
635·0	660·4	685·8	711·2	736·6
889·0	914·4	939·8	965·2	990·6
1143·0	1168·4	1193·8	1219·2	1244·6
1397·0	1422·4	1447·8	1473·2	1498·6
1651·0	1676·4	1701·8	1727·2	1752·6
1905·0	1930·4	1955·8	1981·2	2006·6
2159·0	2184·4	2209·8	2235·2	2260·6
2413·0	2438·4	2463·8	2489·2	2514·6
2667·0	2692·4	2717·8	2743·2	2768·6

211

Inches and eighths of an inch to millimetres

in	ft in	mm	in	ft in	mm	in	ft in	mm	in	ft in	mm
⅛		3·2	9⅛		231·8	18⅛	1 6⅛	460·4	27⅛	2 3⅛	689·0
¼		6·4	9¼		235·0	18¼	1 6¼	463·6	27¼	2 3¼	692·2
⅜		9·5	9⅜		238·1	18⅜	1 6⅜	466·7	27⅜	2 3⅜	695·3
½		12·7	9½		241·3	18½	1 6½	469·9	27½	2 3½	698·5
⅝		15·9	9⅝		244·5	18⅝	1 6⅝	473·1	27⅝	2 3⅝	701·7
¾		19·1	9¾		247·7	18¾	1 6¾	476·3	27¾	2 3¾	704·9
⅞		22·2	9⅞		250·8	18⅞	1 6⅞	479·4	27⅞	2 3⅞	708·0
1		25·4	10		254·0	19	1 7	482·6	28	2 4	711·2
1⅛		28·6	10⅛		257·2	19⅛	1 7⅛	485·8	28⅛	2 4⅛	714·4
1¼		31·8	10¼		260·4	19¼	1 7¼	489·0	28¼	2 4¼	717·6
1⅜		34·9	10⅜		263·5	19⅜	1 7⅜	492·1	28⅜	2 4⅜	720·7
1½		38·1	10½		266·7	19½	1 7½	495·3	28½	2 4½	723·9
1⅝		41·3	10⅝		269·9	19⅝	1 7⅝	498·5	28⅝	2 4⅝	727·1
1¾		44·5	10¾		273·1	19¾	1 7¾	501·7	28¾	2 4¾	730·3
1⅞		47·6	10⅞		276·2	19⅞	1 7⅞	504·8	28⅞	2 4⅞	733·4
2		50·8	11		279·4	20	1 8	508·0	29	2 5	736·6
2⅛		54·0	11⅛		282·6	20⅛	1 8⅛	511·2	29⅛	2 5⅛	739·8
2¼		57·2	11¼		285·8	20¼	1 8¼	514·4	29¼	2 5¼	743·0
2⅜		60·3	11⅜		288·9	20⅜	1 8⅜	517·5	29⅜	2 5⅜	746·1
2½		63·5	11½		292·1	20½	1 8½	520·7	29½	2 5½	749·3
2⅝		66·7	11⅝		295·3	20⅝	1 8⅝	523·9	29⅝	2 5⅝	752·5
2¾		69·9	11¾		298·5	20¾	1 8¾	527·1	29¾	2 5¾	755·7
2⅞		73·0	11⅞		301·6	20⅞	1 8⅞	530·2	29⅞	2 5⅞	758·8
3		76·2	12	1 0	304·8	21	1 9	533·4	30	2 6	762·0
3⅛		79·4	12⅛	1 0⅛	308·0	21⅛	1 9⅛	536·6	30⅛	2 6⅛	765·2
3¼		82·6	12¼	1 0¼	311·2	21¼	1 9¼	539·8	30¼	2 6¼	768·4
3⅜		85·7	12⅜	1 0⅜	314·3	21⅜	1 9⅜	542·9	30⅜	2 6⅜	771·5
3½		88·9	12½	1 0½	317·5	21½	1 9½	546·1	30½	2 6½	774·7
3⅝		92·1	12⅝	1 0⅝	320·7	21⅝	1 9⅝	549·3	30⅝	2 6⅝	777·9
3¾		95·3	12¾	1 0¾	323·9	21¾	1 9¾	552·5	30¾	2 6¾	781·1
3⅞		98·4	12⅞	1 0⅞	327·0	21⅞	1 9⅞	555·6	30⅞	2 6⅞	784·2
4		101·6	13	1 1	330·2	22	1 10	558·8	31	2 7	787·4
4⅛		104·8	13⅛	1 1⅛	333·4	22⅛	1 10⅛	562·0	31⅛	2 7⅛	790·6
4¼		108·0	13¼	1 1¼	336·6	22¼	1 10¼	565·2	31¼	2 7¼	793·8
4⅜		111·1	13⅜	1 1⅜	339·7	22⅜	1 10⅜	568·3	31⅜	2 7⅜	796·9
4½		114·3	13½	1 1½	342·9	22½	1 10½	571·5	31½	2 7½	800·1
4⅝		117·5	13⅝	1 1⅝	346·1	22⅝	1 10⅝	574·7	31⅝	2 7⅝	803·3
4¾		120·7	13¾	1 1¾	349·3	22¾	1 10¾	577·9	31¾	2 7¾	806·5
4⅞		123·8	13⅞	1 1⅞	352·4	22⅞	1 10⅞	581·0	31⅞	2 7⅞	809·6
5		127·0	14	1 2	355·6	23	1 11	584·2	32	2 8	812·8
5⅛		130·2	14⅛	1 2⅛	358·8	23⅛	1 11⅛	587·4	32⅛	2 8⅛	816·0
5¼		133·4	14¼	1 2¼	362·0	23¼	1 11¼	590·6	32¼	2 8¼	819·2
5⅜		136·5	14⅜	1 2⅜	365·1	23⅜	1 11⅜	593·7	32⅜	2 8⅜	822·3
5½		139·7	14½	1 2½	368·3	23½	1 11½	596·9	32½	2 8½	825·5
5⅝		142·9	14⅝	1 2⅝	371·5	23⅝	1 11⅝	600·1	32⅝	2 8⅝	828·7
5¾		146·1	14¾	1 2¾	374·7	23¾	1 11¾	603·3	32¾	2 8¾	831·9
5⅞		149·2	14⅞	1 2⅞	377·8	23⅞	1 11⅞	606·4	32⅞	2 8⅞	835·0
6		152·4	15	1 3	381·0	24	2 0	609·6	33	2 9	838·2
6⅛		155·6	15⅛	1 3⅛	384·2	24⅛	2 0⅛	612·8	33⅛	2 9⅛	841·4
6¼		158·8	15¼	1 3¼	387·4	24¼	2 0¼	616·0	33¼	2 9¼	844·6
6⅜		161·9	15⅜	1 3⅜	390·5	24⅜	2 0⅜	619·1	33⅜	2 9⅜	847·7
6½		165·1	15½	1 3½	393·7	24½	2 0½	622·3	33½	2 9½	850·9
6⅝		168·3	15⅝	1 3⅝	396·9	24⅝	2 0⅝	625·5	33⅝	2 9⅝	854·1
6¾		171·5	15¾	1 3¾	400·1	24¾	2 0¾	628·7	33¾	2 9¾	857·3
6⅞		174·6	15⅞	1 3⅞	403·2	24⅞	2 0⅞	631·8	33⅞	2 9⅞	860·4
7		177·8	16	1 4	406·4	25	2 1	635·0	34	2 10	863·6
7⅛		181·0	16⅛	1 4⅛	409·6	25⅛	2 1⅛	638·2	34⅛	2 10⅛	866·8
7¼		184·2	16¼	1 4¼	412·8	25¼	2 1¼	641·4	34¼	2 10¼	870·0
7⅜		187·3	16⅜	1 4⅜	415·9	25⅜	2 1⅜	644·5	34⅜	2 10⅜	873·1
7½		190·5	16½	1 4½	419·1	25½	2 1½	647·7	34½	2 10½	876·3
7⅝		193·7	16⅝	1 4⅝	422·3	25⅝	2 1⅝	650·9	34⅝	2 10⅝	879·5
7¾		196·9	16¾	1 4¾	425·5	25¾	2 1¾	654·1	34¾	2 10¾	882·7
7⅞		200·0	16⅞	1 4⅞	428·6	25⅞	2 1⅞	657·2	34⅞	2 10⅞	885·8
8		203·2	17	1 5	431·8	26	2 2	660·4	35	2 11	889·0
8⅛		206·4	17⅛	1 5⅛	435·0	26⅛	2 2⅛	663·6	35⅛	2 11⅛	892·2
8¼		209·6	17¼	1 5¼	438·2	26¼	2 2¼	666·8	35¼	2 11¼	895·4
8⅜		212·7	17⅜	1 5⅜	441·3	26⅜	2 2⅜	669·9	35⅜	2 11⅜	898·5
8½		215·9	17½	1 5½	444·5	26½	2 2½	673·1	35½	2 11½	901·7
8⅝		219·1	17⅝	1 5⅝	447·7	26⅝	2 2⅝	676·3	35⅝	2 11⅝	904·9
8¾		222·3	17¾	1 5¾	450·9	26¾	2 2¾	679·5	35¾	2 11¾	908·1
8⅞		225·4	17⅞	1 5⅞	454·0	26⅞	2 2⅞	682·6	35⅞	2 11⅞	911·2
9		228·6	18	1 6	457·2	27	2 3	685·8	36	3 0	914·4

in	ft in	mm	in	ft in	mm	in	ft in	mm	in	ft in	mm
36⅛	3 0⅛	917·6	45⅛	3 9⅛	1146·2	54⅛	4 6⅛	1374·8	63⅛	5 3⅛	1603·4
36¼	3 0¼	920·8	45¼	3 9¼	1149·4	54¼	4 6¼	1378·0	63¼	5 3¼	1606·6
36⅜	3 0⅜	923·9	45⅜	3 9⅜	1152·5	54⅜	4 6⅜	1381·1	63⅜	5 3⅜	1609·7
36½	3 0½	927·1	45½	3 9½	1155·7	54½	4 6½	1384·3	63½	5 3½	1612·9
36⅝	3 0⅝	930·3	45⅝	3 9⅝	1158·9	54⅝	4 6⅝	1387·5	63⅝	5 3⅝	1616·1
36¾	3 0¾	933·5	45¾	3 9¾	1162·1	54¾	4 6¾	1390·7	63¾	5 3¾	1619·3
36⅞	3 0⅞	936·6	45⅞	3 9⅞	1165·2	54⅞	4 6⅞	1393·8	63⅞	5 3⅞	1622·4
37	3 1	939·8	46	3 10	1168·4	55	4 7	1397·0	64	5 4	1625·6
37⅛	3 1⅛	943·0	46⅛	3 10⅛	1171·6	55⅛	4 7⅛	1400·2	64⅛	5 4⅛	1628·8
37¼	3 1¼	946·2	46¼	3 10¼	1174·8	55¼	4 7¼	1403·4	64¼	5 4¼	1632·0
37⅜	3 1⅜	949·3	46⅜	3 10⅜	1177·9	55⅜	4 7⅜	1406·5	64⅜	5 4⅜	1635·1
37½	3 1½	952·5	46½	3 10½	1181·1	55½	4 7½	1409·7	64½	5 4½	1638·3
37⅝	3 1⅝	955·7	46⅝	3 10⅝	1184·3	55⅝	4 7⅝	1412·9	64⅝	5 4⅝	1641·5
37¾	3 1¾	958·9	46¾	3 10¾	1187·5	55¾	4 7¾	1416·1	64¾	5 4¾	1644·7
37⅞	3 1⅞	962·0	46⅞	3 10⅞	1190·6	55⅞	4 7⅞	1419·2	64⅞	5 4⅞	1647·8
38	3 2	965·2	47	3 11	1193·8	56	4 8	1422·4	65	5 5	1651·0
38⅛	3 2⅛	968·4	47⅛	3 11⅛	1197·0	56⅛	4 8⅛	1425·6	65⅛	5 5⅛	1654·2
38¼	3 2¼	971·6	47¼	3 11¼	1200·2	56¼	4 8¼	1428·8	65¼	5 5¼	1657·4
38⅜	3 2⅜	974·7	47⅜	3 11⅜	1203·3	56⅜	4 8⅜	1431·9	65⅜	5 5⅜	1660·5
38½	3 2½	977·9	47½	3 11½	1206·5	56½	4 8½	1435·1	65½	5 5½	1663·7
38⅝	3 2⅝	981·1	47⅝	3 11⅝	1209·7	56⅝	4 8⅝	1438·3	65⅝	5 5⅝	1666·9
38¾	3 2¾	984·3	47¾	3 11¾	1212·9	56¾	4 8¾	1441·5	65¾	5 5¾	1670·1
38⅞	3 2⅞	987·4	47⅞	3 11⅞	1216·0	56⅞	4 8⅞	1444·6	65⅞	5 5⅞	1673·2
39	3 3	990·6	48	4 0	1219·2	57	4 9	1447·8	66	5 6	1676·4
39⅛	3 3⅛	993·8	48⅛	4 0⅛	1222·4	57⅛	4 9⅛	1451·0	66⅛	5 6⅛	1679·6
39¼	3 3¼	997·0	48¼	4 0¼	1225·6	57¼	4 9¼	1454·2	66¼	5 6¼	1682·8
39⅜	3 3⅜	1000·1	48⅜	4 0⅜	1228·7	57⅜	4 9⅜	1457·3	66⅜	5 6⅜	1685·9
39½	3 3½	1003·3	48½	4 0½	1231·9	57½	4 9½	1460·5	66½	5 6½	1689·1
39⅝	3 3⅝	1006·5	48⅝	4 0⅝	1235·1	57⅝	4 9⅝	1463·7	66⅝	5 6⅝	1692·3
39¾	3 3¾	1009·7	48¾	4 0¾	1238·3	57¾	4 9¾	1466·9	66¾	5 6¾	1695·5
39⅞	3 3⅞	1012·8	48⅞	4 0⅞	1241·4	57⅞	4 9⅞	1470·0	66⅞	5 6⅞	1698·6
40	3 4	1016·0	49	4 1	1244·6	58	4 10	1473·2	67	5 7	1701·8
40⅛	3 4⅛	1019·2	49⅛	4 1⅛	1247·8	58⅛	4 10⅛	1476·4	67⅛	5 7⅛	1705·0
40¼	3 4¼	1022·4	49¼	4 1¼	1251·0	58¼	4 10¼	1479·6	67¼	5 7¼	1708·2
40⅜	3 4⅜	1025·5	49⅜	4 1⅜	1254·1	58⅜	4 10⅜	1482·7	67⅜	5 7⅜	1711·3
40½	3 4½	1028·7	49½	4 1½	1257·3	58½	4 10½	1485·9	67½	5 7½	1714·5
40⅝	3 4⅝	1031·9	49⅝	4 1⅝	1260·5	58⅝	4 10⅝	1489·1	67⅝	5 7⅝	1717·7
40¾	3 4¾	1035·1	49¾	4 1¾	1263·7	58¾	4 10¾	1492·3	67¾	5 7¾	1720·9
40⅞	3 4⅞	1038·2	49⅞	4 1⅞	1266·8	58⅞	4 10⅞	1495·4	67⅞	5 7⅞	1724·0
41	3 5	1041·4	50	4 2	1270·0	59	4 11	1498·6	68	5 8	1727·2
41⅛	3 5⅛	1044·6	50⅛	4 2⅛	1273·2	59⅛	4 11⅛	1501·8	68⅛	5 8⅛	1730·4
41¼	3 5¼	1047·8	50¼	4 2¼	1276·4	59¼	4 11¼	1505·0	68¼	5 8¼	1733·6
41⅜	3 5⅜	1050·9	50⅜	4 2⅜	1279·5	59⅜	4 11⅜	1508·1	68⅜	5 8⅜	1736·7
41½	3 5½	1054·1	50½	4 2½	1282·7	59½	4 11½	1511·3	68½	5 8½	1739·9
41⅝	3 5⅝	1057·3	50⅝	4 2⅝	1285·9	59⅝	4 11⅝	1514·5	68⅝	5 8⅝	1743·1
41¾	3 5¾	1060·5	50¾	4 2¾	1289·1	59¾	4 11¾	1517·7	68¾	5 8¾	1746·3
41⅞	3 5⅞	1063·6	50⅞	4 2⅞	1292·2	59⅞	4 11⅞	1520·8	68⅞	5 8⅞	1749·4
42	3 6	1066·8	51	4 3	1295·4	60	5 0	1524·0	69	5 9	1752·6
42⅛	3 6⅛	1070·0	51⅛	4 3⅛	1298·6	60⅛	5 0⅛	1527·2	69⅛	5 9⅛	1755·8
42¼	3 6¼	1073·2	51¼	4 3¼	1301·8	60¼	5 0¼	1530·4	69¼	5 9¼	1759·0
42⅜	3 6⅜	1076·3	51⅜	4 3⅜	1304·9	60⅜	5 0⅜	1533·5	69⅜	5 9⅜	1762·1
42½	3 6½	1079·5	51½	4 3½	1308·1	60½	5 0½	1536·7	69½	5 9½	1765·3
42⅝	3 6⅝	1082·7	51⅝	4 3⅝	1311·3	60⅝	5 0⅝	1539·9	69⅝	5 9⅝	1768·5
42¾	3 6¾	1085·9	51¾	4 3¾	1314·5	60¾	5 0¾	1543·1	69¾	5 9¾	1771·7
42⅞	3 6⅞	1089·0	51⅞	4 3⅞	1317·6	60⅞	5 0⅞	1546·2	69⅞	5 9⅞	1774·8
43	3 7	1092·2	52	4 4	1320·8	61	5 1	1549·4	70	5 10	1778·0
43⅛	3 7⅛	1095·4	52⅛	4 4⅛	1324·0	61⅛	5 1⅛	1552·6	70⅛	5 10⅛	1781·2
43¼	3 7¼	1098·6	52¼	4 4¼	1327·2	61¼	5 1¼	1555·8	70¼	5 10¼	1784·4
43⅜	3 7⅜	1101·7	52⅜	4 4⅜	1330·3	61⅜	5 1⅜	1558·9	70⅜	5 10⅜	1787·5
43½	3 7½	1104·9	52½	4 4½	1333·5	61½	5 1½	1562·1	70½	5 10½	1790·7
43⅝	3 7⅝	1108·1	52⅝	4 4⅝	1336·7	61⅝	5 1⅝	1565·3	70⅝	5 10⅝	1793·9
43¾	3 7¾	1111·3	52¾	4 4¾	1339·9	61¾	5 1¾	1568·5	70¾	5 10¾	1797·1
43⅞	3 7⅞	1114·4	52⅞	4 4⅞	1343·0	61⅞	5 1⅞	1571·6	70⅞	5 10⅞	1800·2
44	3 8	1117·6	53	4 5	1346·2	62	5 2	1574·8	71	5 11	1803·4
44⅛	3 8⅛	1120·8	53⅛	4 5⅛	1349·4	62⅛	5 2⅛	1578·0	71⅛	5 11⅛	1806·6
44¼	3 8¼	1124·0	53¼	4 5¼	1352·6	62¼	5 2¼	1581·2	71¼	5 11¼	1809·8
44⅜	3 8⅜	1127·1	53⅜	4 5⅜	1355·7	62⅜	5 2⅜	1584·3	71⅜	5 11⅜	1812·9
44½	3 8½	1130·3	53½	4 5½	1358·9	62½	5 2½	1587·5	71½	5 11½	1816·1
44⅝	3 8⅝	1133·5	53⅝	4 5⅝	1362·1	62⅝	5 2⅝	1590·7	71⅝	5 11⅝	1819·3
44¾	3 8¾	1136·7	53¾	4 5¾	1365·3	62¾	5 2¾	1593·9	71¾	5 11¾	1822·5
44⅞	3 8⅞	1139·8	53⅞	4 5⅞	1368·4	62⅞	5 2⅞	1597·0	71⅞	5 11⅞	1825·6
45	3 9	1143·0	54	4 6	1371·6	63	5 3	1600·2	72	6 0	1828·8

Feet and inches to metres and millimetres

Feet	Inches											
	0	**1**	**2**	**3**	**4**	**5**	**6**	**7**	**8**	**9**	**10**	**11**
	Metres and millimetres											
0	—	25	51	76	102	127	152	178	203	229	254	279
1	305	330	356	381	406	432	457	483	508	533	559	584
2	610	635	660	686	711	737	762	787	813	838	864	889
3	914	940	965	991	1·016	1·041	1·067	1·092	1·118	1·143	1·168	1·194
4	1·219	1·245	1·270	1·295	1·321	1·346	1·372	1·397	1·422	1·448	1·473	1·499
5	1·524	1·549	1·575	1·600	1·626	1·651	1·676	1·702	1·727	1·753	1·778	1·803
6	1·829	1·854	1·880	1·905	1·930	1·956	1·981	2·007	2·032	2·057	2·083	2·108
7	2·134	2·159	2·184	2·210	2·235	2·261	2·286	2·311	2·337	2·362	2·388	2·413
8	2·438	2·464	2·489	2·515	2·540	2·565	2·591	2·616	2·642	2·667	2·692	2·718
9	2·743	2·769	2·794	2·819	2·845	2·870	2·896	2·921	2·946	2·972	2·997	3·023
10	3·048	3·073	3·099	3·124	3·150	3·175	3·200	3·226	3·251	3·277	3·302	3·327
11	3·353	3·378	3·404	3·429	3·454	3·480	3·505	3·531	3·556	3·581	3·607	3·632
12	3·658	3·683	3·708	3·734	3·759	3·785	3·810	3·835	3·861	3·886	3·912	3·937
13	3·962	3·988	4·013	4·039	4·064	4·089	4·115	4·140	4·166	4·191	4·216	4·242
14	4·267	4·293	4·318	4·343	4·369	4·394	4·420	4·445	4·470	4·496	4·521	4·547
15	4·572	4·597	4·623	4·648	4·674	4·699	4·724	4·750	4·775	4·801	4·826	4·851
16	4·877	4·902	4·928	4·953	4·978	5·004	5·029	5·055	5·080	5·105	5·131	5·156
17	5·182	5·207	5·232	5·258	5·283	5·309	5·334	5·359	5·385	5·410	5·436	5·461
18	5·486	5·512	5·537	5·563	5·588	5·613	5·639	5·664	5·690	5·715	5·740	5·766
19	5·791	5·817	5·842	5·867	5·893	5·918	5·944	5·969	5·994	6·020	6·045	6·071
20	6·096	6·121	6·147	6·172	6·198	6·223	6·248	6·274	6·299	6·325	6·350	6·375
21	6·401	6·426	6·452	6·477	6·502	6·528	6·553	6·579	6·604	6·629	6·655	6·680
22	6·706	6·731	6·756	6·782	6·807	6·833	6·858	6·883	6·909	6·934	6·960	6·985
23	7·010	7·036	7·061	7·087	7·112	7·137	7·163	7·188	7·214	7·239	7·264	7·290
24	7·315	7·341	7·366	7·391	7·417	7·442	7·468	7·493	7·518	7·544	7·569	7·595
25	7·620	7·645	7·671	7·696	7·722	7·747	7·772	7·798	7·823	7·849	7·874	7·899
26	7·925	7·950	7·976	8·001	8·026	8·052	8·077	8·103	8·128	8·153	8·179	8·204
27	8·230	8·255	8·280	8·306	8·331	8·357	8·382	8·407	8·433	8·458	8·484	8·509
28	8·534	8·560	8·585	8·611	8·636	8·661	8·687	8·712	8·738	8·763	8·788	8·814
29	8·839	8·865	8·890	8·915	8·941	8·966	8·992	9·017	9·042	9·068	9·093	9·119
30	9·144	9·169	9·195	9·220	9·246	9·271	9·296	9·322	9·347	9·373	9·398	9·423
31	9·449	9·474	9·500	9·525	9·550	9·576	9·601	9·627	9·652	9·677	9·703	9·728
32	9·754	9·779	9·804	9·830	9·855	9·881	9·906	9·931	9·957	9·982	10·008	10·033
33	10·058	10·084	10·109	10·135	10·160	10·185	10·211	10·236	10·262	10·287	10·312	10·338
34	10·363	10·389	10·414	10·439	10·465	10·490	10·516	10·541	10·566	10·592	10·617	10·643
35	10·668	10·693	10·719	10·744	10·770	10·795	10·820	10·846	10·871	10·897	10·922	10·947
36	10·973	10·998	11·024	11·049	11·074	11·100	11·125	11·151	11·176	11·201	11·227	11·252
37	11·278	11·303	11·328	11·354	11·379	11·405	11·430	11·455	11·481	11·506	11·532	11·557
38	11·582	11·608	11·633	11·659	11·684	11·709	11·735	11·760	11·786	11·811	11·836	11·862
39	11·887	11·913	11·938	11·963	11·989	12·014	12·040	12·065	12·090	12·116	12·141	12·167
40	12·192	12·217	12·243	12·268	12·294	12·319	12·344	12·370	12·395	12·421	12·446	12·471
41	12·497	12·522	12·548	12·573	12·598	12·624	12·649	12·675	12·700	12·725	12·751	12·776
42	12·802	12·827	12·852	12·878	12·903	12·929	12·954	12·979	13·005	13·030	13·056	13·081
43	13·106	13·132	13·157	13·183	13·208	13·233	13·259	13·284	13·310	13·335	13·360	13·386
44	13·411	13·437	13·462	13·487	13·513	13·538	13·564	13·589	13·614	13·640	13·665	13·691
45	13·716	13·741	13·767	13·792	13·818	13·843	13·868	13·894	13·919	13·945	13·970	13·995
46	14·021	14·046	14·072	14·097	14·122	14·148	14·173	14·199	14·224	14·249	14·275	14·300
47	14·326	14·351	14·376	14·402	14·427	14·453	14·478	14·503	14·529	14·554	14·580	14·605
48	14·630	14·656	14·681	14·707	14·732	14·757	14·783	14·808	14·834	14·859	14·884	14·910
49	14·935	14·961	14·986	15·011	15·037	15·062	15·088	15·113	15·138	15·164	15·189	15·215
50	15·240	15·265	15·291	15·316	15·342	15·367	15·392	15·418	15·443	15·469	15·494	15·519
51	15·545	15·570	15·596	15·621	15·646	15·672	15·697	15·723	15·748	15·773	15·799	15·824
52	15·850	15·875	15·900	15·926	15·951	15·977	16·002	16·027	16·053	16·078	16·104	16·129
53	16·154	16·180	16·231	16·231	16·256	16·281	16·307	16·332	16·358	16·383	16·408	16·434
54	16·459	16·485	16·510	16·535	16·561	16·586	16·612	16·637	16·662	16·688	15·713	16·739
55	16·764	16·769	16·815	16·840	16·866	16·891	16·916	16·942	16·967	16·993	17·018	17·043
56	17·069	17·094	17·120	17·145	17·170	17·196	17·221	17·247	17·272	17·297	17·323	17·348
57	17·374	17·399	17·424	17·450	17·475	17·501	17·526	17·551	17·577	17·602	17·628	17·653
58	17·678	17·704	17·729	17·755	17·780	17·805	17·830	17·856	17·882	17·907	17·932	17·958
59	17·983	18·009	18·034	18·059	18·085	18·110	18·136	18·161	18·186	18·212	18·237	18·263
60	18·288	18·313	18·339	18·364	18·390	18·415	18·440	18·466	18·491	18·517	18·542	18·567
61	18·593	18·618	18·644	18·669	18·694	18·720	18·745	18·771	18·796	18·821	18·847	18·872
62	18·898	18·923	18·948	18·974	18·999	19·025	19·050	19·075	19·101	19·126	19·152	19·177
63	19·202	19·228	19·253	19·279	19·304	19·329	19·355	19·380	19·406	19·431	19·456	19·482
64	19·507	19·533	19·558	19·583	19·609	19·634	19·660	19·685	19·710	19·736	19·761	19·787
65	19·812	19·837	19·863	19·888	19·914	19·939	19·964	19·990	20·015	20·041	20·066	20·091
66	20·117	20·142	20·168	20·193	20·218	20·244	20·269	20·295	20·320	20·345	20·371	20·396
67	20·422	20·447	20·472	20·498	20·523	20·549	20·574	20·599	20·625	20·650	20·676	20·701
68	20·726	20·752	20·777	20·803	20·828	20·853	20·879	20·904	20·930	20·955	20·980	21·006
69	21·031	21·057	21·082	21·107	21·133	21·158	21·184	21·209	21·234	21·260	21·285	21·311

Feet and inches to metres and millimetres (continued)

Feet	Inches											
	0	1	2	3	4	5	6	7	8	9	10	11
	Metres and millimetres											
70	21·336	21·361	21·387	21·412	21·438	21·463	21·488	21·514	21·539	21·565	21·590	21·615
71	21·641	21·666	21·692	21·717	21·742	21·768	21·793	21·819	21·844	21·869	21·895	21·920
72	21·946	21·971	21·996	22·022	22·047	22·073	22·098	22·123	22·149	22·174	22·200	22·225
73	22·250	22·276	22·301	22·327	22·352	22·377	22·403	22·428	22·454	22·479	22·504	22·530
74	22·555	22·581	22·606	22·631	22·657	22·682	22·708	22·733	22·758	22·784	22·809	22·835
75	22·860	22·885	22·911	22·936	22·962	22·987	23·012	23·038	23·063	23·089	23·114	23·139
76	23·165	23·190	23·216	23·241	23·266	23·292	23·317	23·343	23·368	23·393	23·419	23·444
77	23·470	23·495	23·520	23·546	23·571	23·597	23·622	23·647	23·673	23·698	23·724	23·749
78	23·774	23·800	23·825	23·851	23·876	23·901	23·927	23·952	23·978	24·003	24·028	24·054
79	24·079	24·105	24·130	24·155	24·181	24·206	24·232	24·257	24·282	24·308	24·333	24·359
80	24·384	24·409	24·435	24·460	24·486	24·511	24·536	24·562	24·587	24·613	24·638	24·663
81	24·689	24·714	24·740	24·765	24·790	24·816	24·841	24·867	24·892	24·917	24·943	24·968
82	24·994	25·019	25·044	25·070	25·095	25·121	25·146	25·171	25·197	25·222	25·248	25·273
83	25·298	25·324	25·349	25·375	25·400	25·425	25·451	25·476	25·502	25·527	25·552	25·578
84	25·603	25·629	25·654	25·679	25·705	25·730	25·756	25·781	25·806	25·832	25·857	25·883
85	25·908	25·933	25·959	25·984	26·010	26·035	26·060	26·086	26·111	26·137	26·162	26·187
86	26·213	26·238	26·264	26·289	26·314	26·340	26·365	26·391	26·416	26·441	26·467	26·492
87	26·518	26·543	26·568	26·594	26·619	26·645	26·670	26·695	26·721	26·746	26·772	26·797
88	26·822	26·848	26·873	26·899	26·924	26·949	26·975	27·000	27·026	27·051	27·076	27·102
89	27·127	27·153	27·178	27·203	27·229	27·254	27·280	27·305	27·330	27·356	27·381	27·407
90	27·432	27·457	27·483	27·508	27·534	27·559	27·584	27·610	27·635	27·661	27·686	27·711
91	27·737	27·762	27·788	27·813	27·838	27·864	27·889	27·915	27·940	27·965	27·991	28·016
92	28·042	28·067	28·092	28·118	28·143	28·169	28·194	28·219	28·245	28·270	28·296	28·321
93	28·346	28·372	28·397	28·423	28·448	28·473	28·499	28·524	28·550	28·575	28·600	28·626
94	28·651	28·677	28·702	28·727	28·753	28·778	28·804	28·829	28·854	28·880	28·905	28·931
95	28·956	28·981	29·007	29·032	29·058	29·083	29·108	29·134	29·159	29·185	29·210	29·235
96	29·261	29·286	29·312	29·337	29·362	29·388	29·413	29·439	29·464	29·489	29·515	29·540
97	29·566	29·591	29·616	29·642	29·667	29·693	29·718	29·743	29·769	29·794	29·820	29·845
98	29·870	29·896	29·921	29·947	29·972	29·997	30·023	30·048	30·074	30·099	30·124	30·150
99	30·175	30·201	30·226	30·251	30·277	30·302	30·328	30·353	30·378	30·404	30·429	30·455
100	30·480	—	—	—	—	—	—	—	—	—	—	—

Feet and inches to metres

Feet	Inches											
	0	1	2	3	4	5	6	7	8	9	10	11
	Metres											
0	—	0·0254	0·0508	0·0762	0·1016	0·1270	0·1524	0·1778	0·2032	0·2286	0·2540	0·2794
1	0·3048	0·3302	0·3556	0·3810	0·4064	0·4318	0·4572	0·4826	0·5080	0·5334	0·5588	0·5842
2	0·6096	0·6350	0·6604	0·6858	0·7112	0·7366	0·7620	0·7874	0·8128	0·8382	0·8636	0·8890
3	0·9144	0·9398	0·9652	0·9906	1·0160	1·0414	1·0668	1·0922	1·1176	1·1430	1·1684	1·1938
4	1·2192	1·2446	1·2700	1·2954	1·3208	1·3462	1·3716	1·3970	1·4224	1·4478	1·4732	1·4986
5	1·5240	1·5494	1·5748	1·6002	1·6256	1·6510	1·6764	1·7018	1·7272	1·7526	1·7780	1·8034
6	1·8288	1·8542	1·8796	1·9050	1·9304	1·9558	1·9812	2·0066	2·0320	2·0574	2·0828	2·1082
7	2·1336	2·1590	2·1844	2·2098	2·2352	2·2606	2·2860	2·3114	2·3368	2·3622	2·3876	2·4130
8	2·4384	2·4638	2·4892	2·5146	2·5400	2·5654	2·5908	2·6162	2·6416	2·6670	2·6924	2·7178
9	2·7432	2·7686	2·7940	2·8194	2·8448	2·8702	2·8956	2·9210	2·9464	2·9718	2·9972	3·0226
10	3·0480	3·0734	3·0988	3·1242	3·1496	3·1750	3·2004	3·2258	3·2512	3·2766	3·3020	3·3274
11	3·3528	3·3782	3·4036	3·4290	3·4544	3·4798	3·5052	3·5306	3·5560	3·5814	3·6068	3·6322
12	3·6576	3·6830	3·7084	3·7338	3·7592	3·7846	3·8100	3·8354	3·8608	3·8862	3·9116	3·9370
13	3·9624	3·9878	4·0132	4·0386	4·0640	4·0894	4·1148	4·1402	4·1656	4·1910	4·2164	4·2418
14	4·2672	4·2926	4·3180	4·3434	4·3688	4·3942	4·4196	4·4450	4·4704	4·4958	4·5212	4·5466
15	4·5720	4·5974	4·6228	4·6482	4·6736	4·6990	4·7244	4·7498	4·7752	4·8006	4·8260	4·8514
16	4·8768	4·9022	4·9276	4·9530	4·9784	5·0038	5·0292	5·0546	5·0800	5·1054	5·1308	5·1562
17	5·1816	5·2070	5·2324	5·2578	5·2832	5·3086	5·3340	5·3594	5·3848	5·4102	5·4356	5·4610
18	5·4864	5·5118	5·5372	5·5626	5·5880	5·6134	5·6388	5·6642	5·6896	5·7150	5·7404	5·7658
19	5·7912	5·8166	5·8420	5·8674	5·8928	5·9182	5·9436	5·9690	5·9944	6·0198	6·0452	6·0706
20	6·0960	—	—	—	—	—	—	—	—	—	—	—

Inches and thirty-seconds of an inch to millimetres

Inches	0	1	2	3	4	5	6	7	8	9	10	11
	Millimetres											
—	—	25·4	50·8	76·2	101·6	127·0	152·4	177·8	203·2	228·6	254·0	279·4
1/32	0·8	26·2	51·6	77·0	102·4	127·8	153·2	178·6	204·0	229·4	254·8	280·2
1/16	1·6	27·0	52·4	77·8	103·2	128·6	154·0	179·4	204·8	230·2	255·6	281·0
3/32	2·4	27·8	53·2	78·6	104·0	129·4	154·8	180·2	205·6	231·0	256·4	281·8
1/8	3·2	28·6	54·0	79·4	104·8	130·2	155·6	181·0	206·4	231·8	257·2	282·6
5/32	4·0	29·4	54·8	80·2	105·6	131·0	156·4	181·8	207·2	232·6	258·0	283·4
3/16	4·8	30·2	55·6	81·0	106·4	131·8	157·2	182·6	208·0	233·4	258·8	284·2
7/32	5·6	31·0	56·4	81·8	107·2	132·6	158·0	183·4	208·8	234·2	259·6	285·0
1/4	6·4	31·8	57·2	82·6	108·0	133·4	158·8	184·2	209·6	235·0	260·4	285·8
9/32	7·1	32·5	57·9	83·3	108·7	134·1	159·5	184·9	210·3	235·7	261·1	286·5
5/16	7·9	33·3	58·7	84·1	109·5	134·9	160·3	185·7	211·1	236·5	261·9	287·3
11/32	8·7	34·1	59·5	84·9	110·3	135·7	161·1	186·5	211·9	237·3	262·7	288·1
3/8	9·5	34·9	60·3	85·7	111·1	136·5	161·9	187·3	212·7	238·1	263·5	288·9
13/32	10·3	35·7	61·1	86·5	111·9	137·3	162·7	188·1	213·5	238·9	264·3	289·7
7/16	11·1	36·5	61·9	87·3	112·7	138·1	163·5	188·9	214·3	239·7	265·1	290·5
15/32	11·9	37·3	62·7	88·1	113·5	138·9	164·3	189·7	215·1	240·5	265·9	291·3
1/2	12·7	38·1	63·5	88·9	114·3	139·7	165·1	190·5	215·9	241·3	266·7	292·1
17/32	13·5	38·9	64·3	89·7	115·1	140·5	165·9	191·3	216·7	242·1	267·5	292·9
9/16	14·3	39·7	65·1	90·5	115·9	141·3	166·7	192·1	217·5	242·9	268·3	293·7
19/32	15·1	40·5	65·9	91·3	116·7	142·1	167·5	192·9	218·3	243·7	269·1	294·5
5/8	15·9	41·3	66·7	92·1	117·5	142·9	168·3	193·7	219·1	244·5	269·9	295·3
21/32	16·7	42·1	67·5	92·9	118·3	143·7	169·1	194·5	219·9	245·3	270·7	296·1
11/16	17·5	42·9	68·3	93·7	119·1	144·5	169·9	195·3	220·7	246·1	271·5	296·9
23/32	18·3	43·7	69·1	94·5	119·9	145·3	170·7	196·1	221·5	246·9	272·3	297·7
3/4	19·1	44·5	69·9	95·3	120·7	146·1	171·5	196·9	222·3	247·7	273·1	298·5
25/32	19·8	45·2	70·6	96·0	121·4	146·8	172·2	197·6	223·0	248·4	273·8	299·2
13/16	20·6	46·0	71·4	96·8	122·2	147·6	173·0	198·4	223·8	249·2	274·6	300·0
27/32	21·4	46·8	72·2	97·6	123·0	148·4	173·8	199·2	224·6	250·0	275·4	300·8
7/8	22·2	47·6	73·0	98·4	123·8	149·2	174·6	200·0	225·4	250·8	276·2	301·6
29/32	23·0	48·4	73·8	99·2	124·6	150·0	175·4	200·8	226·2	251·6	277·0	302·4
15/16	23·8	49·2	74·6	100·0	125·4	150·8	176·2	201·6	227·0	252·4	277·8	303·2
31/32	24·6	50·0	75·4	100·8	126·2	151·6	177·0	202·4	227·8	253·2	278·6	304·0

Cubic feet to cubic metres

Cubic feet	0	1	2	3	4	5	6	7	8	9
	Cubic metres (m³)									
0	—	0·03	0·06	0·08	0·11	0·14	0·17	0·20	0·23	0·25
10	0·28	0·31	0·34	0·37	0·40	0·42	0·45	0·48	0·51	0·54
20	0·57	0·59	0·62	0·65	0·68	0·71	0·73	0·76	0·79	0·82
30	0·85	0·88	0·91	0·93	0·96	0·99	1·02	1·05	1·08	1·10
40	1·13	1·16	1·19	1·22	1·25	1·27	1·30	1·33	1·36	1·39
50	1·42	1·44	1·47	1·50	1·53	1·56	1·59	1·61	1·64	1·67
60	1·70	1·73	1·76	1·78	1·81	1·84	1·87	1·90	1·93	1·95
70	1·98	2·01	2·04	2·07	2·10	2·12	2·15	2·18	2·21	2·24
80	2·27	2·29	2·32	2·35	2·38	2·41	2·44	2·46	2·49	2·52
90	2·55	2·58	2·61	2·63	2·66	2·69	2·72	2·75	2·78	2·80
100	2·83	—	—	—	—	—	—	—	—	—

Square feet to square metres

Square feet	0	1	2	3	4	5	6	7	8	9
	Square metres (m²)									
0	—	0·09	0·19	0·28	0·37	0·46	0·56	0·65	0·74	0·84
10	0·93	1·02	1·11	1·21	1·30	1·39	1·49	1·58	1·67	1·77
20	1·86	1·95	2·04	2·14	2·23	2·32	2·42	2·51	2·60	2·69
30	2·79	2·88	2·97	3·07	3·16	3·25	3·34	3·44	3·53	3·62
40	3·72	3·81	3·90	3·99	4·09	4·18	4·27	4·37	4·46	4·55
50	4·65	4·74	4·83	4·92	5·02	5·11	5·20	5·30	5·39	5·48
60	5·57	5·67	5·76	5·85	5·95	6·04	6·13	6·22	6·32	6·41
70	6·50	6·60	6·69	6·78	6·87	6·97	7·06	7·15	7·25	7·34
80	7·43	7·53	7·62	7·71	7·80	7·90	7·99	8·08	8·18	8·27
90	8·36	8·45	8·55	8·64	8·73	8·83	8·92	9·01	9·10	9·20
100	9·29	9·38	9·48	9·57	9·66	9·75	9·85	9·94	10·03	10·13
110	10·22	10·31	10·41	10·50	10·59	10·68	10·78	10·87	10·96	11·06
120	11·15	11·24	11·33	11·43	11·52	11·61	11·71	11·80	11·89	11·98
130	12·08	12·17	12·26	12·36	12·45	12·54	12·63	12·73	12·82	12·91
140	13·01	13·10	13·19	13·29	13·38	13·47	13·56	13·66	13·75	13·84
150	13·94	14·03	14·12	14·21	14·31	14·40	14·49	14·59	14·68	14·77
160	14·86	14·96	15·05	15·14	15·24	15·33	15·42	15·51	15·61	15·70
170	15·79	15·89	15·98	16·07	16·17	16·26	16·35	16·44	16·54	16·63
180	16·72	16·82	16·91	17·00	17·09	17·19	17·28	17·37	17·47	17·56
190	17·65	17·74	17·84	17·93	18·02	18·12	18·21	18·30	18·39	18·49
200	18·58	18·67	18·77	18·86	18·95	19·05	19·14	19·23	19·32	19·42
210	19·51	19·60	19·70	19·79	19·88	19·97	20·07	20·16	20·25	20·35
220	20·44	20·53	20·62	20·72	20·81	20·90	21·00	21·09	21·18	21·27
230	21·37	21·46	21·55	21·65	21·74	21·83	21·93	22·02	22·11	22·20
240	22·30	22·39	22·48	22·58	22·67	22·76	22·85	22·95	23·04	23·13
250	23·23	23·32	23·41	23·50	23·60	23·69	23·78	23·88	23·97	24·06
260	24·15	24·25	24·34	24·43	24·53	24·62	24·71	24·81	24·90	24·99
270	25·08	25·18	25·27	25·36	25·46	25·55	25·64	25·73	25·83	25·92
280	26·01	26·11	26·20	26·29	26·38	26·48	26·57	26·66	26·76	26·85
290	26·94	27·03	27·13	27·22	27·31	27·41	27·50	27·59	27·69	27·78
300	27·87	27·96	28·06	28·15	28·24	28·34	28·43	28·52	28·61	28·71
310	28·80	28·89	28·99	29·08	29·17	29·26	29·36	29·45	29·54	29·64
320	29·73	29·82	29·91	30·01	30·10	30·19	30·29	30·38	30·47	30·57
330	30·66	30·75	30·84	30·94	31·03	31·12	31·22	31·31	31·40	31·49
340	31·59	31·68	31·77	31·87	31·96	32·05	32·14	32·24	32·33	32·42
350	32·52	32·61	32·70	32·79	32·89	32·98	33·07	33·17	33·26	33·35
360	33·45	33·54	33·63	33·72	33·82	33·91	34·00	34·10	34·19	34·28
370	34·37	34·47	34·56	34·65	34·75	34·84	34·93	35·02	35·12	35·21
380	35·30	35·40	35·49	35·58	35·67	35·77	35·86	35·95	36·05	36·14
390	36·23	36·33	36·42	36·51	36·60	36·70	36·79	36·88	36·98	37·07
400	37·16	37·25	37·35	37·44	37·53	37·63	37·72	37·81	37·90	38·00
410	38·09	38·18	38·28	38·37	38·46	38·55	38·65	38·74	38·83	38·93
420	39·02	39·11	39·21	39·30	39·39	39·48	39·58	39·67	39·76	39·86
430	39·95	40·04	40·13	40·23	40·32	40·41	40·51	40·60	40·69	40·78
440	40·88	40·97	41·06	41·16	41·25	41·34	41·43	41·53	41·62	41·71
450	41·81	41·90	41·99	42·09	42·18	42·27	42·36	42·46	42·55	42·64
460	42·74	42·83	42·92	43·01	43·11	43·20	43·29	43·39	43·48	43·57
470	43·66	43·76	43·85	43·94	44·04	44·13	44·22	44·31	44·41	44·50
480	44·59	44·69	44·78	44·87	44·97	45·06	45·15	45·24	45·34	45·43
490	45·52	45·62	45·71	45·80	45·89	45·99	46·08	46·17	46·27	46·36
500	46·45									

Pounds to kilogrammes

Pounds	0	1	2	3	4	5	6	7	8	9
	Kilogrammes (kg)									
0	—	0·45	0·91	1·36	1·81	2·27	2·72	3·18	3·63	4·08
10	4·54	4·99	5·44	5·90	6·35	6·80	7·26	7·71	8·16	8·62
20	9·07	9·53	9·98	10·43	10·89	11·34	11·79	12·25	12·70	13·15
30	13·61	14·06	14·52	14·97	15·42	15·88	16·33	16·78	17·24	17·69
40	18·14	18·60	19·05	19·50	19·96	20·41	20·87	21·32	21·77	22·23
50	22·68	23·13	23·59	24·04	24·49	24·95	25·40	25·85	26·31	26·76
60	27·22	27·67	28·12	28·58	29·03	29·48	29·94	30·39	30·84	31·30
70	31·75	32·21	32·66	33·11	33·57	34·02	34·47	34·93	35·38	35·83
80	36·29	36·74	37·19	37·65	38·10	38·56	39·01	39·46	39·92	40·37
90	40·82	41·28	41·73	42·18	42·64	43·09	43·54	44·00	44·45	44·91
100	45·36	45·81	46·27	46·72	47·17	47·63	48·08	48·53	48·99	49·44
110	49·90	50·35	50·80	51·26	51·71	52·16	52·62	53·07	53·52	53·98
120	54·43	54·88	55·34	55·79	56·25	56·70	57·15	57·61	58·06	58·51
130	58·97	59·42	59·87	60·33	60·78	61·24	61·69	62·14	62·60	63·05
140	63·50	63·96	64·41	64·86	65·32	65·77	66·22	66·68	67·13	67·59
150	68·04	68·49	68·95	69·40	69·85	70·31	70·76	71·21	71·67	72·12
160	72·57	73·03	73·48	73·94	74·39	74·84	75·30	75·75	76·20	76·66
170	77·11	77·56	78·02	78·47	78·93	79·38	79·83	80·29	80·74	81·19
180	81·65	82·10	82·55	83·01	83·46	83·91	84·37	84·82	85·28	85·73
190	86·18	86·64	87·09	87·54	88·00	88·45	88·90	89·36	89·81	90·26
200	90·72	91·17	91·63	92·08	92·53	92·99	93·44	93·89	94·35	94·80
210	95·25	95·71	96·16	96·62	97·07	97·52	97·98	98·43	98·88	99·34
220	99·79	100·24	100·70	101·15	101·61	102·06	102·51	102·97	103·42	103·87
230	104·33	104·78	105·23	105·69	106·14	106·59	107·05	107·50	107·96	108·41
240	108·86	109·32	109·77	110·22	110·68	111·13	111·58	112·04	112·49	112·95
250	113·40	113·85	114·31	114·76	115·21	115·67	116·12	116·57	117·03	117·48
260	117·93	118·39	118·84	119·30	119·75	120·20	120·66	121·11	121·56	122·02
270	122·47	122·92	123·38	123·83	124·28	124·74	125·19	125·65	126·10	126·55
280	127·01	127·46	127·91	128·37	128·82	129·27	129·73	130·18	130·64	131·09
290	131·54	132·00	132·45	132·90	133·36	133·81	134·26	134·72	135·17	135·62
300	136·08	136·53	136·99	137·44	137·89	138·35	138·80	139·25	139·71	140·16
310	140·61	141·07	141·52	141·97	142·43	142·88	143·34	143·79	144·24	144·70
320	145·15	145·60	146·06	146·51	146·96	147·42	147·87	148·33	148·78	149·23
330	149·69	150·14	150·59	151·05	151·50	151·95	152·41	152·86	153·31	153·77
340	154·22	154·68	155·13	155·58	156·04	156·49	156·94	157·40	157·85	158·30
350	158·76	159·21	159·67	160·12	160·57	161·03	161·48	161·93	162·39	162·84
360	163·29	163·75	164·20	164·65	165·11	165·56	166·02	166·47	166·92	167·38
370	167·83	168·28	168·74	169·10	169·64	170·10	170·55	171·00	171·46	171·91
380	172·37	172·82	173·27	173·73	174·18	174·63	175·09	175·54	175·99	176·45
390	176·90	177·36	177·81	178·26	178·72	179·17	179·62	180·08	180·53	180·98
400	181·44	181·89	182·34	182·80	183·25	183·71	184·16	184·61	185·07	185·52
410	185·97	186·43	186·88	187·33	187·79	188·24	188·69	189·15	189·60	190·06
420	190·51	190·96	191·42	191·87	192·32	192·78	193·23	193·68	194·14	194·59
430	195·05	195·50	195·95	196·41	196·86	197·31	197·77	198·22	198·67	199·13
440	199·58	200·03	200·49	200·94	201·40	201·85	202·30	202·76	203·21	203·66
450	204·12	204·57	205·02	205·48	205·93	206·39	206·84	207·29	207·75	208·20
460	208·65	209·11	209·56	210·01	210·47	210·92	211·37	211·83	212·28	212·74
470	213·19	213·64	214·10	214·55	215·00	215·46	215·91	216·36	216·82	217·27
480	217·72	218·18	218·63	219·09	219·54	219·99	220·45	220·90	221·35	221·81
490	222·26	222·71	223·17	223·62	224·08	224·53	224·98	225·44	225·89	226·34
500	226·80	—	—	—	—	—	—	—	—	—

Pounds force per sq ft to kilonewtons per sq m

lbf/ft:	0	10	20	30	40	50	60	70	80	90
	Kilonewtons per square metre									
0	—	0·479	0·958	1·436	1·915	2·394	2·873	3·352	3·830	4·309
100	4·788	5·267	5·746	6·224	6·703	7·182	7·661	8·140	8·618	9·097
200	9·576	10·055	10·534	11·013	11·491	11·970	12·449	12·928	13·407	13·885
300	14·364	14·843	15·322	15·801	16·279	16·758	17·237	17·716	18·195	18·673
400	19·152	19·631	20·110	20·589	21·067	21·546	22·025	22·504	22·983	23·461
500	23·940	24·419	24·898	25·377	25·855	26·334	26·813	27·292	27·771	28·249
600	28·728	29·207	29·686	30·165	30·643	31·122	31·601	32·080	32·559	33·037
700	33·516	33·995	34·474	34·953	35·431	35·910	36·389	36·868	37·347	37·825
800	38·304	38·783	39·262	39·741	40·219	40·698	41·177	41·656	42·135	42·613
900	43·092	43·571	44·050	44·529	45·007	45·486	45·965	46·444	46·923	47·402
1000	47·880									

Kilogrammes to pounds

KILOGRAMS	0	1	2	3	4	5	6	7	8	9
0		2·205	4·409	6·614	8·818	11·023	13·228	15·432	17·637	19·842
10	22·046	24·251	26·455	28·660	30·865	33·069	35·274	37·479	39·683	41·888
20	44·092	46·297	48·502	50·706	52·911	55 116	57·320	59·525	61·729	63·934
30	66·139	68·343	70·548	72·752	74·957	77·162	79·366	81·571	83·776	85·980
40	88·185	90·389	92·594	94·799	97·003	99·208	101·41	103·62	105·82	108·03
50	110·23	112·44	114·64	116·84	119·05	121·25	123·46	125·66	127·87	130·07
60	132·28	134·48	136·69	138·89	141·10	143·30	145·51	147·71	149·91	152·12
70	154·32	156·53	158·73	160·94	163·14	165·35	167·55	169·76	171·96	174·17
80	176·37	178·57	180·78	182·98	185·19	187·39	189·60	191·80	194·01	196·21
90	198·42	200·62	202·83	205·03	207 23	209·44	211·64	213·85	216·05	218·26
100	220·46	222·67	224·87	227·08	229·28	231·49	233·69	235·89	238·10	240·30

Volume conversions – Imperial gallons, litres, US gallons

Imperial gallons	Litres	US gallons
0·125	0·57	0.15
0·22	1·00	0·26
0·83	3·78	1·0
1·0	4·55	1·2
2	9·09	2·4
3	13·6	3·6
4	18·2	4·8
5	22·7	6.0
6	27·3	7·2
7	31·8	8·4
8	36·4	9·6
9	40·9	10·8
10	45·5	12·0
11	50·0	13·2
12	54·6	14·4
13	59.1	15·6
14	63·6	16·8
15	68·2	18·0
16	72·7	19·2
17	77·3	20·4
18	81·8	21·6
19	86·4	22·8
20	90·9	24·0
50	227	60
100	445	120

219

Speed conversions – knots, mph, kph

Knots	Miles per hour	Kilometres per hour
1	1·152	1·85
2	2·303	3·70
3	3·455	5·55
4	4·606	7·41
5	5·758	9·26
6	6·909	11·13
7	8·061	12·98
8	9·212	14·83
9	10·364	16·68
10	11·515	18·55
11	12·667	20·40
12	13·818	22·25
13	14·970	24·10
14	16·121	25·95
15	17·273	27·80
16	18·424	29·65
17	19·576	31·50
18	20·727	33·35
19	21·879	35·21
20	23·031	36·70
21	24·182	38·91
22	25·333	40·80
23	26·485	42·62
24	27·636	44·50
25	28·788	46·33
26	29·939	48·20
27	31·091	49·03
28	32·242	51·90
29	33·394	53·74
30	34·545	55·60
31	35·697	57·34
32	36·848	59·30
33	38·000	61·15
34	39·152	63·00
35	40·303	64·86
36	41·455	66·70
37	42·606	68·56
38	43·758	70·42
39	44·909	72·27
40	46·061	73·40

Tons per sq in to kg per sq mm – and vice versa

UK Tons per Sq. Inch		Kg. per Sq. mm.	UK Tons per Sq. Inch		Kg per Sq. mm.
0.635	1	1.575	32.38	51	80.32
1.27	2	3.15	33.02	52	81.89
1.90	3	4.72	33.65	53	83.47
2.54	4	6.30	34.29	54	85.04
3.17	5	7.87	34.92	55	86.62
3.81	6	9.45	35.56	56	88.19
4.44	7	11.02	36.19	57	89.77
5.08	8	12.60	36.83	58	91.34
5.71	9	14.17	37.46	59	92.92
6.35	10	15.75	38.10	60	94.49
6.98	11	17.32	38.73	61	96.07
7.62	12	18.90	39.37	62	97.64
8.25	13	20.47	40.00	63	99.22
8.89	14	22.05	40.64	64	100.79
9.52	15	23.62	41.27	65	102.37
10.16	16	25.20	41.91	66	103.94
10.79	17	26.77	42.54	67	105.52
11.43	18	28.35	43.18	68	107.09
12.00	19	30.02	43.81	69	108.67
12.70	20	31.50	44.45	70	110.24
13.33	21	33.07	45.08	71	111.82
13.97	22	34.65	45.72	72	113.39
14.60	23	36.22	46.35	73	114.97
15.24	24	37.80	46.99	74	116.54
15.87	25	39.37	47.62	75	118.12
16.51	26	40.95	48.26	76	119.69
17.14	27	42.52	48.89	77	121.27
17.78	28	44.10	49.53	78	122.84
18.41	29	45.67	50.16	79	124.42
19.05	30	47.25	50.80	80	125.99
19.68	31	48.82	51.43	81	127.57
20.32	32	50.40	52.07	82	129.14
20.95	33	51.97	52.70	83	130.72
21.59	34	53.55	53.34	84	132.29
22.22	35	55.12	53.97	85	133.86
22.86	36	56.70	54.61	86	135.44
23.49	37	58.27	55.24	87	137.01
24.13	38	59.85	55.88	88	138.59
24.76	39	61.42	56.51	89	140.16
25.40	40	63.00	57.15	90	141.74
26.03	41	64.57	57.78	91	143.31
26.67	42	66.14	58.42	92	144.89
27.30	43	67.72	59.05	93	146.46
27.94	44	69.29	59.69	94	148.04
28.57	45	70.87	60.32	95	149.61
29.21	46	72.44	60.96	96	151.19
29.84	47	74.02	61.59	97	152.76
30.48	48	75.59	62.23	98	154.34
31.11	49	77.17	62.86	99	155.91
31.75	50	78.74	63.50	100	157.49

Read known figure in bold typeface. Corresponding figure in kilogrammes per square millimetre will be found in column to the right. Corresponding figure in UK tons per square inch will be found in column to the left.

Weights of materials

See page 70–1 for weights of light materials and page 66 for weights of woods

Material	lb/cu ft	kg/cu m
Aluminium	166	2660
Aluminium bronze	480	7690
Brass	535	8555
Bronze, heavy	525	8410
Cement	183	2930
Concrete	145	2310
Copper	556	8910
Diesel oil fuel	53·3	854
Fibreglass (70% resin, 30% glass)	96	1540
Fibreglass insulation	3·5	56
Glass, plate	161	2580
Ice	44	705
Iron, cast	450	7210
Iron, wrought	485	7770
Lead	710	11370
Lubricating oil	57·5	920
Petrol (gasoline)	46·3	740
Stainless steel	500	8010
Steel bars etc	490	7850
Water, fresh	62·4	1000
Water, sea	64	1025

Wind speeds and pressures

Velocity in metres per second	Pressure in kilos per sq metre	Beaufort Scale	Description	Velocity in knots	Pressure in lbs per sq foot
0	0	0	Calm	0	0
0·5 – 1·5	0·049	1	Light Air	1 – 3	0·01
2·1 – 3·1	0·390	2	Light Breeze	4 – 6	0·08
3·6 – 5·1	1·366	3	Gentle Breeze	7 – 10	0·28
5·5 – 7·5	3·270	4	Moderate Breeze	11 – 15	0·67
8·3 – 10·3	6·393	5	Fresh Breeze	16 – 20	1·31
10·6 – 13·0	11·224	6	Strong Breeze	21 – 26	2·30
13·5 – 16·6	17·575	7	Moderate Gale	27 – 33	3·60
17·2 – 20·1	26·363	8	Fresh Gale	34 – 40	5·40
20·7 – 23·6	37·591	9	Strong Gale	41 – 47	7·70
24·0 – 27·4	51·261	10	Whole Gale	48 – 55	10·50
28·2 – 32·4	68·348	11	Storm	56 – 65	14·00
above 33·5	above 82·994	12	Hurricane	above 65	above 17·00

INDEX